ARAB RESOURCES

ARAB RESOURCES

THE TRANSFORMATION OF A SOCIETY   *I. Ibrahim, Editor*

CENTER FOR CONTEMPORARY ARAB STUDIES, *Washington, D.C.*

CROOM HELM, *London*

© 1983 Centre for Contemporary Arab Studies, Georgetown University
Croom Helm Ltd, Provident House, Burrell Row,
Beckenham, Kent BR3 1AT

British Library Cataloguing in Publication Data

Arab resources.
    1. Arab countries—Economic conditions—Congresses
    I. Ibrahim, I.
    330.9'174927   HC498

    ISBN 0-7099-0727-3

First published in the United States of America in 1983

Library of Congress Cataloging in Publication Data

Main entry under title:

Arab resources.

    Papers from the sixth annual symposium held at the
Centre for Contemporary Arab Studies, Georgetown
University.
    1. Arab countries—Economic conditions—Congresses.
I. Ibrahim, Ibrahim, 1932-
HC498.A717 1982 330.917'4927   82-14785
ISBN 0-932568-07-6

Typesetting by the Graphics Department of
Georgetown University, Washington, D.C.
Printed and bound in Great Britain

CONTENTS

PAGE

INTRODUCTION

Ibrahim Ibrahim. 3

SECTORAL RESOURCES

"Human Resources in the Arab World: The Impact of
Migration" *Ismail Serageldin, James A. Socknat,
and John S. Birks*. 17

"Energy and Arab Development" *Nazli Choucri*. 37

"Arab Financial Resources: An Analysis and Critique
of Present Deployment Policies" *George T. Abed* . . 43

"Arab Agricultural Productivity: A New Perspective"
Atif Kubursi 71

INSTITUTIONAL MECHANISMS FOR RESOURCE DEVELOPMENT

"Institution-Building in Developing Countries"
Hisham M. Nazer. 105

"The Arab Development Funds and Arab Foreign Aid"
Ibrahim M. Oweiss. 115

"Arab Institutions of Higher Learning and Their Own
Manpower Development" *Samir N. Anabtawi*. 125

THE POLITICAL ECONOMY OF DEVELOPMENT

"The Political Environment for Development"
  Roger Owen 139

"A New Framework for Complementarity Among the
  Arab Economies" *Yusif A. Sayigh* 147

"Ideological Determinants of Arab Development"
  Halim Barakat 169

"Case Studies in Technology Transfer in the Arab
  World" *Lawrence L. Edwards* 185

"Administration: The Forgotten Issue in Arab
  Development" *Omar El-Fathaly
  and Richard Chackerian* 193

ASPECTS OF ARAB TRANSFORMATION

"Islamic Revival and the Crisis of the Secular State in
  the Arab World: An Historical Appraisal"
  Philip S. Khoury 213

"Social Implications of Labor Migration in the Arab
  World" *Janet Abu-Lughod* 237

"Modernization, Oil, and the Arab Countries"
  Dankwart A. Rustow 267

"Why Japan?" *Charles Issawi* 283

"The Poor Rich Arabs" *Hisham Sharabi* 301

The editor is pleased to acknowledge the assistance of the many people who contributed to the symposium and to the production of this volume. They include the Center for Contemporary Arab Studies staff and student assistants. Special thanks are for Zeina Azzam Seikaly, symposium manager and coordinator of publication, and Marty Reimer, the Center's secretary. J. Coleman Kitchen, Jr. labored patiently and cheerfully in copy-editing the texts and transcripts.

INTRODUCTION

INTRODUCTION
Ibrahim Ibrahim

Modernization, development, and sociopolitical transformation have been the subjects of intensive study by students of the social and economic sciences. Since the end of World War II this has been particularly true with respect to the Arab world, and interest in the area has intensified further with the so-called "oil revolution." For its sixth annual symposium, the Center for Contemporary Arab Studies at Georgetown University chose the theme "Arab Resources: The Transformation of a Society."

"Human Resources in the Arab World: The Impact of Migration" is discussed by Drs. I. Serageldin, J. Socknat, and J. S. Birks from the World Bank. The authors focus on high growth scenario figures for eighteen Arab countries in the Middle East and North Africa for 1975-85. In the oil-producing countries the demand for migrant labor is projected as increasing to over 4.0 million workers by 1985; the region's needs are expected to shift toward highly skilled manpower. The most important finding, though, is that in the 1950s and 1960s the bulk of migrant workers came from Arab countries, a fact that furthered the advancement of "Arabness" — Arab communication and consciousness. The situation in the 1980s is expected to be different, however, with the number of Arab migrant workers falling from 66 percent of the workforce in 1975 to 48 percent by 1985. Labor from South and South East Asia will have a considerably increased role in the oil-producing Arab countries. An additional factor affecting development is the ratio of expatriates to citizens in most of the oil-producing countries; in the seven rich countries (Bahrain, Kuwait, Libya, Oman, Qatar, Saudi Arabia, and the U.A.E.) the non-nationals in the

Ibrahim Ibrahim earned a PhD in Political Studies from Oxford University. Currently a Research Professor at the Center for Contemporary Arab Studies, Georgetown University, Dr. Ibrahim has also taught at Warwick University (England) and at the American University of Beirut. He has also served for several years as an advisor to the Minister of Foreign Affairs of the United Arab Emirates. Professor Ibrahim has written many articles and monographs on Egypt and the Gulf.

professional and technical fields comprised 65 percent in 1975; by 1985 the number is expected to increase to 71 percent and in the U.A.E. to 98 percent. This dependency must cause serious concern on the part of the governments of these countries. On the other hand, the labor-exporting countries are themselves becoming aware of the serious problems that can result from the loss of their needed human resources; in 1975 Jordan was exporting 40 percent of its national work force, and North Yemen 24 percent. In 1985 these figures will be higher, and this will lead to skilled manpower shortages in these countries. Another aspect of labor importation that can be detrimental to development is the proliferation of sinecure public employment for nationals in the oil-producing countries. Those so employed are effectively withdrawn from the productive work force, and thus dependency on foreign labor is enhanced.

Generally speaking, nations have been always interdependent, and this is particularly so in the Arab world. The two papers presented by Professor Nazli Choucri and Dr. George Abed argue that the resources of the Arab world are highly complementary in terms of population, resources, and technology. Therefore, Arab investment should confine itself first and foremost to the region itself. This would enhance the productive capacity in the economies of the region as a whole. Dr. Abed is rather critical of the way Arab resources have been deployed to date; neither the financial returns from investment in the West nor the political benefits have been that rewarding. To be sure, some individual Arab countries have gained some influence through their investments abroad, but "the gains have been country specific and have not been generalized to the Arab bloc as a whole."

Apart from oil, agricultural production is crucial for development, and this is the subject of Professor Atif Kubursi's paper on "Arab Agricultural Productivity: A New Perspective." Professor Kubursi's concern about the future of development in this very important sector stems from the fact that apart from Lebanon and the Sudan, agricultural productivity per worker in most Arab countries has decreased between 1961-76. This decline is partly due to the heavy emphasis on urban industrial developments at the expense of rural projects. Investment in infrastructure "lured the rural population into urban centers and diverted capital and investment away from agriculture." To be sure, modernization of "inputs" such as tractors and fertilizers has been helpful in certain countries such as Lebanon; nevertheless, Arab agriculture is facing certain difficulties. It is ironical that the massive oil revenues of the 1970s have mostly not been invested in this sector and thus have exacerbated the difficulties facing it in both the non-oil and oil-producing Arab economies. This explains why "between 1970 and 1977 the food imports of nine Arab oil-producing states rose from $850 million to $5.6 billion."

The Arab oil-producing countries have embarked on an unprecedented effort to achieve comprehensive development. One of the most serious problems resulting from such development is the resulting transformation of existing structures and institutions. The paper by Shaykh Hisham Nazer, Saudi Arabia's minister of planning, deals with this problem. It focuses exclusively on Saudi Arabia, the most important Arab oil-producing country. In the author's view, each country has its unique character, which in the case of Saudi Arabia stems from Islam — for the Saudis, a historical institution that cannot be challenged. As Shaykh Nazer puts it, "Islam is a decisive and basic reality. It is an all-embracing value system that permeates and regulates every aspect of public and private life." Another distinctive aspect of the Saudi system of government is tribalism, which Shaykh Nazer considers to be similar to the classical Greek "representative government." Therefore, the introduction of modern institutions such as political parties would lead to instability; it would be divisive in that it would add to the centrifugal energies of the system and indeed threaten the very existence of the state.

Arab development funds and aid disbursements is the subject of Professor Ibrahim Oweiss's paper. Apart from their contributions to the International Monetary Fund and the International Bank for Reconstruction and Development, the major Arab oil-producing countries (Kuwait, Abu Dhabi, Saudi Arabia, and Iraq) have established several funds to help finance economic development projects in Third World countries through concessionary loans. Indeed, the Arab percentage of gross national product allocated to foreign aid is very impressive when compared to those of the advanced industrialized nations such as the United States, Britain, and West Germany.

In his paper on "Arab Institutions of Higher Learning and Their Own Manpower Development," Professor Samir N. Anabtawi argues that the institutions of higher education have always been at the heart of the developmental process. Arab universities are not as one would have expected or hoped, however, and their failures are a reflection of the social and cultural maladies of the Arab world at large. First, the Arab university "is an array of competing, and sometimes incongruous, traditions that have been imported from abroad"; as a result, one finds diverse academic subcultures competing among themselves with hostility and bitterness. Second, Arab universities are alien to their milieu; they "find themselves functioning in a setting within which they have not been assigned, or cannot perceive for themselves, a specified role." That setting's uncongeniality to scholarship and learning is indicated by the fact that half of all Arab science and engineering PhDs have left the Arab world. This state of affairs is attributed by the author to a political scene that breeds value systems unhealthy for universities. It is an "environment of subtle and crass pressures designed to breed a caution that stultifies experimentation, initiative, and creative thought." Professor Anabtawi puts the blame on the ruling elite; they keep the Arab universities on the periphery of governmental undertakings and economic activities and turn instead to western companies and expertise. "Most of the major contracts are awarded to foreign enterprises which, when in need of expertise, turn to their research units and academic institutions back home." Under such unfavorable conditions Arab universities cannot advance; on the contrary, they are reduced to "nothing more than glorified high schools, or even adult day care centers, aimed at occupying and pacifying the youth."

Dr. Roger Owen's paper addresses the question of regime stability in the Arab world. The 1970s was a decade of great stability; whether in monarchical states like Saudi Arabia and

Jordan or "mobilizing" countries like Iraq, Algeria, and Syria, the regimes were able — in spite of economic and political pressures at the intra-Arab and international levels — to stay in power. In the author's view, this "remarkable stability" is related to the growth of the state bureaucracy, its sizeable role in the field of economic activity, and the growth of its security apparatus. To be sure, external pressures and intra-Arab political relations, especially after the signature of the Camp David accord, may affect regime stability; nevertheless, there is an increasing movement toward the reinforcement of Arab integration through many vehicles: labor migration, regional Arab institutions, and banks and development agencies devoted solely to investing Arab capital in Arab countries. Dr. Owen believes, however, that such stability is precarious as long as there is no active political participation; lawyers, journalists, professors, and working men and women are still denied the right to participate in the political process. National development and the protection of Arab national resources call for the involvement of these groups.

Since the birth of the Arab League in the mid-1940s, many supporters of pan-Arabism have stressed the vital importance of economic integration, although at the beginning their call was for cooperation rather than integration. The loss of Palestine in 1948, the tragic collapse of the union between Egypt and Syria in 1961, and the defeat of June 1967 strengthened the conviction within this group that economic planning cannot be successfully implemented under the existing conditions of Arab fragmentation and "provincialism." As a pan-Arab political economist, Dr. Yusif Sayigh argues for "complementarity" among Arab economies as the most profitable course to follow. There are many obstacles to this goal. Arab technocrats present the most important of these by succumbing to the "particular" interest — *qutriyya* — while failing to link it to the general interest. Of course, certain Arab states, particularly those endowed with oil, feel rather "secure" and "self-sufficient," but this is a delusion, for oil is a depletable commodity (in one or two generations there will be no oil to sell), while petrodollar investment in the West is self-defeating for the simple reason that this kind of investment if carried too far, would reduce the Arab world to a "hostage" to the West. Finally, the oil-producing countries belong to the "developing" world and their future lies with the less fortunate Arab countries. It is in their interest, therefore, to embrace a strategy of "complementarity," especially because informed public opinion and the general public are pressing for economic integration and Arab unity.

Representative government has been the aspiration of the emerging classes in the Arab world; since the collapse of the Ottoman Empire and the coming of British and French colonialism, various individuals and groups have called for independence and political participation. In his paper, "Ideological Determinants of Arab Development," Professor Halim Barakat discusses three ideological forces presently at work in the Arab world. The first is a "rightist" ideology of the "privileged class," which prefers an "evolutionary" model of development. The second is the ideology of the middle classes, who are more likely to subscribe to the liberal reformist model because that is more in keeping with their interests and aspirations. Finally, the "deprived classes" tend to adopt a "leftist" progressive ideology and opt for a "revolutionary" model. According to Professor Barakat, both the rightist and centrist groups are entering into their phase of decline, even though they are still holding power in Saudi Arabia, Jordan, and Morocco; they cannot compete with or withstand the pressure of the rising leftist and socialist movements and ideas, which are strong and promising. The prospects of revolutionary change are not as dim as they may seem on the surface. The enemies, the well-wishers, and the pessimists have proved to be wrong in similar situations.

Dr. Lawrence L. Edwards's paper, entitled "Case Studies in Technology Transfer in the Arab World," is based on his experience as a program manager in the Division of International Programs (U.S. National Science Foundation) that was involved with the U.S.-Egyptian Cooperative Science Program. Most of the project consisted of basic and applied research carried out in Egypt since 1972. Many of the projects in this program failed to develop partly because "support for science is not a high priority in Egypt," and partly because of bureaucratic involvement and the large number of parties involved in the decision-making process. In Saudi Arabia joint projects between the Saudi Arabian National Center for Science and Technology (SANCST) and the National Science Foundation are new. Progress in developing capabilities in science and technology is slow, but given the resources and political will of the country, SANCST "will grow slowly but surely into a major research supporter in the world."

Development and change are seriously affected by the existing ineffective administrations in most Arab countries. The paper on "Administration: The Forgotton Issue in Arab Development" by Professors Omar El-Fathaly and Richard Chackerian points out the difficulties facing the development of "efficient" Arab administrative machines. Apart from certain historical-cultural factors affecting the development of bureaucracy, it is the "authoritarian" political system that hinders the establishment of a modern "rational" bureaucracy. The absence of "representative government" and the denial of political participation negates the very idea of serious public institutions. "The citizen in the Arab world (as well as in most other developing countries) often has no say in who gets what and how. He receives public services more as a matter of favor than as a right." Neither monarchies nor party-governments nor military rule are capable of implementing change and modernization as long as they deny their citizenry the right to share in the political life of society.

Islamic revival or resurgence is not something new in the "Islamic world"; there have been Islamic movements protesting — sometimes rebelling — against despotic governments throughout Arabo-Islamic history. The emergence of such movements in recent times can, therefore, be seen partly as a historical continuation of those "protest" or reform movements. But it can also be seen as a by-product of the multifaceted crisis of the contemporary "secular" state in the Middle East. This is the thesis of Professor Philip S. Khoury's paper. In his view, the crisis is related to the failure of the "secular" state in Egypt and Syria to mobilize and assimilate the majority to the new socioeconomic order. Other important factors contributed to the crisis: (1) from the beginning the state was created as a weak economic and political dependency in a world order managed first by Europe and later the United States. (2) There was a wide cultural and economic gap between the ruling elite and the majority of society. (3) The ruling elite was unable to foster confidence in the newly created state, whose legitimacy was being questioned by the ruled majority.

The fall of the old nationalist elite did not alter the critical nature of the situation; by the 1960s the new elites blended into a new "class" which can be termed "the state bourgeoisie." They "stood at a distance from the majority of society" and forced the latter to remain apart from political participation. With the help of the growing repressive apparatus of the state (the security forces) they were able to reinforce the separation of the majority from the state.

In the 1970s the crisis was compounded by the growing pressure from the West on the state to make political and ideological compromises necessary to attract foreign loans to regenerate a sluggish economy; coupled with this was the population explosion and the resulting rapid urbanization since the beginning of the 1960s. (Cairo, for instance, grew from around four million inhabitants in 1960 to eight million in 1979.) Unemployment and other social and economic dislocations were bound to intensify the majority's feelings of uprootedness and eventually reinforce their already existing alienation from the state.

Like many Third World countries, Egypt and most Arab countries are passing through a revolutionary phase, in their case caused in part by wars with Israel, the pressure of Zionism, and the depressing reality faced by the Palestinian people. Other causes can be found in the denial of political participation and the excesses of coercion and repressive government. But, above all, economic hardships, unemployment, and social and cultural alienation could pave the way for fundamentalist Islamic movements. "Islamic fundamentalism" has remained restricted to the "traditionally" oriented sector of society, however, and has been unable to strike deep roots in the modern classes in Arab society, which remain, on the whole, committed to modernization.

As was indicated earlier, Saudi Arabia and the littoral states in the Gulf have been attracting a vast number of Arab and non-

Arab immigrants since the discovery of oil. From the 1950s onward, labor migration has become a significant factor in the economic, social, and political life of the recipient and the exporting countries. Professor Janet Abu-Lughod's paper discusses "Social Implications of Labor Migration in the Arab World." One of the major factors causing Arab out-migration is war; in 1948 Israel drove the majority of Palestinians out of their homeland and some of these displaced people sought refuge in Kuwait and Saudi Arabia. The second Palestinian exodus took place after the June war of 1967, but this time Egyptian "refugees" too started seeking employment in Gulf countries. The war of October 1973 enhanced Arab labor migration indirectly due to the dramatic increase in the demand for labor in the oil-producing countries.

Since the mid-1970s, however, a relative decline in the role of Arab migrant labor reflects a shift in the policy of recipient governments: recently Saudi Arabia and the Gulf states have been recruiting vast numbers of non-Arab Asian laborers. According to Professor Abu-Lughod, this policy was prompted partly by economic needs, but was also intended to minimize the growing contradictions and potential conflict that could arise from the existence of a permanent Arab expatriate community with moral and political claims on the host countries: "Given the ancient values of the Islamic *Umma* and the more recent values of Arab unity, it has become increasingly anomalous to withhold equal opportunities and citizenship from members of permanently-settled Muslim Arab communities." But the new shift to Asian labor cannot solve the problem and will have far-reaching consequences; sooner or later, the recipient countries have to come to terms with the fact that labor cannot be treated as "a rented commodity," especially in societies believing in the ideals of Islam.

In his paper "Modernization, Oil, and the Arab Countries" Professor Dankwart A. Rustow cautions against confusing modernization with westernization. To him, modernization is a learning process — the ability to learn and adapt to new conditions. The Middle East has always played an important role in this process, and "recent learning processes . . . have been rapid and effective beyond all expectations." Having won their political independence, the oil producing countries have been successful in transforming the oil revenues into rapid economic development. At present superpower rivalry and the threat of new imperialism are affecting stability; however, there is every reason to believe that the ruling elites will be able to cope with the challenges of modernization by "combining the social and technological imperatives of today and tomorrow with the timeless Islamic and Arabic values inherited from the past."

Since the emergence of the "developing" nations, Japan as a non-western industrial country has attracted a number of political economists and social historians who have tried to discover the secret behind its success. Nearly two decades ago Robert E. Ward and Dankwart A. Rustow edited an impressive volume of essays (*Political Modernization in Japan and Turkey,* Princeton University Press, 1964) in which specialists discussed and compared the different aspects of development in Japan and Turkey. In his important book, *Cotton and the Egyptian Economy* (Oxford, 1969), Roger Owen sought to compare and contrast development in Japan and Egypt. At this symposium, Professor Charles Issawi has again raised the same question: "Why did Japan alone among the countries of Asia, Africa, and Latin America 'make it' in the nineteenth and early twentieth centuries? Why not the Arabs?" Once more the comparison is between Egypt and Japan. In 1913, Egypt's gross domestic product per capita was slightly higher than that of Japan and its exports and imports per head of population were twice as high; however, the "Japanese miracle" was made possible thanks to certain factors specific to Japan:

(1) A favorable geographical location that reduced the danger of foreign intervention. Egypt, on the other hand, is very close to Europe and thus could not resist the pressure and aggression of European imperialism; indeed, Egypt had to wait until 1937 to get rid of the "capitulations," the imperialist "regulations" that stipulated interference in her fiscal and judicial system.

(2) A social cohesion unmatched in the world. The nobility, the productive middle class, the working class, and the peasantry

were all united, whereas in Egypt there was division: "Egypt imported its middle class *en bloc,* in the form of Europeans, Greeks, Syro-Lebanese, Jews, and Armenians."

(3) Far more developed human resources combined with a high degree of literacy. By 1907 Japan was able to wipe out illiteracy, whereas in Egypt the development of natural resources was not accompanied by a strong development of human resources.

(4) An early orientation toward economic growth and a much greater sense of curiosity. Like Egypt, Japan encouraged foreign investment and high technology foreign firms to come in, but unlike Egypt the Japanese "saw to it that foreigners did not control too large a section of the economy."

(5) Wise leadership with well-defined aims and goals, supported by a cohesive "patriotic" society (see point 2 above).

"The Poor Rich Arabs" is the ironical title of Professor Hisham Sharabi's paper: the Arabs are temporarily rich in cash money, but in terms of their economies they are not. Most of their oil revenues are spent on nonproductive goods and services. The "rich" (perhaps 2 percent) live in luxury; the small middle class (some 10 percent) enjoy some comfort; "the majority, close to 90 percent, struggle for mere survival." Hence the present instability is only to be expected; however, reasons for instability go beyond the disparity between poor and rich, and include external pressures, particularly the hostile attitude of the United States toward Arab aspirations. The cultural backlash and the rise of Islamic fundamentalist movements are witness to the growing revolt against Arab ruling elites friendly to the United States. In conclusion, peaceful transformation is only possible when the wealth of the Arab people is properly used in their service, and when the United States comes to realize that the preservation of the status quo at all costs is self-defeating.

SECTORAL RESOURCES

HUMAN RESOURCES IN THE ARAB WORLD: THE IMPACT OF MIGRATION

Ismail Serageldin, James A. Socknat, and John S. Birks

The book in which this paper appears has as its subtitle "The Transformation of a Society," the implication being that the Arab region as a whole, rather than individual societies or countries, is being assessed. This paper, therefore, takes a systematic approach to the human resources of the Arab world by focusing on the pervasive and increasing linkages generated by international migration for employment. The paper is divided into five portions.

Ismail Serageldin holds a PhD in Regional Planning from Harvard University. Dr. Serageldin worked as a consultant in the United States and the Caribbean before joining the World Bank in 1972. He served as Chief of the Technical Assistance and Special Studies Division in the Projects Department of the Europe, Middle East, and North Africa Regional Office and is currently Chief of the Urban Projects Division of the same regional office at the World Bank.

James A. Socknat earned a JD from Georgetown University and currently holds the position of Manpower Specialist in the Technical Assistance and Special Studies Division, Europe, Middle East, and North Africa Region of the World Bank. Previously he was an Adjunct Associate Professor of Economics at the University of Utah, where he conducted research on human resources development issues in the Arab Middle East. Mr. Socknat also worked as Project Specialist in Manpower Planning with the Ford Foundation in Jordan, Lebanon, and Bahrain during 1969-1975.

John S. Birks holds a PhD in Economics and Social Sciences from Liverpool University. Most recently, Dr. Birks served as Manpower Economist and Labor Market Specialist in the Europe, Middle East, and North Africa Region of the World Bank, and currently he is the coordinator of the Manpower Planning Unit of the Sultanate of Oman's Ministry of Social Affairs and Labor. Dr. Birks has conducted extensive research on economic development in the Arab world. His publications include *Arab Manpower, the Crisis of Development* and *Development, Population and Migration in the Arab World.*

This paper reports on the findings of a major World Bank research project on "International Labor Migration and Manpower in the Middle East and North Africa" (Proj. Nr. 67163). The authors wish to acknowledge their great debt to Bob Li, who was responsible for the design of the model and whose contributions to the study cannot be overstated. The general guidance and support of Vinod Dubey is also gratefully acknowledged. Any shortcomings are purely our own. The views expressed in this paper are those of the authors alone and should not be ascribed to the World Bank or any of its affiliated organizations.

The first section provides some necessary definitions and caveats. The second gives an overview of current levels of, and prospects for, international labor migration in the Middle East and North Africa. The third focuses on the labor-importing countries, whose economies are the central factor in the labor migration process. The fourth examines the challenges faced by the labor-exporting countries, and the final section presents some tentative conclusions.

Some Definitions and Caveats

This paper draws upon the findings of the Research Project on International Labor Migration and Manpower in the Middle East and North Africa, which was funded by the World Bank and carried out over a number of years by the Technical Assistance and Special Studies (T.A.S.S.) Division of the Bank's Europe, Middle East, and North Africa Region. It is impossible in a short paper to do full justice to the methodology, data, and conclusions of a two-volume report utilizing a sophisticated International Migration Model. Interested persons are invited to contact the T.A.S.S. Division at the Bank for further information.

Essentially, the report presents manpower projections made for most of the Arab countries plus Iran using the International Migration Model, which is a modified version of the Integrated Computer Based Manpower Forecasting Model (Compound Model) developed by the T.A.S.S. Division. The projections were made under likely high and likely low growth scenarios representing the upper and lower extremes of a realistic range of achievable growth paths in the countries of the region. This paper will focus throughout on high growth scenario figures. The Middle Eastern and North African countries covered by the report are Algeria, Bahrain, Egypt, Iran, Iraq, Jordan, Kuwait, Lebanon, Libya, Morocco, Oman, Qatar, Saudi Arabia, Sudan, Syria, Tunisia, the United Arab Emirates (U.A.E.), the Yemen Arab Republic (Y.A.R.), and the People's Democratic Republic of Yemen (P.D.R.Y.). For the sake of brevity, these countries will be referred to together in this paper as "MENA" (an acronym for "Middle East and North Africa") or as "the MENA region."

The findings of the report highlight labor market trends in the MENA region from 1975 to 1985 in a manner useful to the region's planners. The projections indicate manpower requirements by broad occupational category, and also the supply of new entrants to the labor force coming from the education and training systems of each state. They therefore form a useful backdrop to work on detailed national or occupation-specific projections of manpower demand and supply.

Figures for 1985 should be taken as orders of magnitude only; they have been rounded to varying extents, according to what the scale of data will bear. They are meant to be illustrative rather than a detailed basis for specific decision-making in a time of great change. While in reality the MENA region is very volatile, the projections were made using the simplifying assumptions that no major internal or international crises would develop to upset the current parameters of the study. (In this connection it should be noted that the Iran-Iraq conflict has had relatively little impact on the migration patterns discussed in this paper.)

Current Levels and Prospects

Total labor requirements for the MENA region under the high economic growth scenario are projected to rise from just under 42 million persons in 1975 to almost 56 million in 1985 — an overall increase of 32 percent, equivalent to an average annual compound growth rate of 2.8 percent. It is worth observing that, despite the rapid economic growth in the oil-rich states, the compound rate of increase in manpower requirements under this scenario is close to the regional rate of population increase.

Against this background, international migration for employment in the Arab region is pervasive and increasing. The nine capital-rich states of Algeria, Bahrain, Iraq, Kuwait, Libya, Oman, Qatar, Saudi Arabia, and the U.A.E. together had imported 1.6 million migrant workers by 1975. By 1985 the stock of migrant workers in these nine states is projected as increasing to over 4.0 million workers (see Table 1). The key to this increasing scale of labor migration is the pace and nature of economic development in the major oil-exporting states.

TABLE 1

MIGRANT WORKERS' STOCKS IN 1975 AND 1985

(In thousands)

Labor-Importing Countries	1975			1985		
	No. of Migrant Workers	Percent of Sub-Total	Percent of Total	No. of Migrant Workers	Percent of Sub-Total	Percent of Total
BAHRAIN	29	1.8	1.8	81	2.3	1.9
KUWAIT	211	13.2	12.9	273	7.7	6.5
LIBYA	280	17.5	17.1	719	20.3	17.2
OMAN	103	6.4	6.3	107	3.0	2.6
QATAR	61	3.8	3.7	117	3.3	2.8
SAUDI ARABIA	668	41.7	40.7	1,680	47.4	40.2
UNITED ARAB EMIRATES	248	15.5	15.1	571	16.1	13.6
(Subtotal)	(1,601)	(100.0)	--	(3,548)	(100.0)	--
ALGERIA	10	100.0	0.6	263	51.5	6.3
IRAQ	0[a]	0.0	0.0	248	48.5	5.9
(Subtotal)	(10)	(100.0)	--	(511)	(100.0)	--
JORDAN[b]	28	93.3	1.7	81	64.8	1.9
YEMEN (Y.A.R.)[b]	2	6.6	0.1	44	35.2	1.1
(Subtotal)	(30)	(100.0)	--	(125)	(100.0)	--
GRAND TOTAL	1,641		100.0	4,184		100.0

Notes: [a] Iraq was importing some labor in 1975, but the numbers involved were small.
[b] Jordan and Yemen (Y.A.R.) import replacement migrants (see text). These are excluded from Tables 2 and 3.

Source: A wide variety of primary and secondary sources have been used in the compilation of the 1975 data in this table. The 1985 figures are based upon the World Bank report's high growth projections.

Total labor requirements in the nine labor-importing countries listed above amounted to 9.7 million persons in 1975 (23
percent of the total for MENA). By 1985, labor requirements in
the nine countries are projected to rise to 15.3 million, an increase
of 58 percent, equivalent to an average annual compound increase
of 4.6 percent. In 1985 these capital-rich states will account for
over 27 percent of the labor requirements of the region. The
projected changes in manpower requirements vary, of course, by
country. For example, under the high growth scenario, manpower
requirements increase 116 percent in the U.A.E. (where rapid oil-
revenue-financed economic expansion was under way from a low
base in 1975), corresponding to an average annual compound
growth rate of 8.0 percent. Almost all other countries experience
overall increases in labor requirements under the high growth
scenario, though compound rates of increase are low in Lebanon
(because of that country's instability, population outflow, and
consumption of capital) and in Sudan (where employment growth
has been constrained by foreign exchange problems and a stag-
nant agricultural sector). The Y.A.R. experiences a fall in overall
labor requirements even in the high growth rate scenario; the
rapid growth in the modern non-agricultural sector (at an average
annual compound rate of 4.8 percent) does not create as much
new employment as is lost due to declining labor requirements in
rural areas. Migration abroad, however, more than accounts for
the surplus labor that would otherwise contribute to Yemeni
unemployment.

Over the 10-year projection period, the sectoral composition
of manpower requirements also evolves markedly. While in 1975
some 45 percent of manpower demand was in agriculture, fishing,
and forestry, by 1985 this sector falls to 35 percent of total requirements. Apart from mining and quarrying, a small sector, the
most rapid increase in manpower demand is in utilities (86 percent), followed by construction (72 percent). Particularly in the
oil-endowed states, this growth reflects the focus on infrastructure, diversification, and modernization that has followed the oil
price rises. Also significant is the growth in services (52 percent).
In the oil states, manpower requirements in services have expand-

ed rapidly with the drive, largely unrestrained by financial considerations, to provide social infrastructure. In the capital-poor
states, especially Egypt, growth in service employment reflects
attempts to "mop up" unemployment, especially that of educated
labor market entrants, by expansion of governmental and quasi-
governmental cadres. Indeed, in the projection the service sector
accounts for 32 percent of the increase in demand for labor in the
region. Manufacturing and construction are projected as each
experiencing an increase in manpower requirements equal to one-
half of that in the sector of services.

The restructuring of the region's economy is also reflected in
the changing occupational composition of manpower requirements. In 1975, professional and technical manpower requirements comprised 1 percent of total requirements; by 1985 this
occupational level accounts for about 2 percent of the greatly
enlarged manpower demand; this implies an annual average compound growth of 9.6 percent in the demand for such workers.
Perhaps this figure, more than any other, reflects the region's
appetite for highly skilled manpower. It also underscores the irony
of the region's being a continuing exporter of high-level Arab
manpower.

In contrast, the share of unskilled manpower requirements
falls significantly from 63 percent in 1975 to about 54 percent at
the close of the projection period. There is an overall increase in
the demand for unskilled workers of 14 percent, corresponding to
an annual compound growth rate of only 1.3 percent.

Here then is a critical challenge to the education systems in
the Arab region: the demand for unskilled workers is projected to
rise at a slower rate than the region's population; at the same time,
the requirements for semiskilled and skilled workers are increasing sharply.

During the last decade, the labor requirements in the oil-
exporting countries far outstripped their domestic labor supplies
both qualitatively and quantitatively; the manpower demands
could be met only by imports of labor, brought about essentially
through high real wages. Consequently, by 1975 some 17 percent
of employment in these oil-exporting states was already accounted

for by non-nationals. By 1985 this proportion is expected to reach 28 percent.

Of the non-national migrant workers employed in 1975, almost 47 percent (763,000) were unskilled. Unskilled and semi-skilled occupations accounted for two-thirds of the total of migrant employment. In 1975, professional and subprofessional groups together accounted for almost 17 percent of the stock of non-nationals in the major labor-importing countries. In contrast, almost 27 percent of 1985's enlarged non-national labor pool of 4.0 million is projected to be professionally and subprofessionally qualified. Requirements for technical professional migrants are expected to more than quadruple over the 10-year period, amounting to an increase in requirements of over 130,000, while the proportion of unskilled workers falls to 35 percent.

In 1975, some 65 percent of the total number of the region's migrant workers were from MENA countries other than Iran. This proportion is projected to fall to 48 percent by 1985, despite an 88 percent increase in the total number of Arab migrant workers. For example, in 1975 Egyptians (354,000 migrants), Yemenis (Y.A.R.) (329,000), and Jordanians (including Palestinians, 139,000), together amounted to over half of the stock of migrant workers in the region. By 1985, their numbers abroad are projected to increase by 73 percent (from 822,000 to 1,426,000) but they would comprise only 35 percent of the 1985 stock of migrant workers (see Table 2).

In contrast to the situation for these Arab migrants, workers from outside the MENA region, especially from South and Southeast Asia, are expected to increase their share in the region's labor market; the proportion of migrant worker stock coming from the group of countries here classified as "Southeast Asian" (including nationals of Burma, Indonesia, the Philippines, South Korea, Taiwan, Thailand, Malaysia, and China (PRC)) rises from a mere 1.3 percent in 1975 to 9.5 percent in 1985.

What one sees, therefore, is an enormous international movement of peoples into and within the Arab MENA region, with the MENA Arab component of this movement falling by 1985 to less than half the total. It should be noted that as a

TABLE 2

STOCKS OF MIGRANT WORKERS IN THE LABOR IMPORTING COUNTRIES (ALGERIA, BAHRAIN, IRAQ, KUWAIT, LIBYA, OMAN, QATAR, SAUDI ARABIA, AND UNITED ARAB EMIRATES), BY NATIONALITY, 1975 AND 1985

(High and Low Growth Rates)

(In thousands)

Nationality	1975		1985 High Economic Growth Rates				1985 Low Economic Growth Rates			
	Number	Percent Shares	Number	Percent Shares	Compound Growth Rate	Increase as Percent of Total Change	Number	Percent Shares	Compound Growth Rate	Increase as Percent of Total Change
EGYPTIANS	353.7	22.0	761.7	18.8	8.0	16.7	616.9	18.2	5.7	14.7
IRAQIS	18.7	1.2	12.4	0.3	-4.0	-0.3	11.6	0.3	-4.7	-0.4
JORDANIANS	139.0	8.6	263.4	6.5	6.6	5.1	267.0	7.9	6.7	7.2
LEBANESE	28.5	1.8	86.1	2.1	11.7	2.4	71.7	2.1	9.7	2.4
MOROCCANS	2.2	0.1	12.5	0.3	19.0	0.4	9.8	0.3	16.1	0.4
OMANIS	30.8	1.9	46.0	1.1	4.1	0.6	44.6	1.3	3.8	0.8
SUDANESE	26.0	1.6	88.1	2.2	13.0	2.5	80.0	2.4	11.9	3.0
SYRIANS	38.1	2.4	113.0	2.8	11.5	3.1	91.8	2.7	9.2	3.0
TUNISIANS	29.8	1.8	94.0	2.3	12.2	2.6	62.2	1.8	7.6	1.8
YEMENIS (YAR)	328.5	20.4	400.8	9.9	2.0	3.0	381.0	11.2	1.5	2.9
YEMENIS (PDRY)	45.8	2.8	84.7	2.1	6.3	1.6	80.9	2.4	5.9	2.0

Sub-total: Arabs	(1,041.1)	(64.7)	(1,962.7)	(48.4)	(6.5)	(37.7)	(1,717.5)	(50.6)	(5.1)	(37.8)
IRANIANS	70.0	4.3	115.6	2.8	5.1	1.9	98.1	2.9	3.4	1.6
INDIANS	141.9	8.8	364.4	9.0	10.0	9.1	291.2	8.6	7.5	6.4
PAKISTANIS	205.7	12.8	555.1	13.7	10.4	14.3	446.0	13.1	8.0	13.5
Sub-total: South Asians	(347.6)	(21.6)	(914.5)	(22.7)	(10.2)	(23.4)	(737.2)	(21.7)	(7.8)	(21.9)
SOUTHEAST ASIANS[ii]	20.5	1.3	383.9	9.5	34.0	14.8	369.9	10.9	33.5	19.6
OTHER NATIONALITIES[iii]	130.8	8.2	677.9	16.6	17.9	22.2	472.8	13.9	13.7	19.1
TOTAL	1,610.0	100.0[i]	4,059.6	100.0	9.7	100.0	3,395.5[i]	100.0	7.7	100.0

Notes: (i) Does not include Algerian migrants within MENA region;
     (ii) "Southeast Asians" includes mainly: South Koreans, Filippinos, Malayans, Indonesians, and Thais (see text);
     (iii) "Other Nationalities" includes only Somalis and Mauritanians from within the Arab world; all other countries or regions except those specifically
        listed are included.

Source: Compiled from World Bank's report "International Labor Migration and Manpower in the Middle East and North Africa."

consequence of the change in the ethnic composition of migrant workers in the Arab world, the character of society in the labor-importing states is also changing, almost as quickly as the labor market, as the dependents of migrant workers settle in ever-increasing numbers. As far as human resources are concerned, the society of the Arab world is indeed being transformed.

Labor-Importing Countries

The nine major labor-importing countries differ in important ways. In particular, Algeria and Iraq stand apart from the other labor-importing states. In 1975, migrants represented only 0.2 percent of their work forces. In 1985, the corresponding figure is projected to just under 6 percent. This relatively limited reliance upon migrant workers means that Algeria and Iraq approach questions of development almost without regard for the implications in terms of imported labor, because they know that the resulting scale of immigration is likely to be small and will not involve reshaping their society to any significant extent. Labor migration is thus not regarded as a problem.

The remaining seven oil-exporting states offer a sharp contrast. In 1975, Bahrain, Kuwait, Libya, Oman, Qatar, Saudi Arabia, and the U.A.E. had work forces which were 44 percent non-national (see Table 3). By 1985, the non-national component of these work forces is projected to be 57 percent. Even in Saudi Arabia and Libya, countries with larger national work forces, the majority of total employment is expected to be accounted for by non-nationals by 1985. The smaller countries of the Arabian Gulf show an even greater dependence on expatriates; by 1985 the non-national share of the work force is expected to be over 90 percent in the U.A.E. and to reach 86 percent in Qatar.

The smallness of the national work forces of these seven oil-exporting states bears stressing. Together, these states' national work forces will only amount to about 2.7 million in 1985, while their total manpower requirements are projected to rise to 6.2 million workers (meaning an average annual compound increase of 5.5 percent between 1975 and 1985). At this rate of growth of employment, further labor importation is inevitable.

TABLE 3

NON-NATIONALS' SHARES OF EMPLOYMENT IN THE LABOR-IMPORTING STATES OF BAHRAIN, KUWAIT, LIBYA, OMAN, QATAR, SAUDI ARABIA, AND THE UNITED ARAB EMIRATES, BY SECTOR AND OCCUPATION, 1975 AND 1985 (PERCENT)

(High Growth Rates)

	Agriculture, Forestry, & Fishing		Mining & Quarrying		Manufacturing		Utilities		Construction		Trade & Finance		Transport & Communications		Services		Total	
	1975	1985	1975	1985	1975	1985	1975	1985	1975	1985	1975	1985	1975	1985	1975	1985	1975	1985
Professional Technical Occupations	56.3	74.6	79.6	83.2	89.5	84.3	80.7	79.5	93.3	91.4	62.4	78.8	79.8	82.7	75.5	81.2	80.6	83.2
Other Professional Occupations	30.7	61.7	74.0	77.2	80.4	80.1	51.3	71.8	85.3	86.5	57.5	70.6	60.6	72.4	66.7	73.5	66.7	74.6
Sub-Professional & Technical Occupations	51.2	75.9	79.2	80.5	80.1	76.3	88.6	82.8	88.8	83.2	78.5	80.6	69.3	78.1	76.4	75.4	79.7	78.4
Other Sub-Professional Occupations	15.5	45.5	47.1	71.4	80.5	65.5	57.8	66.3	74.2	67.5	61.8	67.0	58.9	60.6	44.7	50.8	50.1	56.3
Skilled Office & Manual Occupations	77.4	70.5	51.4	64.3	73.5	70.3	58.3	67.3	74.1	74.4	64.7	71.4	59.7	67.8	51.2	67.1	62.8	70.3
Semi-Skilled Office & Manual Occupations	30.2	42.3	16.0	37.4	61.1	39.9	35.7	43.1	79.9	55.3	52.9	54.8	43.7	51.7	33.5	46.0	47.4	48.3
Unskilled Occupations	6.1	36.9	30.2	50.5	63.4	71.5	37.4	56.4	73.0	69.9	52.4	49.6	44.3	50.4	43.6	55.5	35.2	51.2
TOTAL	9.2	38.5	36.8	54.8	66.8	61.3	46.2	58.9	73.6	69.7	57.5	62.5	48.9	58.3	45.7	36.7	44.0	56.8

Source: World Bank's report "International Labor Migration and Manpower in the Middle East and North Africa."

In 1975, non-nationals held 81 percent of professional technical jobs and 80 percent of subprofessional technical jobs in these seven states. This is well in excess of the 1975 figure for overall non-national employment in the seven countries (44 percent). In all professional and subprofessional occupations taken together, non-nationals held 65 percent of the jobs in 1975. By 1985 this dependence is projected to increase to 71 percent. Reliance on non-nationals in the U.A.E. is particularly startling. Non-nationals held 95 percent of professional technical jobs in 1975, and are projected to hold 98 percent in 1985. Thus, by 1985, for every 20 national professional technical workers in the U.A.E. there will be 1,000 non-nationals. This degree of dependence is causing increasing consternation.

Also causing worry in the labor-importing states is the influx of dependents of non-national workers. In 1975, there were 1.5 million non-national dependents associated with the 1.6 million migrant workers. The total population of the non-national communities in the region is projected to increase in number from 3.1 million in 1975 to as many as 12.0 million by 1985.

The labor-importing states appear able to do little about the inflow of dependents of migrants, and continue to plan for increased labor demand. In the face of these large imports of Arab and Asian labor and dependents, however, the ideal of permitting only such economic development as is compatible with limits on the numbers of resident non-nationals is gaining increasing currency.

Labor-Exporting Countries

The situation has also become more complex in the labor-exporting countries of the MENA region; these include Egypt, Jordan, Lebanon, Oman, Sudan, Syria, Tunisia, and the Yemens. The earlier modest labor movements in the MENA region did not evoke much concern on the part of the labor suppliers. The advantages of supplying workers to oil-rich states include the remittances sent home by the migrants, which were (and are) seen as a valuable source of foreign exchange; in 1977, remittances were equivalent to 38 percent of the value imports in Jordan, 139 percent in the Y.A.R., and 49 percent in the P.D.R.Y.

As the scale of labor movement has grown, the countries supplying labor in the MENA region have become increasingly concerned about the disadvantages associated with their place in the international migration system. In 1975, Egypt was exporting 3.8 percent of its total national work force, the Y.A.R. 24 percent, and Jordan about 40 percent. In 1985, Egypt is projected as exporting almost 6 percent of its total national work force; Jordan 43 percent of its stock; and the Y.A.R. 34 percent (though this figure falls in the late 1970s before rising again). (See Table 4.) Overall, labor exports are expected to increase from 5.3 percent (1975) to 7.9 percent (1985) of the total work forces of the major Arab labor-supplying states.

Labor exports from the modern sector are increasing more quickly than exports from the traditional and rural sectors, a clear reflection of the selectivity of labor migration; the labor-importing countries are increasingly demanding more skilled manpower which is concentrated in the non-agricultural sectors of the labor-sending countries. In 1975, exports of professional technical workers from Egypt, Jordan, Lebanon, Oman, Sudan, Syria, Tunisia, and the Yemens amounted to 13 percent of the total available manpower at that level of qualification; in the same year, only 4 percent of total unskilled worker stocks were exported. By 1985, however, 20 percent of the labor-supplying states' supply of professionals is projected to be exported. In contrast, only 5 percent of unskilled workers are projected as being exported by 1985. This disproportionate draw upon high-level manpower is one of the chief disadvantages attaching to labor migration from the perspective of the labor suppliers. Certain manpower shortages in the better qualified levels of the labor markets in the capital-poor states have actually been caused by migration for employment. In many other cases, shortages of skilled labor in the capital-poor states have been aggravated by exports of labor. This shortage of skills largely explains the shift of the labor-importing states toward Asian labor, which, throughout the 1970s, remained relatively cheap, quickly available, and of reliable quality.

TABLE 4

ARAB LABOR-EXPORTING STATES, TOTAL NATIONAL WORKFORCE, EXPORTS OF EMPLOYMENT, AND DOMESTIC SHORTAGES AND SURPLUS BY OCCUPATIONAL LEVEL, 1985

(High and Low Growth Rates)

(In thousands)

	Professional Technical Occupations		Other Professional Occupations		Sub-Professional & Technical Occupations		Other Sub-Professional Occupations		Skilled Office & Manual Occupations		Semi-Skilled Office & Manual Occupations		Unskilled Occupations		Total	
	No.	Percent	No.	Percent	No.	Percent	No.	Percent	No.	Percent	No.	Percent	No.	Percent	No.	Percent
EGYPT																
Total National Workforce	329.2		574.5		416.4		464.8		1,588.2		3,073.5		6,441.3		12,887.9	
Workers Exported	33.4	10.1	76.3	13.3	27.7	6.6	66.5	14.3	117.0	7.4	88.4	2.9	352.2	5.5	761.5	5.9
Shortfall	0		0	0.0	0	0.0	57.9	12.5	820.9	51.7	0		0		878.8	6.8
Surplus	53.0	16.1	1.7	0.3	298.7	71.7	0		0		1,291.4	42.0	1,982.9	30.8	3,627.7	28.1
JORDAN																
Total National Workforce	35.7		84.5		54.8		98.1		87.2		117.6		198.6		676.5	
Workers Exported	26.7	74.8	52.9	62.6	29.3	53.5	44.1	44.9	40.6	46.6	21.5	18.3	48.3	24.3	263.4	38.9
Shortfall	5.8	16.2	18.4	21.8	11.2	20.4	20.5	20.9	17.3	19.8	7.0	5.9	30.6	15.4	110.8	16.4
Surplus	0	0.0	0	0.0	0	0.0	0	0.0	0	0.0	0	0.0	0	0.0	0	0.0
LEBANON																
Total National Workforce	28.3		62.9		47.9		97.2		84.5		122.6		229.2		672.6	
Workers Exported	14.3	50.5	13.6	21.6	10.0	20.9	19.7	20.3	12.1	14.3	5.0	4.1	11.3	4.9	86.0	12.8
Shortfall	4.4	15.5	8.0	12.7	0	0.0	0	0.0	0	0.0	0	0.0	0	0.0	12.4	1.8
Surplus	0	0.0	0	0.0	1.4	2.9	0.4	0.4	8.3	9.8	69.5	56.7	32.5	14.2	112.1	16.7
OMAN																
Total National Workforce	1.4		2.3		1.8		1.6		17.2		45.7		125.8		195.8	
Workers Exported	0.4	28.6	0.4	17.4	0.4	22.2	0.9	56.2	5.8	33.7	17.6	38.5	20.5	16.3	46.0	23.5
Shortfall	4.6	328.5	4.4	191.3	16.1	894.4	8.9	556.2	29.8	173.3	25.3	55.4	17.9	14.2	107.0	54.6
Surplus	0	0.0	0	0.0	0	0.0	0	0.0	0	0.0	0	0.0	0	0.0	0	0.0

SUDAN															
Total National Workforce	11.0	67.3	47.8	21.1	39.0	13.1	87.4	176.8	12.1	313.2	7.0	3,116.8	0.6	3,792.0	2.3
Workers Exported	7.4	261.8	10.1	54.2	5.1	97.4	10.6	14.2	88.6	21.8	0.0	18.8	0.0	88.0	5.1
Shortfall	28.8	0.0	25.9	0.0	38.0	0.0	77.4	23.9	0.0	634.8	202.6	214.4	6.9	194.0	22.4
Surplus	0													849.2	
SYRIA															
Total National Workforce	64.8	12.2	93.5	34.0	61.3	10.8	73.7	208.8	20.3	709.8	2.8	1,212.4	2.2	2,424.3	4.7
Workers Exported	7.9	0.0	21.8	4.5	6.6	0.0	15.0	15.5	41.8	19.8	0.0	26.4	0.0	113.0	2.6
Shortfall	7.2	11.1	4.2	0.0	29.4	48.0	30.8	29.0	0.0	524.0	73.8	257.5	21.2	64.0	33.7
Surplus														818.1	
TUNISIA															
Total National Workforce	27.5	27.3	34.7	22.2	92.0	8.7	63.9	207.8	18.1	524.6	1.6	1,265.5	1.4	2,216.0	4.2
Workers Exported	7.5	78.5	7.7	62.8	8.0	15.3	11.6	33.3	97.2	8.6	0.0	17.0	0.0	94.1	5.4
Shortfall	21.6	0.0	21.8	0.0	14.1	0.0	62.1	24.2	0.0	199.0	37.9	104.3	8.2	119.6	14.8
Surplus														327.5	
YEMEN (YAR)															
Total National Workforce	2.2	13.6	11.4	13.2	2.5	20.0	11.8	42.7	16.1	137.7	70.0	1,347.2	19.7	1,555.5	25.8
Workers Exported	0.3	386.4	1.5	41.2	0.5	412.0	1.9	34.5	129.7	96.4	19.7	265.6	0.0	400.7	7.2
Shortfall	8.5	0.0	4.7	0.0	10.3	0.0	15.3	46.5	0.0	27.1	0.0	34.8	2.6	112.4	2.2
Surplus														34.8	
YEMEN (PDRY)															
Total National Workforce	2.6	46.1	6.2	17.7	3.6	25.0	20.6	44.8	11.2	87.1	40.8	359.0	1.9	523.9	16.2
Workers Exported	1.2	265.4	1.1	145.2	0.9	200.0	2.3	36.7	60.7	35.5	0.0	6.8	0.0	84.5	13.4
Shortfall	6.9	0.0	9.0	0.0	7.2	0.0	12.5	34.6	0.0	67.0	76.9	172.0	47.9	70.2	45.6
Surplus														239.0	
TOTAL															
Total National Workforce	502.7	917.8	917.8	20.2	719.3	12.3	919.1	2,458.0	18.8	5,131.8	6.1	14,295.8	5.4	24,944.5	7.8
Workers Exported	99.1	19.7	185.4	10.5	88.5	13.5	172.6	309.7	31.0	314.6	1.2	767.3	0.3	1,937.2	6.9
Shortfall	80.6	16.0	96.4	0.2	96.9	45.8	285.4	1,002.0	0.0	59.4	54.3	48.5	19.6	1,669.2	24.1
Surplus	60.2	12.0	1.7	10.3	329.5	0.4	285.0	32.5	1.3	2,785.7		2,798.4	19.6	6,008.4	0.0
Net Shortfall	20.4	4.1	94.7	0.0	232.6	32.3	285.0	969.5	39.4	2,726.3	53.1	2,749.9	19.2	4,339.2	17.2
Net Surplus		0.0	0.0	0.0				0.0							

Source: World Bank's report "International Labor Migration and Manpower in the Middle East and North Africa."

In the face of skilled labor shortages, the benefits of remittances to the economies of the labor-exporting states are no longer seen as clear-cut. In any case, the period of rapid growth in remittances to the labor exporting Arab states generally appears to have ended; the unskilled, who have a high propensity to remit, comprise a falling proportion of migrants, and increased numbers of dependents are moving to the countries of employment.

Conclusion

Through international migration of labor the oil-endowed economies of the Arabian Peninsula and Libya are being transformed. Yet with international migration has come a series of unforeseen economic and social consequences for both labor receivers and labor senders. Both parties find aspects of the process disagreeable and difficult to accommodate. Indeed, there is arguably a very real sense in which the economic development of the oil-exporting states is forging ahead at the expense of a fundamental distortion of the labor markets and economies of some of the Arab countries supplying migrant workers.

In the labor-importing countries, oil revenues, investment, and employment of imported labor have generated a standard of living for nationals that is remarkably high, as well as an expectation that, when migrants have completed their work, most will depart, leaving behind an idyllic capital-rich state. Only now is this perception altering, as the dependents of migrant workers begin to arrive in larger numbers. The size and the rapidity of demographic evolution of the immigrant communities will surprise policymakers. Yet the capital-rich states are set upon a path of growth alterable only in detail in the medium-run. Expansions of social infrastructure to cater to non-nationals do require a considerable increase in government expenditure, but compared with the productive capacity of immigrant labor these additions are quite small.

A profound and unforeseen consequence of labor importation has been stunted development of indigenous human resources; migration permits a proliferation of sinecure public sector employment for nationals in the capital-rich states, causing their withdrawal from the productive work force. The education systems in these states prepare nationals for this sinecure employment rather than for productive tasks. Thus, migration has distorted the development of human capital and its deployment throughout the economy. Nevertheless, the current pattern of economic development ensures reliance on increasing amounts of migrant labor. The capital-rich states thus face the danger of domestic human capital being underutilized at a time of expanding migrant employment, just when concerns about the rising tide of immigrants are growing more acute.

The capital-rich states are, however, fortunate in the opportunities they have for manipulation of their labor markets. Policies which they utilize include encouraging greater use of female labor (non-national as well as national), both in presently acceptable occupations and in a wider reach of the economy; using new salary structures and a reduction in public sector nonproductive sinecure positions to redistribute national manpower throughout the economy; changing the emphasis of their education systems and utilizing more appropriate and innovative instruction techniques in order to produce graduates better prepared to fill the labor requirements of the economy at large (e.g., by expanding vocational training courses and providing better rewards for the enrollees); carefully monitoring productivity trends; increasing further the capital/labor ratio; and adopting more stringent immigration policies in respect of dependents.

Notwithstanding the impact of such policies, there is no doubt that planners in the capital-rich states are going to question the pursuit of economic diversification in those instances when it requires large numbers of extra migrants. It may be these societies' finite ability to absorb non-nationals which, in the final reckoning, becomes the limit to economic growth.

In the case of the labor-exporting capital-poor states, there is undoubtedly a wide divergence between the social and individual economic return from international labor migration. Private returns are high; for most migrant workers, migration for employment is a rewarding and fulfilling experience, notwithstanding any discrimination that they may suffer. Once labor exports increase

beyond a modest percentage, however, the consequences for supplying economies involve harm as well as benefit.

Unemployment in labor-exporting countries is probably not
much eased by international migration. The selectivity of international migration (those in employment tend to migrate), inflexi-
bility within the domestic labor market (which limits the domestic
reshuffling of labor following a migrant's departure), and the
rigidity of these capital-poor states' educational and training systems, combined with the usual lead time before newly-trained
manpower reaches the market place, all seriously limit the scope
for filling gaps in the labor force left by large-scale labor migration.

The impact of these critical skill shortages is not likely to be
transient. Education, particularly at the higher echelons, has a
high financial and opportunity cost in poor Arab countries. By
making the domestic developmental payoff from investment in
education less certain, out-migration for employment has made it
harder for the capital-poor states to decide on the share of scarce
resources to be allocated to education.

Remittances are the most tangible benefit from labor migration, yet even they have a dark side. They have proved difficult to
harness for investment purposes, and appear to substantially contribute to demand-led inflation, which is often aggravated by cost-
push inflation caused by skilled labor shortages. There is evidence
that they have sometimes stimulated booms in consumer imports,
to the detriment of agriculture and domestic industries. The
apparent fall in real terms of remittances to Arab countries may
therefore ease inflationary pressures.

Overall, migration for employment on the scale of the 1970s
cannot be seen as having contributed greatly to accelerated long-
term economic growth among the labor-supplying countries. Its
benefits appear to have been outweighed by the costs incurred. In
particular, the modern sector, to which so much of the development effort of these governments has been directed, has been
poached of its most expensive and scarce skills. Yet an even
greater absolute and relative withdrawal of workers in the higher
occupational levels is expected. The labor exporters in the MENA

region stand to fare less well, rather than better, from international migration over the next five years.

At least, this is the case under the present style of management of migration for employment by the labor-exporting country governments. The difficulties of intervening effectively in the labor market in the face of the manpower requirements generated by the exceptional investment spending (and consumption expenditures) of the oil-rich states should not be minimized. However, even the most obvious ways to control the labor market through manipulation of rewards and promotion opportunities have not been widely tested. Flexible short-term training schemes of low cost and short lead time should be urgently investigated. Ways of transferring monies from capital-rich states to pay for education in the capital-poor countries could be explored. Positive action either in liaison with labor importers or unilaterally, through incentive exchange rates, bond issues, and customs relief on migrants' imports of goods, should enable better control of remittances, and their direction into investment expenditure. The unpredictability of remittance flows should nevertheless always be borne in mind.

More generally, the governments of the labor-exporting states should address their new situation in respect of economic development; the most active labor exporters have, paradoxically, become almost capital-rich, with labor shortages and ample foreign exchange supplies. Under these circumstances, they should be exploring anti-inflationary policies with more energy, rather than remaining so preoccupied with stimulating further economic growth.

In short, the time for a laissez-faire attitude on the part of the labor exporters toward migration for employment is over. But whatever policies are chosen must be strong yet flexible in action; the international labor market forces which these controls are to influence are at once powerful and volatile. Above all, the labor-exporting states must always be prepared to reassess their policies, and in particular need to be ready for any downturn in the international demand for labor to which their dependence upon the capital-rich states leaves them exposed.

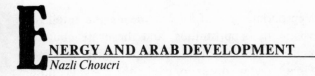

ENERGY AND ARAB DEVELOPMENT
Nazli Choucri

Introduction

The purpose of this paper is to highlight the basic issues for Arab energy policy in both the short and the long run. Decisions made in the short-term often have affected long term consequences. Policies made today will determine opportunities and growth paths of tomorrow.

In the short run, energy in the Arab world means oil. Critical policy issues pertain to prices, production, investments in exploration and development, and expansion of production capacity and capacity utilization. The energy agenda of today includes the disposition of oil related revenue (income) and allocations to extensive development programs in conjunction with expansion of a varied portfolio of investment and assistance programs to developing countries. Two underlying objectives will determine economic investments: concern for balanced growth and a commitment to diversification of economic activity.

In the longer run, energy in the Arab world means the following: development of alternative sources of energy, acquisition of knowledge and skills necessary for expansion of resource base, conservation of fuels, diversification of energy uses, and expansion of technology required for economic diversification. The future will, by necessity, be shaped by policies made today.

The capital of the Arab world is not limited to oil. The resources of the Arab world are highly complementary in terms of population, resources, and technology. There is wealth in such

Nazli Choucri holds a PhD from Stanford University and is presently Professor of Political Science and Associate Director of the Technology Adaptation Program, Massachusetts Institute of Technology. Dr. Choucri has served in an advisory function to a number of governmental and international organizations, and has written on a wide variety of topics, including public and population policy in developing countries, energy politics, and international conflict studies. Her books include *International Energy Futures: Petroleum Prices, Power and Payments* and *The International Politics of Energy Interdependence.*

diversity. The appropriate use of capital means the intelligent selection of investment opportunities, and these are abundant within the region itself. The rate of return on potential investment must be viewed in a broader context of explicit risk and economic prospects in the countries where such investments are made. Despite the Iran-Iraq war, the opportunities for investment in the Arab world are increasing, and the risks are declining. It is becoming apparent that everyone gains from expansion of productive capacity in the economies of the region. Central to this expansion is the role of oil and energy.

The Short Run

The most important short-term energy issues in the Arab world are the pricing and production of petroleum.

Though the price increases of 1973 were regarded as dramatic and excessive, in today's context — even after one corrects for inflation — they appear quite moderate. Yet these increases signalled more than simply a change in the terms of exchange. They signified that these terms would henceforth be strongly influenced, if not set, by the oil-exporting countries. The price of oil also reflected changes in power relations. It can be regarded as a political statement made possible by prevailing market conditions and economic relations. Thus, the initial price increases had profound consequences for the structure of the oil market and for world politics more broadly defined.

Relations between producer and consumer countries changed, and the role of the international oil companies adjusted accordingly. Although these companies retain their position as global regulators of the industry, their immediate influence has been reduced, partly by the emergence of direct producer-consumer interactions and partly by the establishment of national oil companies. The assumption by national oil companies of responsibilities that had previously belonged to the international concerns is also helping to reduce the relative technological superiority of the global companies. In Europe, too, state-owned oil enterprises are becoming more important in their respective economic and political contexts.

If maximizing the present discounted value of future income streams were the only objective of the oil-exporting countries, then setting the optimal price of oil would be a fairly straight-forward proposition. But governments, unlike firms, seek to attain (not necessarily maximize) numerous objectives, only one of which involves profit. In Arab countries political memories are strong; the memory of past events influences current decisions. Goals are national, but their international effects are also scrutinized. The constituencies for political decisions include present and future populations for each state, as well as the broader Arab world and the Islamic community at large.

Thus, claims and claimants on oil revenues are great. There is no historical precedent in which countries, on such short order, have embarked on such ambitious political and economic programs with such massive resources available.

The immediate energy issues facing the Arab world have less to do with price alone than with quantities; specifically, how much petroleum should be produced and with what ceilings, at what price, and, to some extent, for whom. The balance between those factors encouraging the expansion of production and production capacity and those factors leading to production cuts and constraints on the use of capacity will give some indication as to whether the oil-exporting countries will tend to increase or decrease actual production.

To a considerable extent, production levels are chosen by the respective governments, but some influences are outside their control. Actual production may be constrained by interruptions or damage. In some cases, interruptions have also occurred for political purposes. Moreover, decisions in the energy field must take into account changes in the oil market as a whole as well as factors internal to the oil-exporting countries themselves. To the extent that production decisions are under government control, it goes without saying that individual countries in the Arab world will respond to their own priorities. Nevertheless, they will be increasingly constrained by market conditions and shifts in demand.

While new entrants — such as the United Kingdom or capital-poor oil-exporting countries like Egypt and Mexico — may not have fundamental long-term effects on the market, they do act as residual suppliers to assist adjustment between OPEC supplies and global demand. They will, in fact, serve to clear the market.

In the short run, price changes send different messages to different producers. For small producers and exporters (Egypt and Mexico), higher prices are an incentive for increased exploration and development. For the established producers (major OPEC countries), higher prices encourage production cutbacks. Finally, for all producers, prices mean revenue. Oil revenue provides investment funds for development and thus makes it possible to move away from an oil-dependent economy.

The Long Run

In coming decades, the Arab world must turn to such alternative energy sources as natural gas, hydroelectric power, nuclear power, and solar technology. Coal is not abundant in the Arab world and its prospects as an alternative source of energy are dim. While development of some of these new energy sources is already under way, these alternatives (with the exception of hydroelectricity) are not yet commercially viable. Thus, the Arab countries, like the rest of the world, will remain dependent upon petroleum for some uses well into the next generation.

In the future — more than today — power will be defined in terms of autonomy in decision-making: the capacity to make decisions largely on the basis of national objectives and priorities, rather than having to shape them in response to external considerations. Oil-related decisions are increasingly in the hands of the governments of oil-exporting countries, those which own and control the resources. Yet decision-making with respect to the development of other sources of energy remains outside the control of Arab governments since they have neither access to the technology nor the ability to develop alternatives unilaterally. If long-term Arab energy security is to be achieved, it is imperative that autonomy in decision-making about energy alternatives be attained and then maintained. The ability to choose, and to implement that choice, is the single most important policy issue for energy in the long run. Thus, the diversification of the Arab economies and Arab access to advanced technology are critical concerns. The expansion of Arab technical skills is the key to Arab freedom of choice about the region's energy future.

ARAB FINANCIAL RESOURCES: AN ANALYSIS AND CRITIQUE OF PRESENT DEPLOYMENT POLICIES *George T. Abed*

Introduction

The financial wealth under the control of the oil surplus Arab countries represents a major source of economic and political power. The bulk of these financial resources has been generated by the cumulative effects of successive balance of payments surpluses. More fundamentally, the accumulation of financial wealth by the Arab oil surplus countries (AOSCs) is part of a process of converting physical assets, namely the exhaustible oil resources, into financial assets through the extraction and sale of petroleum and related products. Although public discussion of an "oil weapon" has been a constant underlying theme of most analyses of Arab policymaking, the question of using Arab *financial* resources to achieve specific political ends has not been as widely debated. Thus, there is a need to explore the nature and potential efficacy of the "financial power" of the Arab countries — the purposes it has served to date, and the broader developmental objectives it could serve in the future. The general thesis of this paper is that the manner in which the Arab financial resources have been deployed to date has produced only modest and fragmentary rewards. The financial returns have generally not been high, while the broader political and strategic benefits have been minimal. While there has been some visible improvement in international understanding of the position of certain Arab countries, this can-

George T. Abed received a PhD in Economics at the University of California at Berkeley. He has held several economics-related posts, including those of professor, consultant, and researcher. Dr. Abed has written numerous analytical studies on the economics of the oil-exporting countries, finance, labor, and planning. Currently Division Chief of the International Monetary Fund's Middle Eastern Department, Dr. Abed also serves as senior consultant for the Kuwait Institute for Scientific Research.

The views expressed in this paper are strictly those of the author and in no way reflect the views or policies of the International Monetary Fund (IMF).

not be wholly attributed to a recognition of the Arab countries' newfound financial power. Even in the economic and financial arena, Arab investments in many countries in the West (and especially in the key U.S. market) are received with resentment bordering on hostility, while on the key political questions that are vital to the Arab world as a whole (e.g., the question of Palestine) the possession of considerable financial resources does not appear to have made a *critical* difference, although it admittedly has made *some* difference. This paper examines some relevant questions bearing on the strength and credibility of the Arab countries' financial resources, especially their potential deployment in a more purposeful strategy aimed at promoting the broader developmental goals and objectives of the Arab region and, to the extent possible, those of the Third World without necessarily compromising the more universalist goal of international financial stability.

Financial resources in the Arab countries are largely concentrated in the oil-exporting countries and more specifically in the six surplus countries of Iraq, Kuwait, Libya, Qatar, Saudi Arabia, and the United Arab Emirates.[1] The discussion will therefore be limited to the financial resources of these six countries. The ability of these countries to generate financial surpluses permits them, at least in principle, considerable leverage in the financial world. Under certain circumstances, this leverage can be translated into financial power which in turn can be utilized to promote specific economic or political objectives. In this sense, these countries possess a potentially powerful "financial weapon."

Financial Resources Of The Surplus Countries: 1974-1980

The origin of the financial resources of the Arab oil surplus countries is of course oil, although Iraq, and to a much lesser extent Saudi Arabia and Libya, possess other resources that could generate significant export receipts. In 1970, the oil production of the AOSCs amounted to 12.7 million barrels per day (mbd), equivalent to about 56 percent of OPEC production at the time and about 28 percent of total world supply. By 1980, AOSC oil output had risen to 18.2 mbd or 30 percent of the world total.

During this period oil prices rose more than 15 times to an average of about US$30 per barrel in 1980. As a result, export receipts soared from a mere US$10 billion in 1970 to US$195 billion in 1980. The latter figure may be compared to the US$220 billion of exports of the United States or the US$500 billion of combined exports of the four major European countries (France, Germany, Italy, and the United Kingdom) in the same year.

The rapid growth of export receipts, coupled with low absorptive capacity in most of the surplus countries, led to the generation of annual financial surpluses which translated into the accumulation of large financial assets in the period 1974-80. As expected, however, the capacity of the AOSCs to absorb the oil revenues expanded considerably during the period and the external surpluses declined with surprising speed through 1978, before rising again as a result of a new round of price adjustments in 1979 and 1980. Specifically, the combined current account (annual) surplus (excluding official transfers), which was only US$6.7 billion in 1973, soared to US$43.4 billion in 1974 but then declined steadily to about US$18.6 billion in 1978. As the price of oil rebounded in 1979, total export receipts rose again and the combined current account surplus in that year amounted to US$57.8 billion. The continued strength of the oil export market in 1980 contributed to a further increase in the surplus to about US$102 billion in that year. The surplus was expected to decline to an estimated US$76 billion in 1981 as excessive oil supplies, generated in part by Saudi Arabia's oil production policy, weakened an already soft world oil market and led to widespread price and output reductions. It is worth noting that in 1980 the six AOSCs accounted for more than 90 percent of the total current account surplus of all OPEC countries.

In the seven-year period 1974-80, total exports of the AOSCs amounted to US$691 billion while their commodity imports amounted to US$255 billion.[2] In addition, the AOSCs ran large deficits on service payments and private transfers abroad, totaling US$115 billion. Thus, the combined current account surplus accumulated by the AOSCs in the period 1974-80 amounted to about US$321 billion.

In order to arrive at an estimate of the AOSCs' foreign asset position, however, we need to make some adjustments to this figure. In the first place, the amount has to be reduced to account for the foreign aid provided by these countries, estimated at about US$25 billion during the period. In addition, the gross figure includes privately held foreign assets which, strictly speaking, are not under the direct control of the governments in question; approximately 25-30 percent of the total may be assumed to be in this category, reducing the gross figure by a further US$90 billion. Thus, the total *official* foreign assets accumulated during the period 1974-80 (inclusive) may be estimated at about US$208 billion. If we then add to this figure the initial stock position in 1973, which was about US$14 billion, *we obtain a figure for the net foreign asset holdings of the six surplus countries at the end of 1980 of about US$222 billion.*[3]

Before discussing the composition of the AOSCs' external assets, it might be useful to dwell on a couple of points regarding the nature of these assets and the circumstances surrounding the persistence of external surpluses. As representatives of these countries have often emphasized, the rapid accumulation of external assets in the mid-1970s was largely a short-term phenomenon. It was due primarily to the limited absorptive capacities of these countries — limited, that is, if measured against the enormous revenues that accrued to them. These countries' primitive infrastructure (physical, human, institutional, etc.) made it difficult for them to absorb the sizable revenues in a short time. "Absorptive capacity" is not static, however; it affects and is affected by rising investment expenditures. By rapidly increasing investment in infrastructure and by maintaining a liberal policy toward labor inflows from other countries, the oil-exporting states were able to expand their absorptive capacities considerably. As noted earlier, not only did the combined current account surplus of the six AOSCs decline rapidly through 1978, but the bulk of this annual surplus was concentrated in the so-called "low absorbing" countries of Kuwait and the U.A.E. Indeed, even Saudi Arabia, the trumpeted perennial surplus country, ran a balance of payments deficit in 1978. Thus, it is worth emphasizing that the position of a balance of payments surplus should not be viewed as a permanent feature of these or any other group of countries. It is in the nature of economic laws that systems that suffer temporary imbalances tend to move toward some sort of equilibrium in the long run.

The other point that needs emphasis is that whereas most countries generate exports in order to finance imports needed for their own consumption or investment purposes, the oil-exporting countries, and especially the surplus countries of the Gulf, generated surpluses in their external accounts largely to accommodate an expanding world demand for energy. Most of them produced and exported oil beyond their domestic financial needs and were therefore left with the sole option of accepting financial assets in exchange for their depletable petroleum assets. This is not to deny that at least some of the AOSCs found it in their own interests to pursue a high production, moderate pricing strategy during the later 1970s, thereby advancing their own political or other objectives in the process; it is only to note that, objectively, the AOSCs could have managed with lower oil production levels, as will be explained in greater detail later on in this presentation.

Detailed statistics on the composition of the oil-exporting countries' external assets are not available and what exists is largely derived from aggregate data on initial placements, and is incomplete. Nevertheless, there appears to be a consensus about the broad features and dimensions of the oil-exporting countries' external assets. The following discussion is restricted to the disposable surpluses of the six AOSCs, and more specifically to the 70-75 percent of the total held by official institutions, i.e. central banks and ministries of finance or their designated agents. The vast bulk of these funds was initially placed in the Eurodollar market or in financial instruments of the industrial countries, particularly the United States and the United Kingdom. Of these flows, about one-half went into bank deposits while the other half was placed in short-term government securities, mainly U.S. and U.K. Treasury bills.[4] The remaining 10-15 percent of the accumulated surplus was placed in longer-term securities, corporate equities, bonds, and direct investments primarily in the industrial countries, although much smaller amounts also found their way to the developing countries. From a global perspective, the surpluses of the oil-exporting countries were necessarily matched by deficits elsewhere in the world, and the financial flows representing these surpluses were matched by borrowing by the deficit countries. This recycling process was accomplished largely by the international commercial banking system, although the international and regional organizations, as well as bilateral arrangements, also facilitated these flows.

The vast bulk of these external assets has been held in dollar-denominated assets. Although the proportion of these assets so held has been declining in recent years, it is reported to have been about 80 percent at the end of 1978; it declined to 75 percent at the end of 1979 and stood at about 70 percent at the end of June 1980.[5] Since then, and despite the rising strength of the dollar, the oil-exporting countries have continued to diversify away from the dollar. The reasons for this development are not clear, but it appears that the oil-exporting countries made a conscious effort not to destabilize the international financial markets by adding further strength to the dollar at the expense of other reserve currencies. The surplus countries have also been gradually diversifying their portfolio across a wider spectrum of assets, in part to protect their wealth from unpredictable, and often costly, currency fluctuations but also in order to improve the long-term yield of these assets. The tendency to diversify both away from a single currency and away from short-term financial assets has been most evident in the cases of Kuwait, Libya, and the U.A.E. Both Kuwait and Libya have developed institutions that have been instrumental in carrying out this diversification strategy, especially in terms of increasing the ratio of real investments in the overall portfolio. More recently, these countries have placed an increasing share of their wealth in equities, especially in the United States, the United Kingdom, Germany, and Japan. In addition, they have made bilateral arrangements to lend to Germany (through the purchase of government bonds in an amount of US$6-8 billion) as well as to the IMF (Saudi Arabia in 1981 made a commitment of SDR 9.0 billion over two years).

By and large, however, the AOSCs managed their external financial assets quite conservatively through the end of 1980. They generally shied away from shifting assets among currencies or among geographic financial centers to achieve short-term gains. The AOSCs also fashioned their trade and aid policies in a manner conducive to the recycling process through the existing international financial system. Thus, the AOSCs expanded their imports and augmented their spending levels enormously, thereby helping to absorb exports from the industrial and, to a much lesser extent, the developing countries at rates that are almost unprecedented in recent times. In addition, these countries maintained liberal exchange and trade systems and permitted sizable outflows of capital as well as private transfers, in the form of remittances from workers, thereby facilitating the external adjustment process on the global scale. Foreign aid was also provided in sizable amounts: between 2.5 percent and 5 percent of the combined GDP of these countries (in contrast to the ratio of 0.34 percent applicable to the OECD countries during the same period). Finally, these countries helped establish and effectively participated in international and regional financial and aid-giving institutions, thereby facilitating the process of transferring resources to the developing countries. Through 1980, nearly US$8 billion was provided to the IMF and a large amount, nearly US$3.8 billion, was also provided to the World Bank. Several regional institutions — the Arab Fund for Economic and Social Development, the Arab Monetary Fund, the Arab Bank for Economic Development in Africa, the Islamic Development Bank, the OPEC Fund for International Development, and some others — were also established to assist in the process of channeling aid resources to the poorest countries. Finally, most of these surplus countries, particularly Saudi Arabia, have maintained a fairly "moderate" stance on the question of price increases in the petroleum market, thereby easing the burden of adjustment by the industrial, as well as the developing, oil-importing countries.

These policies of the AOSCs have been particularly helpful to the industrial countries, which managed a remarkable turnaround in their external payments position following the 1973-74 oil price increases. The combined current account deficit of the industrial countries, which amounted to US$12.4 billion in 1974, was transformed into a surplus of US$17 billion in the following year. In the eight-year period 1973-80, the industrial countries' combined current account deficit averaged only US$1 billion per year. The less developed oil-importing countries, on the other hand, less equipped to deal with the aftermath of the oil shocks, experienced a serious widening of their combined current account deficit, from US$11.5 billion in 1973 to US$36.8 billion in 1974, and have remained in deficit since then. Their combined current account deficit in the period of 1973-80 averaged a staggering US$41.4 billion per year.[6]

It is also important to point out that, as many observers in the developing countries have noted, the manner in which the surpluses were recycled through the international financial system served to reinforce the existing economic order and further strengthen its institutions. The unprecedented increase in bank deposits in the multinational banks of the United States and Europe (generated by the oil-induced surpluses of the AOSCs) was translated, almost instantaneously, into the most torrential outflow of international bank lending in history. A considerable portion of the loans went to the oil-importing developing nations, whose total long-term indebtedness to the international commercial banks rose from US$45 billion in 1973 to US$235 billion by the end of 1980.[7] The recent rise in international interest rates, which came in the wake of the large increases in the price of oil in 1979 and 1980, only served to dim even further the economic prospects of the poorer developing countries. It is estimated that for every one percentage point increase in the relevant interest rate, the developing countries incur an additional cost (or an increase in their debt burden) of nearly US$2 billion. Moreover, it was widely perceived that the recycling process itself further reinforced the existing power structure in the international financial and aid-giving institutions, and that the parallel institutions established by OPEC and the Arab countries failed to provide a viable alternative for the oil-importing developing countries. This led to demands from representatives of the developing countries for structural reforms in existing international organizations —primarily the World Bank and the IMF — so as to permit the poorer countries a greater share in decision-making.

Arab Financial Resources In The 1980s

Although the AOSCs accumulated considerable external assets in the past seven years, some observers question whether this trend will continue into the 1980s. They point to the expanded absorptive capacity of these countries, to the depressed world oil market and the resulting downward pressure on oil prices, and to the disruptions caused by the Iraq-Iran war as signs that the rapid accumulation of financial resources may not continue, at least not at the same pace as in the recent past. With regard to the longer run, they argue, the sharp increases in oil prices since 1974 have so altered the structure of production, especially in the industrial countries, that there is no expectation of a return to the high energy consumption rates of earlier years. In addition, they note that oil production from non-OPEC and non-Arab sources has been increasing and is likely to continue to increase in the near future. The substitution for oil of coal and other sources of energy is also expected to increase. These observers believe that the total oil exports of the six AOSCs are not likely to increase significantly, while oil prices will remain flat (at least in real terms) over the next few years. If one includes in this scenario continued rapid growth of imports and capital outflows in the AOSCs, the conclusion would be that the sizable financial surpluses achieved in the period 1974-80 are not likely to be repeated in the decade of the 1980s.

The difficulty with making projections of the balance of payments positions of the AOSCs for the 1980s lies in the fact that the world economy is currently digesting the shocks of the price adjustments of 1973-74 and 1979-80 and is therefore undergoing substantial structural changes that will undoubtedly affect energy demand in ways that are still poorly understood. Thus, although prices have been stable in the past year and in general have declined from the peaks reached in the first half of 1980, no one can say for certain that this condition will prevail beyond the next year or two.[8] Part of the decline in oil consumption in the industrial countries has been the result of genuine conservation measures.[9] On the other hand, a still undetermined part of the reduction in oil use can be attributed to the sluggish economic conditions in the industrial countries. As the economies of the oil-importing nations rebound to somewhat higher growth rates (perhaps by mid-1982), it is quite likely that the demand for oil will begin to rise again.

Nevertheless, one can begin with certain indisputable facts. Oil production of the AOSCs declined measurably in 1981 and for the year as a whole is not expected to exceed 15.5 mbd as compared with just over 18 mbd in 1980. In 1982 it is quite likely that oil exports (which are slightly less than oil production because of domestic consumption and changes in stocks) will not rise in volume terms. The modest increase in world demand for OPEC oil, caused in part by the expected economic recovery, is likely to be offset by some increases in non-OPEC oil and, as far as the AOSCs are concerned, restoration of higher output levels by the non-Arab members of OPEC. In addition, there may be some drawdown of inventories and marginal gains due to continued conservation efforts.

Beyond 1982, the single most important factor in the development of oil demand will be the rate of growth of GDP in the oil-importing countries. The impact of price-induced conservation measures is likely to be negligible as the effects of price increases have been largely internalized during the past seven years. According to current projections, the rate of growth of real GDP in the oil-importing countries (industrial and developing) is expected to be in the range of 2.5-3 percent per year through 1985 (the rate is somewhat higher for the developing countries). With lower GNP energy coefficients prevailing during this period, as compared with the 1970s, the world demand for oil may not grow by more than 2 percent. Furthermore, the strongest growth of demand will come from the oil-importing developing countries. Demand for oil in the AOSCs themselves will grow the fastest, but their overall impact on the world markets will remain small through 1985.

In any case, assuming that the AOSCs' share in total world oil supply does not change materially in the coming years, a reasonable working assumption would be that the volume of exports from the AOSCs will grow by about 5 percent per year through 1985, the rates being somewhat lower or possibly zero in 1982 and 1983 but higher in subsequent years. On the other hand, it is reasonable to assume that the export price of oil will move with the average inflation rate in the industrial countries, i.e. there should be no real increases in the export price of oil for the period. Again, prices through 1982 may not rise much even in nominal terms, but may be expected to resume their upward trend thereafter. One may assume that other exports of the AOSCs will maintain their historical rates of growth, but their impact on overall export proceeds is likely to remain small. Import payments by the AOSCs can be expected to rise by about 20 percent per year in value terms, while service payments and private transfers will continue to increase at comparable rates. Of course, these average rates conceal wide variations among countries within the AOSC group as well as fluctuations over time. The AOSCs will probably continue to be net exporters of private capital as well as an important source of official capital transfers to the developing countries.

On the basis of these assumptions, one may reasonably estimate that the cumulative export receipts of the AOSCs during the period 1981-85 would amount to about US$1,130 billion. Imports, on the other hand, would amount to US$600 billion, while service payments and private transfers net would total US$195 billion. According to these calculations, the cumulative current account surplus of the six AOSCs may be expected to amount to about US$335 billion. Of this total, approximately US$25 billion might be used for aid and other unrequited official transfers, leaving about US$310 billion to be added to the external asset holdings of official and private Arab investors. The current account surplus, exclusive of external aid transfers, is expected to decline from just over US$100 billion in 1980 to about US$76 billion in 1981 and to about US$60 billion in 1982. Beyond 1982, the investable surplus could rise, albeit moderately, through 1985.

Although the total cumulative surplus during the period

1981-85 is similar in magnitude to that of the period 1974-78 in nominal terms,[10] the course of its development over time is distinctly different. During the period 1974-78 the current account surplus declined steadily as the initially limited absorptive capacity of the AOSCs was ultimately expanded, leading to higher rates of absorption of oil revenues. In the first half of the 1980s it is quite likely that the depressed oil market in the early part of this period, coupled with the slow growth of oil output and oil prices in the latter part of the period, will govern the development of the current account surplus. Taking into account the US$300 billion (the cumulative current account surpluses less foreign aid) accrued in the period 1974-80 and the US$310 billion that is expected to accumulate in the period 1981-85, total financial resources of the six AOSCs by the end of 1985 should amount to about US$610 billion. If we assume that the same distribution of resources between official and private investors will prevail as in the past, the officially held portion of the prospective total for 1981-85 would be about US$213 billion. If this is then added to the US$222 billion of previously held official assets, then *the governments of the six surplus countries will directly control about US$435 billion by 1985,* while the private sector will have in its possession the remaining amount equivalent to about US$175 billion (although this figure may also include certain unidentifiable flows as well).

In order to place these numbers in perspective one may compare them to more familiar global magnitudes. For example, total external reserves of the industrial countries (the sum of SDR holdings, IMF reserve positions, and foreign exchange holdings exclusive of gold) amounted to US$218.4 billion at the end of June 1981.[11] The size of the Eurocurrency market (as measured by the sum of all external liabilities of banks in the BIS reporting area) at the end of 1980 was US$810 billion, while in the same year the total assets of the 500 largest industrial corporations in the United States (the Fortune 500) was US$1,176 billion.

It should be emphasized, however, that not all the foreign assets of the AOSCs can be considered as reserves to be used at will. A considerable proportion of the external assets of these countries is held in equities, in real investments, in participation shares in international and regional organizations, and in other more complicated financial arrangements. Even those assets that may be considered reserves are largely held in geographic money centers and in forms that render them vulnerable to arbitrary action (such as happened in the case of Iranian deposits in U.S.-based banks and their branches). Thus, under present circumstances the AOSCs would not have complete freedom in mobilizing their financial resources for specific objectives even if they were able to unite on the pursuit of such objectives.

Arab Financial Power

Nevertheless, if they were to develop a well-conceived strategy of financial resource utilization, the AOSCs could wield enormous power in the international economic arena. To get an idea of the magnitude of this "financial clout," let us examine the degree of flexibility the AOSCs have in managing their financial resources. Clearly, a certain proportion of these resources is needed to meet basic economic requirements and cannot be mobilized for extra-economic objectives. The question then is: what portion of these financial resources is needed for these "basic" requirements and what portion may be deployed in the service of broader developmental objectives?

These issues may be pursued by examining these countries' needs for external reserves. Although countries have traditionally held foreign exchange reserves for specific financial purposes (i.e. to support an exchange rate under a fixed exchange rate regime, or more generally to meet balance of payments requirements), the question as it relates to the oil surplus countries is somewhat more complex. Looking at the current and prospective balance of payments positions of the surplus countries, one would be hard pressed to see an urgent need (except in the temporary cases of Iraq and Libya) to hold large reserves to cover balance of payments deficits. Nevertheless, in view of the uncertainties prevailing in the region and the extent to which the oil-exporting countries' economies are dependent on exogenous factors, a case could be made for these countries to hold substantial foreign exchange reserves for balance of payments purposes.[12] In addition, the special circumstances of the oil-exporting countries give rise to a broad spectrum of responsibilities and obligations borne by their governments that go beyond the mere management of the balance of payments, and therefore imply a need to hold larger than normal levels of external reserves.

Let us consider, in greater detail, the main elements of the AOSCs' financial wealth. This wealth may be described in terms of two variables: the *stock position,* which is the accumulated total of net official foreign assets at any given time, and the *flow position,* namely the annual accrual of additional foreign assets (net of changes in liabilities). In principle, the stock of wealth held by the Arab oil-exporting countries is usable on relatively short notice, as it is held in liquid and semi-liquid instruments. As indicated above, however, access to these resources is in practice not so easy and, with an increasing share of the new wealth going into nonfinancial instruments, the stock of external assets is becoming, on average, less liquid. Furthermore, the annual increments of additional wealth arising from the balance of payments surpluses can only be mobilized gradually, and may be subject to a host of complex external and domestic considerations.[13]

As for the stock position, it was indicated earlier that the total official foreign asset holdings of the six AOSCs amounted to about US$222 billion at the end of 1980 and were projected to rise to about US$450 billion by the end of 1985. In order to determine how much flexibility the oil surplus countries have in the management of their external financial resources we need to examine more carefully the uses to which these funds may be put. According to a classification scheme suggested by an official of one of these countries,[14] the stock of financial assets may be viewed as serving the following functions:

(a) meeting occasional balance of payments needs when, because of a sharp increase in imports or a sudden drop in exports, an oil country may run a balance of payments deficit (for example, as happened to Saudi Arabia in 1978);

(b) meeting the requirements of deferred expenditures on imports which cannot be received immediately for whatever reason, but which may have been contracted for, or otherwise managing deferred payments for services and for financing capital outflows;[15] and

(c) providing future generations with an inheritance in the form of income-producing assets designed to generate revenues when the direct oil revenues alone are no longer sufficient to finance rising levels of imports and other expenditures.

Clearly, these factors are of different importance to different countries but are generally applicable to the surplus countries. We will examine each of these factors in turn.

Balance of payments requirements are generally measured in terms of the number of months of imports that external reserves can finance. In the case of the industrial countries, the average holding of external reserves in the five years ending in 1980 was equivalent to just over 22 percent of their combined total annual imports (the equivalent of about two and a half months). For the non-oil developing countries, the corresponding ratio for the five years ending in 1979 (the 1980 data are unavailable) was 26 percent (the equivalent of just over three months). A case can be made that in view of the oil countries' unique dependence on a single resource to generate their exports, as well as other special considerations, their reserve holdings may need to be somewhat larger than those of either the industrial or the non-oil developing countries. If, for the sake of argument, we assume that the equivalent of six months of imports would be sufficient, then on the basis of their most recent level of imports they would have needed approximately US$53 billion of reserves for that particular purpose in 1980.

The question of holding at least some external reserves to meet deferred payments for development imports is essentially one of cash flow management, and the appropriate course of action is determined by the schedule of project implementation and disbursements associated with development projects. In 1979, total development spending by the six countries in question amounted to about US$58 billion; the 1980 figure may have been as high as US$75 billion. If we assume that approximately one-third of that total involves deferred payments (an admittedly arbitrary but perhaps generous assumption) then these countries would have needed to hold, in 1980, an amount equivalent to about US$25 billion to meet deferred payments for external expenditures associated with their development plans.

The remainder of the foreign assets would then represent the "trust fund" that is held by these countries to generate income in the future once oil exports are no longer adequate to meet their import or budgetary requirements. The amount held in the trust fund may be estimated by deducting from the total official external assets the two elements relating to the immediate balance of payments need and deferred payments on imports. At the end of 1980 the size of the trust fund held by the six surplus countries would have been about US$144 billion or approximately 65 percent of the total official assets of the AOSCs. The interesting feature of this trust fund concept, in contrast to the other two uses of external assets mentioned earlier, is that financial resources held in this trust fund would normally be invested in longer-term assets. In this sense, the investing country has greater flexibility in selecting channels for its investment so as to satisfy broader developmental objectives that go beyond the question of short-run financial rate of return.

The stock of assets held by the six surplus countries is not the only financial resource available to them. These countries can be expected to continue to add to their financial resources through the accumulation of surpluses in their balance of payments. The degree of flexibility possessed by these countries in managing their balance of payments may be deduced by calculating the excess volume of oil that is being exported beyond their immediate financial requirements, on the assumption of no reduction in their stock of external financial reserves. In 1980 the six countries in question had a combined current account surplus of just over US$100 billion and, given the effect of other transactions and capital flows, probably experienced an increase in net foreign assets of about US$70 billion. These additional financial resources may be viewed as equivalent to a certain volume of excess production of oil at the then prevailing prices. *More specifically, in 1980 the six oil-producing countries could have met their balance of payments requirements by producing much less oil — approximately 6.4 mbd less than was produced, or just under 12 mbd instead of the 18.2 mbd that was actually produced.*

An alternative measure of the flexibility available to the six oil-exporting countries may be obtained by examining their budgetary requirements for both development and current purposes. In contrast to a balance of payments need, budgetary requirements need to be measured in terms of both foreign exchange and domestically generated resources. For 1980, total capital expenditures by the six countries in question are estimated to have amounted to about US$75 billion. In addition, current outlays were in the neighborhood of US$55 billion, so that total spending requirements were around US$130 billion. Because of the small size of their domestic production base (which means that their domestic tax base is limited), the six oil-exporting countries depend largely on external receipts to finance their budgetary expenditures. If we assume that 10 percent of their combined expenditure needs can be met from domestic sources, then the foreign exchange component of their budgetary requirements would be 90 percent of the total, or about US$117 billion (0.90 times US$130 billion). If, in addition to their budgetary needs, we allow US$20 billion for extra-budgetary expenditures, then total foreign exchange requirements for development as well as current outlays would be around US$135 billion. However, the combined external budgetary receipts of these countries amounted to US$207 billion in 1980,[16] so that in the foreign-exchange arena the excess of revenues over budgetary requirements in 1980 would have been about US$70 billion, the same figure obtained through the balance of payments calculation. Using the same procedure as indicated above, one can estimate any past year's discretionary oil output (i.e. oil produced by the AOSCs beyond their immediate balance of payments needs); this turns out to have been about 6 mbd for each of the seven years 1974-80.[17]

Underlying these calculations is the assumption that all the expenditures undertaken or planned by the AOSCs are indeed necessary and do not involve discretionary elements. This is a generous assumption. If, on the other hand, one were to assume a greater degree of selectivity in development projects and a more sensible approach to other expenditures, the financial requirements of these countries would be even smaller than calculated above and the volume of discretionary oil exports would be higher. Thus, in some respects the 6.4 mbd volume of discretionary oil output for 1980 represents a lower limit. This implies that throughout the period 1974-80 the AOSCs possessed considerable flexibility in fashioning their oil production and export policies to suit their own national objectives and requirements.

It should be noted, however, that in light of the present softness of the oil market and the continued increase in imports and budgetary expenditures of the AOSCs, the size of the discretionary oil output produced by the six surplus countries may have declined in 1981 and could decline further in 1982. Applying balance of payments calculations to 1981 similar to those outlined above, one finds that the discretionary oil output may be in the neighborhood of 4.0-4.5 mbd in that year. Similarly, on the basis of the previously mentioned projections of the balance of payments of the AOSCs for the period beyond 1981, the average annual volume of discretionary oil output during that period can be estimated at about 4.0 mbd.[18]

What these calculations mean is that the AOSCs possess considerable flexibility in the management of their oil production and pricing policies as well as in the deployment of their financial resources. Even under the most generous assumptions about financial requirements, the AOSCs as a group have the option, at least in principle, of reducing oil production by 4 mbd over the foreseeable future. Such a capability need not be exercised in order to be effective. The mere fact that such a step is possible, if appropriately communicated, should be sufficient to impress the countries with which the AOSCs have economic and political relations. Any action to reduce output would have serious implications for the international price of oil and would therefore carry serious consequences for the economies of the oil-importing countries. In addition, the AOSCs can manage their financial assets so as to achieve broader economic and political gains. Even after allowing for their immediate balance of payments and development needs, the size of the remaining stock of external assets controlled directly by the governments of the AOSCs was estimated earlier at US$144 billion at the end of 1980; it is likely to amount to nearly US$290 billion by the end of 1985. The financial resources represented by these figures need not be invested in short-term assets and could clearly be diversified so as to achieve broader strategic objectives for the Arab region as a whole. Furthermore, this could be done without compromising the more limited financial objective of attaining reasonable returns on the investments over the long run.

Before considering some elements of an alternative deployment strategy for Arab financial resources, it may be useful to take a look at the performance of the present deployment strategy, if one indeed can call present investment policies a "strategy" of deployment. Limiting the discussion first to the more narrowly focused considerations of financial rate of return and security of these investments, one would have to conclude that the performance of present investment policies has not been very satisfactory. It is difficult to obtain direct information on the financial returns on official Arab investments abroad. However, on the basis of existing aggregate data on the overall size of these official assets and the investment return flows reported in the balance-of-payments statistics, it appears that the average rate of return on official assets ranged from just over 5 percent in 1974 to about 9.5 percent in 1980. The average for the seven-year period was about 7.5 percent. Although this rate of return would not be as low as has been commonly thought, it is still considerably lower than rates of return available on assets of this size. One should recall, however, that governments do not only seek the highest return in managing their external assets, in part because of the importance of other considerations not immediately linked to short-term gains. Nevertheless, even after such considerations are taken into account it does not appear that the management of that portion of the AOSCs' external assets which should be managed on a commercial basis has been particularly successful.

The question of the security of these assets has two aspects. The first is that of financial security, i.e. minimization of financial risk, while the second is that of political security, i.e. freedom from politically motivated actions to constrain the mobility of the funds. Concerning the first aspect of security, we noted earlier that the bulk of the AOSCs' external assets is held in financial instruments in a few industrial countries and in a small number of currencies. Although this high degree of concentration has been reduced somewhat in recent years, it is still significant and is likely to subject these assets to sudden and sharp fluctuations in value as a result of inflation and exchange rate changes.

To be sure, this high degree of concentration is in part due to the conservative investment policies of the AOSCs, but it is also the result of specific actions and policies of the industrial countries where the bulk of these assets is held. In general, and despite the universal recognition that the AOSCs' financial surpluses would have to be recycled through the institutions of the industrial countries, these countries have not been receptive to allowing large AOSC investments to be made in their economies according to a more flexible strategy. Indeed, one detects a certain degree of antagonism on the part of the public and the press (often fueled by unfortunate official statements and reinforced by laws and regulations) toward Arab investment in these countries. This has been particularly evident in the United States, even though Arab investments have comprised less than three-quarters of 1 percent of total foreign investment in the U.S. economy. Arab investments in the United States have therefore been largely restricted to official financial instruments and have been placed only marginally in equities and other real investments. Similarly, Arab investments in the Federal Republic of Germany have brought about hostile reactions from official sources as well as the banking community. Following the purchase by Kuwait of certain equity shares in Daimler Benz in 1974-75, and an attempt by Iran to acquire a significant portion of the equity of the same company, the Deutsche Bank intervened in the market and the German government drew up a list of 700 key companies which it classified as sensitive to the economic security of the country and where foreign investment would henceforth require government approval. Italy responded in a similar way after the acquisition by Libya of a 10 percent share in Fiat.

Eventually, the Arab funds placed in the financial institutions of the industrial countries were recycled to deficit oil-importing countries. Although the bulk of the recycling was carried out by the international commercial banking system, other institutions also played an important role. As indicated above, the AOSCs participated in a substantial way in the special facilities established in the IMF for the assistance of countries that suffered balance of payments deficits in part as a result of higher oil import payments. The AOSCs also had their quotas increased in the IMF and thereby made available additional resources to be used by this international institution. In addition, some AOSCs purchased substantial amounts of World Bank bonds and augmented their participation in the Bank's capital, thus making possible an increase in bank lending to developing countries. The capital of the OPEC Fund for International Development was also increased, largely through the help of the AOSCs, and its lending operations to developing countries expanded considerably. Regional development institutions were also established in the Middle East, with the bulk of the capital subscribed by the AOSCs.

In addition to helping these regional and international financial intermediaries, the surplus countries also made bilateral arrangements to lend to deficit countries and to conclude long-term trade accords whereby oil would be exchanged for technology. Iraq, for example, made such arrangements with France and Brazil, while Saudi Arabia concluded a number of agreements with the United States (in the area of petrochemical industries), Germany, and France. The AOSCs also provided substantial amounts of aid on a bilateral basis to a number of developing countries and especially certain Arab countries.

The deployment of Arab financial resources in the recycling process was not restricted to official funds, however. Both private and joint private-public capital also played an important role. A large number of multinational banks and investment houses were established, largely with Arab capital, and these institutions participated effectively in the recycling process through the international banking system. In addition, both the public and private sectors in the surplus countries have financed direct investment projects in the less developed countries. This help, however, has been limited for the most part to short- or medium-term project financing in tourism and, to a lesser extent, in mineral extraction.

It is clear, therefore, that funds from the Arab surplus countries played an important role in the recycling and adjustment process that followed the oil price increases of the early and late 1970s. The question that needs to be asked in the context of this analysis is: to what extent has this participation of Arab financial resources in the international financial system been reflected in an enhanced degree of Arab power or influence?

Although individual Arab countries appear to have made some gains in this regard, it is not clear that the Arab world as a whole has derived substantial economic or strategic benefits commensurate with the resources deployed. The increased participation of the AOSCs in the international financial and development institutions (i.e. the IMF and the World Bank) has brought about an enhancement of the influence of one or two of the countries in question but has not led to any major gains on the more critical pan-Arab issues. Thus, although the Arab countries as a group sponsored the admission of the Palestine Liberation Organization (PLO), with observer status, to the annual meetings of the two institutions, the Arab states were ultimately rebuffed on this issue despite the (nominally) large increase in the voting share of key Arab countries in the two institutions. The AOSCs perhaps gained the most, in terms of influence in the international economic community, from the regional development aid institutions established in the past decade. The financial resources transferred by these institutions have been substantial in relative terms and have benefited most of the poorer developing countries. Even in this case, however, the gains have been country specific and have not been generalized to the Arab bloc as a whole. Other forms of deployment of Arab resources through Arab-controlled multinational banks and investment houses have not yielded any discernible strategic benefits, as these forms of investment are largely motivated by the hope of commercial gain and their impact is diffused through the international banking system.

Without prescribing how the AOSCs should manage their external assets, one could usefully point to some possibilities for investment of the surplus funds that would better serve the broader strategic and developmental objectives of the region, without neglecting the need to achieve reasonable financial returns. In the first place, more of the Arab resources could be used to facilitate the integrated development of the Arab region as a whole. Because of the existing complementarity between the oil surplus and the other Arab countries, there are immense opportunities for more effective utilization of capital and labor for the rapid social and economic transformation of the Arab region. Intra-Arab trade has increased in absolute terms since 1973 but its share in total Arab external trade has remained minuscule. Direct investment by the AOSCs in other Arab countries has been marginal, probably much less than 5 percent of the total foreign investment undertaken by the AOSCs. To be sure, large flows of capital and labor have taken place within the region in the past decade, with the oil surplus countries exporting capital and importing labor while the other Arab countries did the reverse. However, this exchange of resources, which on the surface appears substantial, has not led to a fuller integration of the economies of the Arab countries. Indeed, it appears that the intraregional differences and disparities in the Arab world have widened, and this phenomenon may be attributed to the sudden increase in the wealth of certain countries.

Similarly, greater inflows of investment capital from the oil surplus countries to developing countries outside the Arab region can be justified in economic terms. Because of the paucity of food resources in the oil countries, there is merit in channeling a larger share of the surplus funds into investment in those developing countries with a rich agricultural potential. In this connection, bilateral or multilateral arrangements could be made to exchange oil supplies or financial capital for a secure supply of food over the long run. A greater diversification of investment by the AOSCs into the Arab and other developing countries would not only be consonant with the long-term interests of the oil surplus countries, but could also improve the financial performance of their assets. It would allow greater diversification over different maturities and across geographic regions, and would therefore reduce the political risks associated with the present concentration of Arab financial holdings.

Other objectives that could be advanced through a well-conceived financial deployment strategy include the enhancement of the economic and technological independence of the Arab region through the acquisition and diffusion of modern technology in the development process, and through the accelerated development of indigenous institutions and manpower resources. Although Iraq and Saudi Arabia have both pursued some elements of such a strategy, there is no doubt that more can be done in this regard. Moreover, the exchange of energy supplies (or financial capital) for technology could be carried out more selectively and under improved terms than has been the case to date.

Conclusion

The importance of the Arab countries of the Middle East, in terms of their market size and their possession of a considerable share of the world's energy supplies, is indisputable. Equally significant has been the rapid accumulation of financial wealth by the surplus countries in the region since 1973. By the end of 1980 the total external assets of the six oil surplus countries was no less than US$320 billion, of which about US$220 billion was controlled by the governments themselves. It is quite likely that these assets will double by 1985, and will continue to represent a substantial share of total assets in the international financial markets.

This paper has argued that the accumulation of financial resources by the AOSCs over the 1974-80 period was simply a reflection of a policy of excessive production of oil to help accommodate the world demand for energy. The AOSCs possessed considerable flexibility in their oil production policy but chose to overproduce and thereby accept financial assets in exchange for oil. Furthermore, the AOSCs reinvested the funds they received in existing financial institutions in the industrial countries, although a small portion was recycled directly by institutions they themselves established for the purpose. The question which this paper addressed was: have the AOSCs (and the Arab countries in general) exploited this position of power in the existing international economic order to promote genuinely Arab goals and objectives? More specifically, have the economic and political rewards of the existing financial resource deployment policies of the surplus Arab countries been commensurate with the relative size of their resources? Have the gains been sufficient to offset the "sacrifices" made by the Arab countries in giving up "extra" oil in exchange for financial assets and in placing the management of the bulk of their financial resources under the effective control of the international banking system of the industrial countries?

One must conclude that neither on the basis of strictly financial considerations nor on the basis of a broader set of political and strategic criteria does it appear that the present financial resource deployment policies of the Arab surplus countries have yielded enough permanent benefits to the Arab world as a whole. The benefits that have arisen have been country specific and have been limited in scope. Thus, despite an unprecedented increase in the economic and financial weight of the Arab countries over the past decade, this remarkable rapid transformation has not elevated the Arabs to the status of a cohesive and purposeful political force in the world arena. To be sure, the Arab states have made some gains, in terms of enhancing their influence and advancing their cause in Europe and in the Third World, but on the vital issues that affect the broader strategic interests of the Arab world these improvements have been minor. The problem does not lie only with the investment policies of the AOSCs nor is it even restricted to the economic and financial environment in which these resources are deployed. More important, the absence of a coherent financial deployment strategy also reflects the state of political fragmentation and institutional underdevelopment in the Arab world, which has prevented even the articulation of a coherent view of the Arab strategic interests which the resources are presumed to serve.

NOTES

[1] Because of presumably temporary factors, Iraq and Libya (for somewhat different reasons) are likely to experience some weakening in their external payments position in 1981. However, because of the inherent strength of their oil reserves position, they are included in the group of Arab oil surplus countries.

[2] The augmented absorptive capacity of the AOSCs is indicated by the fact that the value of their imports rose nearly tenfold during this period — from US$6.8 billion in 1973 to US$66.2 billion in 1980.

[3] No distinction needs to be made between the "net" and "gross" external asset position of these countries as their external liabilities are negligible.

[4] The main sources of these data are the Bank of England's *Quarterly Bulletin* and the Bank of International Settlements' (BIS) *Annual Reports*. See also the analysis by Sharif Ghalib, "The U.S. Gets the Money Bank," *Euromoney* (April 1980).

[5] As reported by *Middle East Economic Survey*, August 17, 1981.

[6] International Monetary Fund, *World Economic Outlook*, Occasional Paper No. 4, Washington, D.C. (June 1981), Table 14, p. 123.

[7] IMF, *International Financial Markets*, Occasional Paper No. 7, Washington, D.C. (August 1981), Table 33, p. 76.

[8] It is worth noting that following the output reductions implemented by several OPEC countries in the spring of 1981, the world oil market began to firm up somewhat in the third quarter of the year.

[9] See, for example, the World Bank, *World Development Report, 1981*, pp. 36-38.

[10] If the cumulative surplus during the period 1981-85 were adjusted for inflation (however measured), its real value would naturally be much smaller than its counterpart in the 1974-80 period.

[11] International Monetary Fund, *International Financial Statistics*, October 1981.

[12] The question of demand for external reserves is a widely debated issue among economists and a number of hypotheses have been postulated and tested in this regard. Our concern is, however, a more practical one and the theoretical aspects will therefore not be discussed here.

[13] This complexity is mitigated somewhat by the fact that the oil surplus countries can increase their output of oil rather effortlessly, and by their ability to influence world prices. Hence the flow element of their wealth position can also be managed, within certain broad constraints, to meet certain objectives.

[14] Sheikh Ahmed Abdullatif, "A Strategy for Investing the OPEC Surplus," *Euromoney* (August 1980).

[15] The first and second functions overlap to some extent and their combined requirements for reserves may therefore be somewhat less than the arithmetic sum of the two.

[16] Total *budget* receipts from oil exports were about US$187 billion or US$10 billion less than the export receipts of US$197 billion, but this reduction was

more than offset by external budget receipts from foreign investment of about US$20 billion.

[17] One measure of the sacrifice provided by the six surplus countries in terms of the loss of value during the period 1974-80 due to "over-production" may be obtained by calculating what the present value of the extra oil produced would have been if it had been left in the ground. According to this hypothetical calculation, had the oil been left in the ground and had the prices risen at the historical rates during the period (if less oil had been produced, prices would probably have risen much faster), then the value of this extra oil would have been about US$470 billion, far in excess of the US$320 billion for which the excess oil was essentially exchanged.

[18] These calculations assume that Iraq's oil production will slowly recover during this period so that it would approach near normal levels sometime in the second half of the projection period.

ARAB AGRICULTURAL PRODUCTIVITY: A NEW PERSPECTIVE *Atif Kubursi*

Agriculture in the Arab world is not performing as well as it should or could. The rate of growth of agricultural production has hardly kept up with the rate of population growth in general or with that of the active population in agriculture.

Between 1961 and 1976 agricultural production increased at the high average annual rates of 4.6 percent in Sudan and 4.1 percent in Lebanon, whereas it increased at the low rates of 1.7 percent in Syria and 1.6 percent in Saudi Arabia, and declined at the rate of 4.1 percent in Jordan (which lost the fertile West Bank to Israel in 1967).

Productivity (agricultural production per worker) growth rates over the same period reveal a more disturbing picture. Syria, Egypt, and Jordan show negative growth rates (declines), whereas Algeria, Iraq, and Saudi Arabia show low growth rates that are almost negligible. Lebanon and Sudan, on the other hand, have experienced significant growth rates in agricultural productivity. (See Table 1.)

An immediate consequence of this poor performance record has been the serious deterioration in the food security position of the Arab world, particularly in the 1970s. As the data in Table 2 indicate, the self-sufficiency ratio (SSR) for wheat declined from

Atif Kubursi earned a PhD in Economics at Purdue University. Presently a Professor of Economics at McMaster University (Ontario), Dr. Kubursi also serves as a consultant for the Economic Commission for Western Asia and the United Nations Industrial Development Organization. He has taught at Cambridge University and held several academic fellowships. Dr. Kubursi has also published several monographs on general economic theory and development planning as well as articles in *Regional Science, Public Finance,* and the *Journal of Developing Areas.*

This work was supported in part by the Social Sciences and Humanities Research Council of Canada Grant No. 410-78-0417. I would like to acknowledge the helpful comments and insights of my colleague Dr. Syed Ahmad and the excellent research assistance of Karen Scott and Betty May Lamb.

TABLE 1

GROWTH RATES OF SELECTED INDICATORS OF ARAB AGRICULTURE

1961 - 1976

(Percent)

	Algeria	Egypt	Iraq	Jordan	Lebanon	Syria	Saudi Arabia	Sudan
Production	2.00	2.22	2.33	-4.11	4.06	1.72	1.58	4.64
Arable Land	0.28	0.82	0.58	0.66	0.76	-1.25*	0.34	0.13
Agricultural Land	0.19	0.97	0.34	0.95	1.84	-0.29*	0.03	0.28
Active Population in Agriculture	0.39	2.38	1.51	0.09	-4.47	3.61	0.53	1.43
Arable Land per Worker	-0.11	-1.56	-0.92	0.57	5.22	-4.86*	2.91	-0.12
Productivity per Hectare of Arable Land	1.73	1.39	1.74	-4.77	3.31	2.97	-1.85	3.34
Productivity per Worker	1.62	-0.17	0.82	-4.20	8.53	-1.89	1.05	3.22
Number of Tractors	5.00	4.93	1.17	9.30	6.08	9.03	n.a.	12.4
Nitrogen Use	9.94	5.25	23.87	8.22	6.94	9.50	4.46	9.91

*These numbers are for 1963-1974.

Source: Official publications.

TABLE 2

ANNUAL CHANGE IN PER CAPITA CONSUMPTION AND SELF-SUFFICIENCY RATIOS FOR MAJOR FOOD COMMODITIES IN THE ECWA (Economic Commission for Western Asia) REGIONS 1970 - 1977

Commodity	Self-sufficiency ratio †					Per capita consumption	
	Average 1970-77	1970	1976	1977	Growth Rate 1970-77*	Growth Rate 1970-77*†	1977††
Wheat	57	69	54	39	-4.2	4.0	134
Rice	20	24	13	15	-13.6	2.6	21
Pulses	92	92	90	98	-0.7	6.0	10
Sugar	6	8	6	5	-6.2	4.6	35
Vegetable oils	51	50	64	37	-1.7	-0.3	6.6
Red meat	54	58	55	50	-1.8	1.3	14
Poultry	64	81	36	38	-4.7	16.1	6.7
Hen eggs	74	78	67	74	-1.5	3.8	3.4
Milk	61	65	60	56	-2.3	2.4	115.6
Fish	102	101	99	99	-0.6	-0.4	9.3

Source: Compiled and calculated from Food and Agricultural Organization printouts of agricultural production, December 1978 (unpublished).

* Exponential
† Percent
†† Kilograms

69 percent in 1970 to 39 percent in 1977 and that for rice dropped from 24 percent to 15 percent over the same period. Indeed, the trend of the self-sufficiency ratios for all major food items appears to be negative. These declines in SSRs were the result of both high per capita consumption demands for these products and other food items and low domestic capacity to produce them.[1] At present, only about half of the region's food requirements are met from domestic sources.[2] Between 1970 and 1977, the food imports of nine Arab oil-producing states rose from $850 million to $5.6 billion.[3]

Massive food imports sold at subsidized prices depressed local production because domestic farmers were unable to compete with the flood of imports. Arab farmers also faced higher production costs, as the heavy emphasis on urban industrial development and on infrastructural investments lured the rural population into urban centers and diverted capital and investment away from agriculture. The figures in Table 3 clearly indicate the rapid and unbalanced (unsynchronized) urbanization going on in the Arab world and those in Table 4 point to an obvious tilt away from agriculture in investment planning. South Yemen and Somalia are the only Arab states where investment allocations to agriculture exceeded the share of any other single sector.

The importance of agriculture to the Arab economies (oil-exporting or otherwise), however, is not to be underestimated. Improvements in the food security position of the Arab world have obvious implications for a number of critical issues, not least of which is the bargaining power of OAPEC vis-à-vis the western oil-importing nations. Besides, agriculture is the major foreign exchange earner for most of the Arab non-oil-producing states and accounts for a significant share of income and employment in these states. It is also worth noting that the economic development of the United Kingdom, the United States, Japan, and almost all other present-day industrial countries began in the sector of agriculture, which in due course provided a marketable surplus of raw materials for their industry and of food for their industrial workers, as well as the purchasing power that enabled the rural areas to buy the industrial goods produced. Thus,

TABLE 3

ARAB URBAN POPULATION
SHARE IN TOTAL POPULATION

(Percent)

Country	1970	1977
Algeria	49.1	53.7
Egypt	42.3	43.9
Iraq	58.4	65.7
Jordan	49.6	52.9
Kuwait	--	--
Lebanon	61.8	69.8
Libya	33.2	44.0
Morocco	34.6	37.4
Oman	--	--
Qatar	79.7	83.7
Saudi Arabia	48.7	59.0
Syria	43.5	46.7
Tunisia	44.0	48.0
UAE	57.4	65.3
North Yemen	6.0	7.9
South Yemen	32.1	34.4
Mauritania	12.8	23.1
Somalia	23.1	27.0
Sudan	16.0	20.0

Source: World Bank, Social Indicator Data Sheet, August, 1979.

explaining the poor performance of agricultural productivity assumes special significance.

Elements of Agricultural Labor Productivity

Generally, the agricultural output per worker may be expressed as the product of two components, namely land area per worker and land productivity, as follows (in this paper, "agricultural land" means any land that is suitable for agriculture, while

TABLE 4

INVESTMENT ALLOCATIONS IN ARAB COUNTRIES ACCORDING TO CURRENT DEVELOPMENT PLANS*

Country	Plan Duration	Total Invest. (million$)	Average Annual Invest. (million$)	Sectoral Share in Investment (%)				
				Agriculture	Mining & Manufacture	Construction	Transport & Communication	Other Sectors
Jordan	1976-80	2,308	464	5.2	30.1	11.1	19.0	34.6
UAE	1977-79	4,385	1,462	--	--	--	--	--
Tunisia	1977-81	9,790	1,958	11.9	47.3	1.2	13.6	26.0
Algeria	1974-77	27,575	6,894	11.0	24.5	8.8	9.6	46.1
Saudi Arabia	1975-80	140,346	23,391	0.9	9.6	14.6	8.1	67.3
Sudan	1977-83	6,030	1,005	22.6	28.6	--	23.7	25.0
Syria	1976-80	13,712	2,742	23.9	20.8	14.9	10.4	29.9
Somalia	1974-78	615	123	36.6	16.4	4.0	24.5	18.5
Iraq	1976-80	45,561	9,112	23.6	24.2	17.4	17.4	17.4

TABLE 4 (Continued)

Country	Plan Duration	Total Invest. (million$)	Average Annual Invest. (million$)	Sectoral Share in Investment (%)				
				Agriculture	Mining & Manufacture	Construction	Transport & Communication	Other Sectors
Oman	1976-80	3,922	784	--	--	--	--	--
Kuwait	1976-80	16,609	3,322	0.7	20.5	30.8	16.0	32.1
Lebanon	1972-77	539	90	--	--	--	--	--
Libya	1976-80	24,219	4,844	17.6	15.4	11.2	14.2	41.5
Egypt	1976-80	20,407	4,081	3.5	22.1	16.0	31.1	27.3
Morocco	1973-77	6,179	1,236	16.3	5.4	2.7	13.9	61.7
Mauritania	1976-80	206	41	--	--	--	--	--
North Yemen	1976-80	3,500	700	14.2	22.2	2.8	30.8	29.9
South Yemen	1974-79	216	43	35.0	10.0	--	25.0	30.0

*This distribution is according to the preliminary plans, i.e. before the final adjustments took place.
Note: There are no development plans in Djibouti, Bahrain, or Qatar.
Source: Official publications.

"arable land" means land that is actually used for agricultural purposes):

$$Y/L = (A/L)\ (Y/A)$$

where

Y = Agricultural output	Y/L = Labor productivity
L = Labor	A/L = Land area per worker
A = Agricultural or Arable Land	Y/A = Land productivity

Thus, labor productivity in agriculture can be improved by the use of two different sets of methods: those (e.g., mechanization and land reclamation techniques) that increase the land available for farming per worker, and/or those (e.g., the use of fertilizer and new seed varieties) that increase output per unit of land.

The relative contributions of these two productivity components in the Arab world may be assessed from Table 1 above. Thus, the high agricultural labor productivity growth rate in Lebanon is the result of strong growth in both factors, but the first factor is more prominent. Sudan's moderately high growth rate, however, is the result of higher yield per hectare. Syria's problems are the result of the decrease of its land area per worker, as land productivity is relatively acceptable. However, slow growth in agricultural labor productivity in Algeria, Egypt, and Iraq is due to poor performances in both factors.

The Hayami-Ruttan Findings

In a number of influential studies, Hayami and Ruttan (H-R) (1971, 1973) have argued with the help of the theory of induced innovation, using the concept of the "innovation possibility curve" developed by Ahmad (1966, 1967A, 1967B), that the success of the United States' and Japan's initial as well as later development of agriculture can be attributed to the way in which innovation occurred in response to the relative factor scarcities in each of the two economies. This paper will discuss the extent to which the H-R hypothesis is consistent with the experience of

Arab agriculture. In particular we wish to examine: (a) the extent of induced innovation that has taken place in agriculture in some of the Arab countries, (b) the extent to which these countries have been successful in their agricultural development, and (c) whether (a) can explain (b). For this let us first present the major findings of H-R.

Japan and the United States are characterized by extreme differences in factor endowments. In 1880, the total amount of agricultural land per male farm worker was 36 times larger in the United States than in Japan. This difference has widened over time with the opening of more land in the western United States for agricultural purposes. By 1960, the total amount of agricultural land per male farm worker was 97 times larger in the United States than in Japan. Naturally, the relative prices of land and labor differed in the two countries. In 1880, a Japanese farm worker had to work 9 times as many days as a U.S. farm worker in order to purchase a hectare of arable land. This difference has also widened over time, particularly between 1880 and 1920, when the wages of labor rose more sharply relative to the price of land in the United States. By 1960, a Japanese farm worker had to work 30 times as many days as his U.S. counterpart to acquire a hectare of arable land.

Despite these marked differences in factor endowments and factor prices, both countries experienced rapid and persistent rates of growth in agricultural productivity throughout the entire period of eighty years between 1880 and 1960. This has been ascribed by Hayami and Ruttan (1971, 1973) to the two nations' remarkable adaptation of agricultural technology to suit their contrasting factor endowments. Japan employed biological (including chemical) innovations, whereas U.S. farmers focused more on mechanical methods. In both cases, the process of innovation increased the efficiency of whichever factor was scarce in the given country. Only in the last several decades has there been technological convergence of the two countries, with the United States making greater use of biological methods and Japan rapidly assimilating mechanical technology.

Hayami and Ruttan marshall two types of evidence to support

their contentions. First, they show that there is a link between high agricultural productivity and high output per hectare in Japan and between high productivity and a high land area per worker in the United States. The second type of evidence comes from the results obtained by testing the hypothesis that variations in factor proportions (land-labor, power-labor, and fertilizer-land ratios) are explained by variations in factor price ratios.

Although H-R place strong emphasis on the ability of Japan and the United States to acquire the appropriate "modern" technology to expand productivity in agriculture, they do not distinguish between "modern" (e.g., machinery/power and fertilizer) and "traditional" (e.g., land and labor) inputs. Furthermore, because they were considering two highly developed and more or less "market-oriented economies," they felt no need to distinguish between market prices and true scarcity prices.

In dealing with the various countries of the Arab world, or with any developing country for that matter, this distinction cannot be avoided. The divergence of existing prices from "optimal prices" and the differences in responses of farmers to variations in traditional as opposed to modern factor proportions and their corresponding prices must be considered if one is to have a full understanding of the problems of development. In this paper emphasis will be placed on the analysis of the problem of response. Four types of responses are distinguished. First, there is the response of traditional factors to their own factor price ratios. Second, there is the response of traditional factors to the modern factor price ratios. Third, there is the response of modern factors to their own prices, and fourth, there is the response of modern factors to the factor price ratios of traditional inputs. The first and third type of responses are referred to as direct and the second and fourth type of responses are referred to as indirect.

Generally, one expects to find the following pattern of responses of factor proportions to changes in factor price ratios (see Table 5). If the relative cost of a given, say, traditional factor goes up, it seems reasonable that its use would decrease relative to that of other factors; similar considerations would hold for modern factors. If the relative cost of, say, a traditional factor were to soar,

TABLE 5

Response to / Response of	Traditional Factor Price Ratio		Modern Factor Price Ratio	
Traditional Factor Ratio			(substitute)	(complement)
	−		+	−
		(1)	(2)	
Modern Factor Ratio	(substitute)	(complement)		
	+	−	−	
		(4)	(3)	

then one would think that farmers would step up their use of those modern factors that are substitutes for the now-expensive traditional input, and decrease their use of modern inputs that are complements to the costly factor. A similar argument is obtained by exchanging the words "traditional" and "modern" for each other in the preceding sentence.

The following results emerge when these predictions are compared to the H-R findings for the United States and Japan. For the United States, all responses are generally as expected as far as the signs are concerned, but the statistical significance of the results is more notable in cases (2) and (3) than in cases (1) and (4), and invariably (4) dominates (1).

In the case of Japan, there is a striking difference between the results for modern and for traditional inputs. The sign of the responses (traditional factor proportion to traditional factor's own relative price) is the opposite of what Table 5 predicts, whereas all the other types of responses have correct signs and are generally statistically significant.

This result lends support to a stronger (more specific) version of the H-R hypothesis, namely, that agricultural productivity depends primarily on induced adjustment in modern inputs. This new formulation is especially important from the perspective of the developing countries which must compare their current performances and strategies not with the current performances and strategies of the developed economies, but with the strategies and performances of these countries when they were on the threshold of modern economic development.

Arab Agriculture

As revealed in Table 1, great disparities in productivity growth rates exist among the various Arab countries. Lebanon is at the top of the continuum, whereas Algeria, Saudi Arabia, and Iraq lie around the middle. Syria, Egypt, and Jordan are at the bottom.

The decomposition of the agricultural productivity per worker into the two components discussed earlier makes it possible to identify four distinct groups of countries each sharing roughly similar situations with respect to the two components. Thus, we shall first discuss Lebanon separately, then Alergia, Iraq, and Sudan as a group, then Egypt and Syria as another group, and finally Jordan and Saudi Arabia as a fourth group.

The rest of the tables in this paper give the results of a series of regression analyses carried out on agriculture-related annual data for the countries in these groups. Factor proportions are considered dependent variables and relative prices independent variables. Dummy variables are used to correct for the effects of major structural changes (e.g., Israeli occupation of the West Bank in 1967 and the sharp increase in oil prices in 1973). In these tables, the numbers in parentheses are t-statistics (each one is a measure of the statistical significance of the regression coefficient above it), R^{-2} is the coefficient of multiple determination corrected for degrees of freedom (a measure of the goodness of fit of an assumed model as a whole), SEE is the standard error of estimate, and DW(d) is the Durbin-Watson statistic (the value of which indicates the presence or absence of serious autocorrelation). Except where we state otherwise, we will be referring only to the ordinary least squares (OLS) regression results. Statistical significance of regression coefficients will be determined by two-tailed t-tests at the 10 percent level of significance.

Lebanon. The high rate of growth of productivity in Lebanese agriculture separates Lebanon from the rest of the Arab countries. Lebanon is a small country that has a decentralized open economy with limited government intervention in agricultural decision-making processes, a relative abundance of water, a temperate climate, high educational levels, and extensive western connections. Thus, it is to be expected that farmers in Lebanon would assimilate proper modern inputs promptly and efficiently.

The regression results for Lebanon in Tables 6-9 indicate rather clearly that variations in relative prices of inputs explain much of the variations in factor proportions. Almost 93 percent of the variations in agricultural land per worker in Lebanon are explained by variations in the price ratios of tractors to labor and of fertilizers to labor.

The results in Tables 6 and 7 indicate that the use ratios of traditional inputs seem to respond to variations in the prices of modern inputs in ways consistent with the usual concepts of rational economic behavior. However, the statistical significance of the regression coefficients linking factor proportions to relative prices is not uniform. For instance, the coefficient of the effect of the ratio of the price of tractors to wages on the amount of agricultural land per worker has a small t-statistic (indicating statistical insignificance), whereas the corresponding coefficient for the ratio of the price of fertilizers to wages is just barely significant, with a t-statistic of about 2.

Modern inputs such as tractors and fertilizers are shown in Tables 6 and 7 as responding correctly but weakly to their own relative prices and generally wrongly to competitive modern inputs. Specifically, the number of tractors per worker responds correctly to its own price ratio, but the response is not statistically significant (the t-statistic is below 1). More disturbing, however, is the fact that the response of tractors per worker to the price of fertilizer (a competitive input) relative to wages is not only in the opposite direction from what is expected but has a coefficient that is statistically significant. The same sign results hold for the use of

TABLE 6
LEBANON 1961-1974

NATURAL LOG DATA	COEFFICIENTS OF PRICE OF:			R^2	R^{-2}	SEE	DW
	TRACTORS RELATIVE TO WAGES	FERTILIZER RELATIVE TO WAGES	INTERCEPT	ORDINARY LEAST SQUARES REGRESSION			
Agricultural Land Relative to Labor	-.14290 (.392)	-.40876 (2.022)	2.9944 (1.267)	.935	.923	.064	.950
Arable Land Relative to Labor	-.13221 (.284)	-.50768 (1.967)	3.5452 (1.174)	.926	.913	.082	.806
Number of Tractors Relative to Labor	-.60448 (.914)	-.70535 (1.922)	9.9898 (2.327)	.952	.943	.117	1.723
Fertilizer Relative to Arable Land	-1.3374 (.913)	-.15056 (.185)	15.391 (1.619)	.748	.703	.258	1.432

TABLE 7
LEBANON 1961-1974

NATURAL LOG DATA	COEFFICIENTS OF PRICE OF:			COCHRANE ORCUTT REGRESSION			
	TRACTORS RELATIVE TO WAGES	FERTILIZER RELATIVE TO WAGES	INTERCEPT	R^2	R^{-2}	SEE	DW
Agricultural Land Relative to Labor	.81156E-01	-.37512E-01	1.0018	.058	-.131	.021	.965
	(.781)	(.516)	(1.408)				
Arable Land Relative to Labor	.45005E-01	-.24315E-01	2.1189	.014	-.183	.024	.965
	(.374)	(.290)	(2.555)				
Number of Tractors Relative to Labor	-.11598	-1.0682	7.1212	.977	.972	.088	2.184
	(.229)	(3.666)	(2.182)				
Fertilizer Relative to Arable Land	-1.7929	.55787E-01	18.451	.603	.524	.255	1.679
	(1.167)	(.062)	(1.858)				

fertilizers per hectare — the relationship to the factor's own relative cost is negative and insignificant, and the relationship to the cost of the other modern factor is negative (it should be positive) but insignificant.

Since Lebanon is small, land scarcity is bound to be very important in explaining farmers' responses. The regression results in Tables 8 and 9 take this influence into account. They indicate that there are significant and correct responses in the use of tractors (a modern input) to the proxy variable measuring land scarcity (land area per worker). Specifically, the number of tractors per worker is positively related to the land per worker variable and the coefficient linking these two variables is highly significant statistically. Over 97 percent of the variation in the dependent variable here is explained by the model associated with Table 8. Moreover, the signs of the response of tractors per worker to relative price changes in fertilizer and tractors are now correct, although the t-statistics are not very large.

This model goes a long way in explaining the Lebanese success in agriculture. The successful introduction of mechanization explains much of the high growth rate of productivity in Lebanese agriculture. The growth rate of land yield in Lebanon was relatively high during 1961-76 (see Table 1), but did not contribute to the growth in output per worker as much as did the growth in land area per worker, where mechanization played a significant role.

The second model (the one including land per worker as an independent variable) dealing with the use of fertilizers per hectare (see Table 8) does not appear to be as good as the second model dealing with tractors per worker. Only 27 percent of the variations in the dependent variable are explained by the model, and the signs of the relevant response coefficients are inconsistent with economic theory.

Algeria, Iraq, and Sudan. This group of countries is characterized by relatively high rates of growth of total agricultural production and only moderate growth rates in agricultural productivity. Furthermore, they are characterized by falling land area per worker and modest productivity growth rates of yield per hectare (see Table 1).

TABLE 8

LEBANON 1961-1974

NATURAL LOG DATA	COEFFICIENTS OF PRICE OF:			ORDINARY LEAST SQUARES REGRESSION				
	TRACTORS RELATIVE TO WAGES	FERTILIZER RELATIVE TO WAGES	ARABLE LAND RELATIVE TO LABOR	INTERCEPT	R^2	R^{-2}	SEE	DW
Number of Tractors Relative to Labor	-.46004	-.15073	1.0925	6.1168	.980	.974	.078	2.274
	(1.032)	(.526)	(3.794)	(2.000)				
Fertilizer Relative to Arable Land	-1.2002	.37648	1.0381	11.710	.776	.708	.255	1.487
	(.825)	(.402)	(1.104)	(1.173)				

TABLE 9

LEBANON 1961-1974

NATURAL LOG DATA	COEFFICIENTS OF PRICE OF:				COCHRANE ORCUTT REGRESSION			
	TRACTORS RELATIVE TO WAGES	FERTILIZER RELATIVE TO WAGES	ARABLE LAND RELATIVE TO LABOR	INTERCEPT	R^2	R^{-2}	SEE	DW
Number of Tractors Relative to Labor	-.52013E-01	-.59898	.79932	4.4351	.995	.993	.054	1.538
	(.184)	(3.120)	(4.678)	(2.350)				
Fertilizer Relative to Arable Land	-1.8656	.65587	.89256	16.393	.618	.490	.261	1.577
	(1.187)	(.545)	(.742)	(1.545)				

The (OLS) regression models not employing land-per-worker as an independent variable seem to fit best for Iraq out of the three countries. For example, 96 percent of the variation in arable land per worker is explained by variations in relative factor prices. Changes in the relative price of tractors seem to induce the correct response in arable land per worker but the statistical significance of the coefficient is rather low. Fertilizer price changes invoke the wrong response and have a statistically significant coefficient. Thus, this traditional input ratio seems to be sensitive to price variations of the modern inputs, but when the response appears correct the statistical significance of the relevant coefficient is small and when the response is incorrect the statistical significance of its associated coefficient is very high.

The response of modern inputs in Iraq to their own prices is mixed. Tractors appear to respond positively and thus incorrectly to their own prices but the coefficient has little statistical significance, whereas fertilizer responds correctly to its own price and the coefficient has high statistical significance. The cross-price elasticity results for the modern inputs are also problematic. The cross-price elasticity of demand for tractors per worker with respect to the relative price of fertilizer appears negative, suggesting that tractors and fertilizer are complements; but the cross-price elasticity of demand for fertilizers per hectare with respect to the relative price of tractors appears positive, suggesting that the two commodities are substitutes. However, the statistical significance of the first result is high while that of the second result is very low.

In the case of Algeria, the observed responses of factor proportions to price changes in these factors are mostly weak, usually statistically insignificant, and generally of the wrong sign. The R^{-2} of the agricultural land per worker model is negative and so is that for the arable land per worker model. The R^{-2} values for the models dealing with use variations in modern inputs with respect to modern input prices are at least positive but still quite low. None of the coefficients in the model for tractors per worker is statistically significant. The model for fertilizer per hectare has somewhat better fit (R^{-2} is close to 56 percent); most of the coefficients have correct signs, and the coefficient of the "own-price" variable is statistically significant.

In Sudan, the reverse situation is observed. Traditional inputs appear to respond correctly to variations in modern input prices and some of the coefficients linking these variables are statistically significant. R^{-2} is nearly 72 percent in the model for arable land per worker. However, in the case of the models for the responses of modern inputs to their own prices or those of substitutes, the R^{-2} values are low and the signs are generally wrong. For instance, tractors per worker seem to respond positively to increases in their own relative price and negatively with respect to increases in the relative price of fertilizers; the R^{-2} is below 32 percent. Fertilizer per hectare exhibits a correct and statistically significant response to variations in its own price but reacts wrongly to the relative price of tractors. The R^{-2} of this model is barely above 30 percent.

Summarizing our findings for this group, we find the following general pattern of responses by factor proportions to variations in relative factor prices. Tractors per worker appear to be the variable that is frequently responding wrongly to its own relative price or to the relative prices of competitive and complementary inputs. However, the response of fertilizer per hectare appears generally correct and the associated regression coefficients are sometimes statistically significant. These results are consistent with the observed relative success in increasing yield per hectare and the declines in land area per worker in these states. Sudan's success as indicated by its respectable growth rate in land productivity is also partly due to the clear and systematic response of traditional inputs to changes in the relative prices of modern inputs.

Syria and Egypt. Syria and Egypt are characterized by extreme differences in their relative endowments of land and labor. Syria, which in 1963 had thirty-four times more land per worker than Egypt, also had about three times as many tractors per worker, but was using only one-fiftieth as much fertilizer per hectare in the same year. In the late 1960s, however, Syria experienced a rapid deterioration in its ratio of land per worker and this was accompanied by a rise in fertilizer per hectare from one-fiftieth of the Egyptian use per hectare to one-twentieth.

Egypt's agricultural output grew at an average annual rate of 2.2 percent between 1961 and 1976, whereas that of Syria only grew at the rate of 1.7 percent (see Table 1). Productivity fell in both countries, however, as the number of agricultural workers increased more rapidly than output. This suggests that these countries' difficulties in the agricultural sector may be due in part to problems outside agriculture, namely the failure of other sectors to absorb the increasing population. As far as farmers' responses to market prices are concerned, Egypt presents an interesting case. Traditional input proportions appear to be insensitive to modern input relative prices. However, the use of modern inputs such as tractors and fertilizer seems to respond to modern-input prices. More than 87 percent of the variation in the number of tractors per worker is explained by variations in the price of tractors relative to wages and of fertilizer relative to wages. The sign of the response of tractors per worker to the price of tractors relative to wages is correct but the coefficient is statistically insignificant, whereas the sign of the response coefficient of tractors per worker to the price of fertilizer relative to wages is wrong but highly significant.

The amount of fertilizer used per hectare appears sensitive to the relative prices of modern inputs; 58 percent of the variation in the former are explained by the latter. Morever, the sign of the response of the quantity of fertilizer per hectare to the price of fertilizers relative to wages is correct, and the associated coefficient is statistically significant. The sign of the coefficient of fertilizer-usage response to the relative price of tractors is correct but the coefficient is statistically insignificant.

In view of the high rate of population growth in Egypt, the relative fixity of the amount of land available for agricultural use, and the unavailability of a reliable data series on the price of land, land per worker was used ás a proxy variable in the second set of regression models for modern factor proportions. The results indicate that the explanatory power of the tractors per worker model falls whereas that for fertilizer per hectare rises. The R^{-2} of the former falls to 86 percent (the coefficient for land per worker is statistically insignificant), whereas the R^{-2} of fertilizer per worker rises to 80 percent (the sign of the land per worker coefficient is correct and its statistical significance is high).

The Syrian results presented in Tables 10-13 reveal a somewhat different pattern. Agricultural land per worker responds correctly to the price of fertilizer relative to wages and to the price of tractors relative to wages. However, whereas the former coefficient is statistically significant, the latter is not.

Tractors per worker respond incorrectly to the price of tractors relative to wages and correctly to the price of fertilizer relative to wages. Both coefficients are statistically significant. On the other hand, the ratio of fertilizer per hectare responds correctly to the relative prices of both tractors and fertilizer and both coefficients are almost statistically significant at the 10 percent level of significance.

The coefficients for the political dummy variable introduced in all the models of Table 10 are statistically insignificant, which indicates that political influences had no serious impact on farmers' decision-making processes.

The introduction of land per worker as a proxy variable for land scarcity into the modern input models improves the statistical and economic properties of the models (see Table 12). Tractors per worker appear to respond positively to an increase in land per worker and the coefficient is almost significant at the 10 percent level of significance. Fertilizer per hectare responds negatively to greater availability of land per worker and the coefficient is almost statistically significant at the 10 percent level of significance.

The Syrian pattern of response is one of sensitivity of traditional inputs to modern input prices and limited response of modern inputs to modern-input relative prices, with tractors representing the input that is generally the basic source of the response incongruities. In Egypt, traditional inputs appear to be insensitive to variations in relative prices of modern inputs, but the use of fertilizer per hectare is fairly strongly related to modern input prices. Tractors again are the major source of confusion in the results.

TABLE 10
SYRIA 1963-1976

NATURAL LOG DATA	COEFFICIENTS OF PRICE OF:			ORDINARY LEAST SQUARES REGRESSION				
	TRACTORS RELATIVE TO WAGES	FERTILIZER RELATIVE TO WAGES	DUMMY	INTERCEPT	R^2	R^{-2}	SEE	DW
Agricultural Land Relative to Labor	-.86213 (.838)	.63086 (3.042)	-.72333E-01 (.180)	5.7767 (1.743)	.617	.503	.206	1.172
Arable Land Relative to Labor	-.11073 (.102)	.63476 (2.887)	-.10862 (.255)	3.9901 (1.136)	.502	.352	.219	1.170
Number of Tractors Relative to Labor	1.9068 (2.142)	.34931 (1.946)	.19211 (.553)	3.5537 (1.239)	.744	.668	.178	1.417
Fertilizer Relative to Arable Land	2.9049 (1.441)	-.58273 (1.433)	-.32280 (.410)	-10.091 (1.553)	.514	.368	.404	.508

TABLE 11
SYRIA 1963-1976

NATURAL LOG DATA	COEFFICIENTS OF PRICE OF:			COCHRANE ORCUTT REGRESSION				
	TRACTORS RELATIVE TO WAGES	FERTILIZER RELATIVE TO WAGES	DUMMY	INTERCEPT	R^2	R^{-2}	SEE	DW
Agricultural Land Relative to Labor	-.16760 (.182)	.36448 (1.497)	-.11208 (.352)	2.9743 (.989)	.236	-.018	.174	1.744
Arable Land Relative to Labor	.85042 (.932)	.34744 (1.443)	-.24617 (.794)	.25998 (.087)	.223	-.036	.173	1.837
Number of Tractors Relative to Labor	1.9332 (2.040)	.34434 (1.513)	-.20259 (.587)	-3.6490 (1.178)	.651	.535	.181	1.956
Fertilizer Relative to Arable Land	-.13550 (.113)	-.39566 (1.449)	-.12440 (.410)	1.4131 (.339)	.315	.086	.197	1.027

TABLE 12

SYRIA 1963-1976

NATURAL LOG DATA   COEFFICIENTS OF PRICE OF: ORDINARY LEAST SQUARES REGRESSION

	TRACTORS RELATIVE TO WAGES	FERTILIZER RELATIVE TO WAGES	ARABLE LAND RELATIVE TO LABOR	DUMMY	INTERCEPT	R^2	R^{-2}	SEE	DW
Number of Tractors Relative to Labor	1.9503	.99658E-01	.39329	-.14939	-5.1230	.804	.716	.165	1.083
	(2.371)	(.444)	(1.649)	(.464)	(1.820)				
Fertilizer Relative to Arable Land	2.8202	-.96990E-01	-.76523	-.40592	-7.0372	.597	.418	.388	.786
	(1.457)	(.184)	(1.364)	(.536)	(1.062)				

TABLE 13

SYRIA 1963-1976

NATURAL LOG DATA	COEFFICIENTS OF PRICE OF:				COCHRANE ORCUTT REGRESSION				
	TRACTORS RELATIVE TO WAGES	FERTILIZER RELATIVE TO WAGES	ARABLE LAND RELATIVE TO LABOR	DUMMY	INTERCEPT	R^2	R^{-2}	SEE	DW
Number of Tractors Relative to Labor	.11736	.33922E-01	.93023	.22967E-01	.45624		.899	.848	.076	1.068
	(.242)	(.303)	(7.625)	(.194)	(.273)				
Fertilizer Relative to Arable Land	-.36345	-.50588	.38144	-.47493E-01	.91044		.398	.098	.193	1.072
	(.302)	(1.742)	(1.180)	(.153)	(.229)				

Thus, although traditional input proportions in Egypt may justifiably be treated as exogenous given their lack of response to other input prices, there appears to be a significant adjustment in Syria and Egypt to modern input prices, particularly to the relative price of fertilizer. The ability of farmers to adjust their use of tractors in response to their relative price appears questionable in both countries but it should be recalled that farmers in Syria and Egypt during the study period had limited ownership of these machines, which are primarily owned by the government and often improperly allocated.

The poor record of agricultural productivity in both countries appears therefore to be related to the disproportionate rise in agricultural laborers (3.61 percent per year in Syria and 2.38 percent per year in Egypt; see Table 1) and the failure of other sectors in the economy to absorb them; the decline in productivity may also be partly due to poor pricing and management of modern inputs by cooperatives and governments.

Saudi Arabia and Jordan. The loss of the relatively fertile West Bank to Israeli occupation brought about a severe decline in agricultural output in Jordan. Agricultural production fell at an average annual rate of 4.1 percent between 1961 and 1976. In Saudi Arabia, agricultural production appears to have increased at a rate of 1.6 percent per year over the same period, but to have declined at a rate of 6.9 percent per year between 1965 and 1972.

Jordan's agricultural output declines are also related to land yield declines, and the same is true for Saudi Arabia. The latter country, however, has experienced rapid increases in arable land per worker (about 2.9 percent per year between 1961 and 1976), and a high rate of growth in tractors (more than 9.5 percent per year between 1965 and 1972).

Generally, agricultural input proportions in Saudi Arabia appear to move in directions opposite to those predicted by economic theory when land scarcity is not introduced into the regression models. Perhaps more important is the fact that this incorrect behavior is sometimes statistically significant. Instances of incorrect behavior appear for both modern and traditional inputs, although it is more evident for traditional inputs.

When a Cochrane-Orcutt adjustment for serial autocorrelation is carried out and land per worker is included as an independent variable, significant changes emerge in the regression results. First, some modern inputs respond correctly to relative prices. Second, the equation for tractors per worker displays excellent statistical properties with R^{-2} approaching 99 percent. However, the coefficient for land per worker has an extremely high statistical significance and a wrong sign in both the tractors per worker and the fertilizer per hectare models.

The Jordanian results are less meaningful than those for the other countries in view of the major shock in 1967. We have tried to account for this by using a dummy variable; its coefficient turned out to be significant in some of the models tested. Generally, Jordanian farmers appear to respond weakly but often correctly to relative price changes.

Conclusion

The record of agricultural productivity in the Arab world during the 1960s and 1970s is mixed. The massive oil revenues of the 1970s appear to have exacerbated the difficulties of Arab agriculture in both the oil-producing and the non-oil Arab economies.

The most important influences can be grouped into two categories: those from within the agricultural sector itself and those arising outside agriculture.

The success of Lebanese agriculture is attributable mainly to successful mechanization and the rapid decline in the active population in agriculture. On the other hand, the modest performance of agriculture in Algeria, Iraq, and Sudan is explained by the successful adoption of fertilizers and chemicals (which raised the productivity of land) and the simultaneous failure to extend the area of cultivation per worker, due perhaps to tractorization policies that were improperly applied and/or to the unmanaged increase in the pressure of the rural population on agricultural land.

The productivity declines in Egypt and Syria are again attributable to difficulties in assimilating tractors and to increased population sizes. Egypt appears to have adjusted rather successfully in its use of fertilizers, whereas Syria was only partially successful in this regard. Finally, Saudi Arabia and Jordan appear to suffer from a number of difficulties that have compromised their productivity performance. Jordan lost the fertile land of the West Bank in 1967 to Israeli occupation, whereas limited water supplies in Saudi Arabia place a choking constraint on its ability to increase agricultural production.

In general, however, Arab farmers, whether in Egypt, Sudan, Syria, or Jordan, appear to respond correctly and clearly to a subset of factor prices. When their response is not correct or clear, factors outside agriculture appear to have precluded correct behavior on their part.

NOTES

1 These figures are for the ECWA (Economic Commission for Western Asia) region only, but are indicative of the situation in the Arab world as a whole. The ECWA region includes the Fertile Crescent, the Gulf states, Saudi Arabia, and the two Yemens.
2 Economic Commission for Western Asia, "Regional Food Security," *Agriculture and Development,* No. 2 (May 1979), pp. 71-76.
3 U.S. Department of Agriculture as quoted in the *Middle East Economic Digest,* Vol. XXII, No. 30 (July 28, 1978), p. 13.

REFERENCES

Ahmad, Syed (June 1966), "On the Theory of Induced Invention," *The Economic Journal,* 76, pp. 344-357.

Ahmad, Syed (September 1967A), "Reply to Professor Fellner," *The Economic Journal,* 77, pp. 664-665.

Ahmad, Syed (December 1967B), "A Rejoinder to Professor Kennedy," *The Economic Journal,* 77, pp. 960-963.

Ahmad, Syed and Atif Kubursi (1978), "Induced Adjustment and the Role of Agriculture," in *Technology Transfer and Change in the Arab World,* (A.B. Zahlan ed.) Oxford, Pergamon Press, pp. 293-315.

Arrow, Kenneth (June 1968), Comment, *American Economic Review,* 58, pp. 532-539.

Drandakis, E.M. and E.S. Phelps (December 1966), "A Model of Induced Invention, Growth and Distribution," *The Economic Journal,* 76, pp. 832-840.

Fellner, William (June 1961), "Two Propositions in the Theory of Induced Innovations," *The Economic Journal,* 71, pp. 305-308.

Hayami, Yujiro and Vernon Ruttan (1971), *Agricultural Development: An International Perspective,* The Johns Hopkins Press, Baltimore, Maryland.

Hayami, Yujiro and Vernon Ruttan (September-October 1970), "Factor Prices and Technical Change in Agricultural Development: The United States and Japan 1880-1960," *Journal of Political Economy,* 78, pp. 1115-1141.

Hayami, Yujiro and Vernon Ruttan (1973), "Induced Innovation in Agricultural Development," in Eliezer B. Ayal (ed.) *Micro Aspects of Development,* Praeger, N.Y., pp. 181-208.

Hicks, John R. (1932), *The Theory of Wages,* Macmillan Press, London.

Hicks, John R. (1969), *A Theory of Economic History,* Oxford University Press, London.

Kennedy, Charles (September 1964), "Induced Bias in Innovation and the Theory of Distribution," *The Economic Journal,* 74, pp. 541-547.

Kennedy, Charles (December 1967), "On the Theory of Induced Invention: A Reply," *The Economic Journal,* 77, pp. 442-444.

Mansfield, Edwin (1962), "Does the Market Direct the Relative Factor-Saving Effects of Technological Progress?," in *Rate and Direction of Inventive Activity: Economic and Social Factors,* a Report of the NBER, Princeton University Press, Princeton, New Jersey.

Rosenberg, Nathan (October 1969), "The Direction of Technological Change: Inducement Mechanisms and Focussing Devices," *Economic Development and Cultural Change,* 18, pp. 1-24.

Salter, W.E.G. (1960), *Productivity and Technical Change,* Cambridge University Press, Cambridge.

United Nations, Economic Commission for Western Asia (May 1979), "Regional Food Security," *Agriculture and Development,* No. 2, pp. 71-76.

INSTITUTIONAL MECHANISMS FOR RESOURCE DEVELOPMENT

INSTITUTION-BUILDING IN DEVELOPING
COUNTRIES *Hisham M. Nazer*

Every academic discipline has its share of confusing and contro-versial terms. A case in point is the word "institution" as it is used in the context of social science. By "institutions" is meant a social system — a (sometimes loosely structured) practice, relationship, or organization significant in a given society. The values on which such a system is based are not only subject to change, but may derive from processes which are not always rational. Indeed, the people holding the values may not even be conscious of them.

Despite their changeable and ambiguous nature, however, institutions have always played a central role throughout human history, and no one argues that they are not needed. People can be at peace with their fellows only if they are at peace with them-selves in the first place; they can be at peace with themselves only if their social relationships are governed by systems of values that are either accepted by them or forced upon them. The disintegra-tion of institutions without the evolution of new ones to replace them may cause social disruptions, sometimes culminating in war.

The need for study of the dynamics of institutions has never been more compelling. The entire world is feeling the impact of the emergence of new states, shifts in the control of resources and production, the aging of traditional values, and the birth of new ones. In such a milieu of blinding change, a better understanding of institutional developments can help enhance appreciation by one society of the actions of another more or less unfamiliar

Shaykh Hisham M. Nazer is the Minister of Planning of the Kingdom of Saudi Arabia. Educated in Egypt and the United States, Shaykh Nazer holds an MA in Political Science from UCLA. He has served with distinction in various posts in the Saudi Arabian government, including Minister of State and President of the Central Planning Organization. He has also served as Saudi Arabia's representa-tive to the Board of Governors of OPEC, and as Deputy Minister to the Ministry of Petroleum and Mineral Affairs. As President of the Central Planning Organiza-tion, Shaykh Nazer was responsible for the preparation of the first and second five-year development plans in Saudi Arabia.

society. Indeed, without a sound grasp of institutional developments an intelligent foreign policy simply cannot be constructed.

Theory vs. Reality

The relationship between the actual evolution of social entities and the theoretical analysis of social issues is not a constant one. There are times when the realm of ideas is well ahead of social realities, and then there are those times when social theories have not yet quite caught up with sweeping changes that have already taken place. In the long run, the theoretical and the real seem to balance out. In the short run, however, the pressing need to comprehend and make practical decisions about the shape and the meaning of change in the middle of change itself cannot be met by theories that may dazzle all observers by their internal consistency but are totally inapplicable to a given historical situation.

The above seemingly obvious comment points to a methodological problem of utmost theoretical and political significance. Many otherwise perceptive academics and practitioners often forget their deductive consistency is only a *necessary* condition, not a *sufficient* one, for a theory to be useful. A social theory can only be considered worthwhile if one can demonstrate that the explicit or implicit assumptions on which it is built and from which the deductive process starts are not only consistent but also relevant. Thus these assumptions must be carefully and painstakingly researched. The data on which they are based must be in hand, evident and demonstrable. Only then can a social theory have value for those eager to apply it to a specific real problem.

Needless to say, a lack of congruity between the built-in assumptions of a social theory and social reality can result in more than mere false conclusions. A mistake in the laboratory or the library is one kind of mistake. A mistake in the world outside such protected enclaves is another matter entirely. An incongruous theory can result in misery and suffering for vast numbers of people and destroy what has been gained through generations of struggle.

The foregoing criticisms extend not only to the many dangerous utopian theories for shaping societies, which are filled with assumptions utterly without basis, but also to the equally dangerous tendency to apply a theory that makes perfect sense in one society, in one set of historical conditions, to some other society where the theory is not only inappropriate but often outright harmful because of that society's different historical context. With this last point in mind, let us turn now to what can be called the era of developing countries.

The Era of Developing Countries

In the wake of World War I came the disintegration of the great European and Near Eastern empires — the Austro-Hungarian Empire, the German Empire, Tzarist Russia, and the Ottoman Empire — and the emergence of a considerable number of states, some already independent and some under the tutelage of one or another of the great powers. This process of decolonization reached its full momentum after World War II. This ushered in a period of rapid institution-building in nations that were undeveloped countries (or, as it is more often put these days, "developing countries") in terms of technology and economy.

Of course, this institution-building did not take place in a historical vacuum. On the contrary, the colonial powers had not only introduced but had actually encouraged political systems modelled more or less upon their own. Thus the polity of the Philippines closely resembled the presidential system of the United States; Kenya and Nigeria were given institutions similar to those in the United Kingdom; Vietnam, Senegal, and the Ivory Coast adopted institutions patterned after those of France.

What happened when the colonial powers left their institutional legacies and departed is only too well known. When the institutions that were so effective in London, Paris, and Washington were applied in the very different environments of the newly independent countries, chaos often resulted. Severe incongruities between so-called "general theories" and the realities of specific cases created a breach in the institutional continuity necessary for societal peace.

Reputable social scientists now see the process of institution-building in developing states in a new light. They are challenging the validity of ideological absolutism as it is manifested in the solutions imposed in many developing countries and are emphasizing the fact that the utility of any model, system, or theory varies depending on the place and time to which one is considering applying it. Unfortunately, some theoreticians are still over-eager to apply concepts developed in a particular milieu to an entirely different (and often unsuitable) arena.

Ethnocentrism

Probably the clearest demonstration of the self-satisfied myopia mentioned above can be found in the tendency of some otherwise bright students of society to judge social behavior and structures with an ethnocentric concentration on their own values and experiences. For example, there are those who decree that a "democratic" system of government is appropriate for all states at all times. Such an assumption subjects the victimized country to a variety of assaults on its legitimacy, sometimes amounting to ostracism. To express the situation in Hegelian terms, the idea of democracy was part of the objective spirit of the period following World War II, when democracies of all kinds sprang to life. Almost no government would admit that it was not "democratic" in some sense or another. A nation with alleged shortcomings in this area would feel compelled at least to demonstrate that it had plans for moving toward a democratic form of government. In this atmosphere there was hardly room for elaborating a political system for a developing country unless in some way it could be labeled as "democratic."

In view of its sometimes strident use by theoreticians, it is worth asking just what the term "democratic" really means. Our world is not uniform. Nations differ in size, culture, stage of development, age, degree of self-assertion, and so forth. Small wonder, therefore, that one finds more than one form of government that can legitimately be described as "democratic" to some degree. There appears to be broad agreement among social scientists on two almost axiomatic statements: first, that all persons are created equal; second, that governments exist to protect their citizens in the exercise of certain basic rights.

The moment that one turns from these axioms to operating norms, however, the historical dimension assumes significance. No political system has a definitive form at the moment of its inception. Change occurs over time. To reject absolutism in any form by stating that there should not be inequality, injustice, or coercion has always been only the first step in a normative approach toward making a system more humane. This is followed by a long-term evolutionary process whereby the "should-not-be" is slowly brought into the realm of the "could be." Take the example of the United Kingdom. It is reasonable to say that British democracy started with the Glorious Revolution of 1688 when Parliament established its supremacy over the King. At that time, Parliament was certainly an oligarchic institution. The landed gentry was its controlling force. It took nearly one and a half centuries of development before the Reform Act of 1832 could be passed, and it was not until 1918 that universal suffrage was achieved. Another three decades passed before plural voting was abolished. Thus the evolution of a polity often described as an exemplary democracy extended over more than two and a half centuries, and is still going on.

Even a cursory look at the widely differing forms of democracy and the evolution of political institutions in such countries as the United Kingdom enhances one's awareness of the connection between the evolution of a given political system and that system's environment. Take the factors of territorial size and population size. In the city-states of Greece these factors, among others, rendered the direct democracy system feasible. This also applies in some ways to the tribes in Saudi Arabia. Here, every man has an equal say in his tribe's general assembly. In this particular case, most observers agree that the introduction of political parties into the existing tribal system would over-strengthen the centrifugal aspects of the system and thus jeopardize the security of the state itself.

Also important to the nature and form of political systems is the fact that human beings — including scholars and politicians —

grow up in different cultures and act and react accordingly. For example, in the latter half of the nineteenth century capitalism took root in Japan without the social strife, disruption, and misery so much in evidence during the same period in England. Laissez-faire Manchester liberalism, with its attendant circumstances of worker layoffs caused by severe structural and cyclical changes, was simply unthinkable in Japan. There, entrepreneurs held a high degree of authority over the workmen, but this was coupled with responsibility for their fate and well-being. Similarly, a comparison of the family as an institution in the Middle East and in the West reveals differences that are wide and deep.

What does this mean? Institutions must be in harmony with the existing social and cultural base. Any attempt to superimpose alien economic, social, or legal structures upon indigenous cultural patterns is bound to fail; moreover, such efforts can cause severe harm and disruption in the country victimized by such imposition.

Yet another area where ethnocentric barriers can impede understanding is that of the role of religion and its relation to the state. In Saudi Arabia, Islam is a decisive and basic reality. It is an all-embracing value system that permeates and regulates every aspect of public and private life. The Koran defines and limits the powers of the public authority. Religion and the state are intimately linked in such a way that they cannot be separated. It is not surprising that the nuances of this system are poorly understood in places like Europe, much of whose constitutional history involved the struggle for the separation of the church as an institution from the state as an institution.

One more ethnocentric pitfall is provided by the issue of "freedom of the press." This freedom is only a specific form of the freedom to express opinions and concerns about subjects of public interest. In a society where most people are illiterate, freedom of the press certainly only amounts to a mere formality. Thus, what is called for is an investigation of those social institutions that take the place of the Western press in whatever culture one is studying. To what extent are people there allowed to voice opinions without prior restraint and without sanctions? This is a much more pertinent question than the one of whether or not the people have freedom of the press.

The Pitfalls of Analogizing

Everyone is familiar with arguments based on analogy. Such an argument starts with one situation (call it A), demonstrates the existence of some similarities between this situation and some other situation B, and then claims that the *exhibited* similarities between A and B justify a conclusion that certain *other* similarities also exist between A and B. This form of reasoning can be abused to make situations that are in fact very different appear similar. A case in point is the predilection of journalists to predict a dire future for Saudi Arabia on the basis of the upheaval in Iran. They usually bring up the following so-called facts in their effort to establish the similarity of Saudi Arabia and Iran: both countries were monarchies engaged in rapid modernization financed by oil resources with severe disruption of the social fabric. But consider these ways in which Iran is unlike Saudi Arabia:

(1) The population of Iran is composed of different peoples — Persians, Kurds, Arabs, Baluchis, Azerbaijanis, to name only the main ethnic groups — each speaking its own language, with only the Persians evidencing a commitment to the State of Iran.

(2) During World War II, Iran was invaded and occupied by both the Soviet Union and the Western Allies. One of the first confrontations of the Cold War took place on Iranian soil when the Soviet Union attempted to set up a Soviet Republic of Azerbaijan. By the time the attempt was aborted, a strong pro-Soviet party had been planted that was always ready to challenge the legitimacy of the rule of the Shah.

(3) Under the Shah, a political system was introduced under advice from abroad which was unable to cope with the heterogeneous political and ethnic forces in the country.

(4) The Shah alienated the *Ulema,* the *Basaris,* and finally large sections of the people.

All these factors, which contributed decisively to the political changes in Iran, are noticeably absent in Saudi Arabia. This is not to say that Saudi Arabia has no problems of its own. But to make an analogy with conditions or events in Iran does little to promote understanding of the unique character of the Saudi Arabian situation.

One could present many more modern and historical examples of poor analysis based on attempts to compare situations that are essentially incomparable. In particular, a tendency on the part of some toward careless comparisons between the People's Republic of China and socialist republics like Poland or socialist states in Africa should not go unmentioned.

Some Final Observations

What follows is a number of generalizations about institution-building in the developing world:

(1) Societies are not static. They are dynamic entities that respond to the need to adapt to changing conditions and, with them, changing priorities. Most of today's stable societies, anywhere in the world, have attained that stability over time by accommodating to change.

(2) No matter what the orientation of a country's political system, changes in social institutions normally affect their periphery, leaving the core of the institutions intact. (This is especially evident in societies where religion plays a major structural role.) For example, while the extended family may be largely replaced by the nuclear family, the obligations imposed by society on a family are likely to remain intact.

(3) In developing societies, new administrative and economic institutions seem to be the ones most likely to emerge early in the process of national development, gain immediate acceptance, and prove their worth as essential parts of the system. This process may include the usual bureaucratic struggles, but it is likely to be expedited because of compelling economic conditions or the exercise

of authority by an indigenous elite who happen to find the institutions useful.

(4) Because of the emergence of new administrative and economic institutions, a *de facto* power-sharing system evolves without formal recognition. This power-sharing may favor regionalism as opposed to centralism, or technocracy as opposed to the traditional lines of authority.

(5) An all-embracing political system that is responsive to local needs and that is a part of the indigenous culture is normally the last institution to evolve. This is not a historical accident, but rather a reflection of the dynamics of social evolution. Many ingredients are essential to the development of a mature political system; a few of the most vital are an adequate level of public education, the diffusion of power among interest groups, and an enlightened leadership. The failure of the political system to evolve, however, may lead to an upheaval that could have been avoided with more foresight.

In conclusion, it should be understood that policy decisions affecting the relationship between two societies with different cultures and configurations of institutions can only be beneficial when each of the peoples obtains an understanding of the other culture before rendering judgment. In this context, moreover, the investigation of the other culture must be more than a search for evidence to justify the assumptions of the investigator.

THE ARAB DEVELOPMENT FUNDS AND ARAB FOREIGN AID *Ibrahim M. Oweiss*

This paper will discuss the eight major Arab Funds for Third World economic development in the context of overall Arab foreign aid. The Funds are not the only developmental institutions in the Arab world. For one thing, a number of Arab nations have created banks to finance their own internal development programs. In Egypt, for example, the Agricultural Credit Bank was established in the early 1930s because the existing financial institutions, composed mainly of branches of foreign banks, were refraining from extending loans to small farmers while reaping substantial profits from a concentration on short-term financing of foreign trade. Another example is the Industrial Bank of Egypt, created after World War II to extend medium- and long-term loans to industrial projects. Other such institutions are the Industrial Bank of Kuwait, the Public (or General) Investment Fund of Saudi Arabia, the Saudi Agricultural Credit Bank, and the Saudi Real Estate Development Fund. The key difference between these institutions and the Arab Funds is the latter's focus on providing financial assistance to more than one nation.

Even in the realm of Arab foreign aid, the Funds do not stand alone. Official Development Assistance (ODA) flows from Arab donor nations to recipient countries in a variety of ways. First, there are bilateral arrangements based on direct transactions between donor and recipient authorities, i.e. between heads of state, finance or economic ministers, central banks, or even special envoys. Second, there are certain multilateral arrangements such as the Gulf Organization for the Development of Egypt

Ibrahim M. Oweiss earned a PhD in Economics at the University of Minnesota. He is presently an Associate Professor of Economics at Georgetown University. Dr. Oweiss is a member of the Board of Experts of the League of Arab States and serves as an advisor to the Arab International Bank. During 1978-79 he headed the Egyptian Economic Mission to the United States. Dr. Oweiss is the editor and a contributing author of *Energy, Oil and the Middle East* (forthcoming).

115

(GODE) established in 1977 by Saudi Arabia, Kuwait, Qatar, and the United Arab Emirates. In the same year, its total capital of $2 billion was transferred to Egypt, which was experiencing serious balance of payments deficits and even more serious problems in keeping up with interest payments on its loans. The country was as much as 120 to 180 days behind in these payments, and had been forced to borrow in the short-term capital market at rates of interest as high as 18 to 20 percent in order to be able to pay off the interest on the previous loans. GODE eased Egypt's financial crisis and helped the country to move from short-term borrowing to long-term financing at significantly lower interest rates. Third, a portion of Arab aid is provided through the intermediation of permanent national, regional, and international organizations, including the Arab Funds. Table 1 summarizes recent ODA flows from Saudi Arabia, Kuwait, Iraq, the United Arab Emirates, Libya, and Qatar to Third World countries.[1]

According to the figures provided by the World Bank, the total ODA provided by capital-surplus oil exporters was over three and a half times greater in 1979 than it had been just six years earlier; this corresponds to an average annual rate of increase of approximately 25 percent. However, ODA as a percentage of the combined gross national products of the six Arab oil-exporting countries listed above held steady at 4.5 percent in 1973 and 1974, increased to 5.8 percent in 1975 and steadily declined thereafter to 2.9 percent in 1979. The largest GNP share allocated to foreign aid was that of U.A.E. in 1973 (16 percent), followed by Qatar in 1973 and 1975 (15.6 percent), U.A.E. in 1975 (14.1 percent), U.A.E. in 1976 (11 percent), and Kuwait in 1977 (10.6 percent). By way of comparison, the share of U.S. GNP earmarked for ODA is less than 1 percent and has generally declined in recent years, going from .58 percent in 1965 to .32 percent in 1970 to .27 percent in 1975 to .19 percent in 1979.[2] For France, the corresponding figures are .76 percent, .66 percent, .62 percent, and .59 percent. In Germany and the United Kingdom, foreign assistance was between .32 and .52 percent of GNP during the same years. It should be noted that in spite of the low percentage of U.S. GNP allocated to aid, the United States still provides the highest abso-

TABLE 1

ODA FLOWS FROM CAPITAL-SURPLUS OIL EXPORTERS
TO DEVELOPING COUNTRIES

	1973		1974		1975		1976		1977		1978		1979	
	$m.	% of GNP	$m.	% of GNP	$m.	% of GNP	$m.	% of GNP	$m.	% of GNP	$m.	% of GNP	$m.	% of GNP
Saudi Arabia	305	4.0	1,029	4.5	1,997	5.4	2,407	5.7	2,410	4.3	1,470	2.8	1,970	3.1
Kuwait	345	5.7	622	5.7	976	8.1	615	4.4	1,518	10.6	1,268	6.4	1,099	5.1
Iraq	11	.2	423	4.0	218	1.7	232	1.4	61	.3	172	.8	861	2.9
U.A.E.	289	16.0	511	7.6	1,046	14.1	1,060	11.0	1,177	10.2	690	5.6	207	1.6
Libya	215	3.3	147	1.2	261	2.3	94	.6	115	.7	169	.9	146	.6
Qatar	94	15.6	185	9.3	339	15.6	195	8.0	197	7.9	106	3.7	251	5.6
	1973		1974		1975		1976		1977		1978		1979	
TOTAL	1,259	4.5	2,917	4.5	4,837	5.8	4,603	4.6	5,478	4.5	3,875	3.0	4,534	2.9

Note: Data for 1978 and 1979 are provisional.

lute amount of ODA in the world due to the huge and unmatched size of its GNP.

Turning now to the permanent institutions created by the capital-surplus oil-exporting Arab nations to channel funds to Third World countries, one finds first the Arab Funds, which offer concessionary loans to developing countries and may be institutionally divided as follows: four of these funds are directly administered by the country of origin and four are administered collectively by groups of donor countries. The former are the Kuwait Fund for Arab Economic Development, the Abu Dhabi Fund for Arab Economic Development, the Saudi Fund for Development, and the Iraqi Fund for External Development. The latter are the Arab Fund for Economic and Social Development, the Arab Bank for Economic Development in Africa, the Islamic Development Bank, and the OPEC Special Fund. (Even though the OPEC Special Fund established in 1976 is not an exclusively Arab institution, the bulk of its capital has been subscribed by capital-surplus Arab countries. Its administration and policymaking decisions are predominantly affected by Kuwait, Saudi Arabia, Qatar, U.A.E., and other Arab members of OPEC.)

Investment banks comprise a second institutional source of funds for the developing countries. These include the Arab Latin American Bank (ARLABANK) and the Saudi International Bank as well as the Union de Banques Arabes et Françaises (UBAF). This group of banks and many other American, European, and Japanese banks are commissioned with investments of Arab petrodollar surpluses. These banks do not provide concessionary loans to Third World countries but can participate in syndicated commercial loans to these countries based on competitive market rates of interest.

In addition to the above two groups, one can identify a third group through which part of Arab petrodollar surpluses is recycled. They are principally the International Monetary Fund (IMF) and the International Bank for Reconstruction and Development (World Bank). Loans extended to these organizations, which use the funds to ease severe balance of payments deficits and meet some long-term developmental needs, are not presently considered concessional because the terms and interest rates associated with such loans are comparatively close to those of the commercial loans raised by the IMF and the World Bank.

It should be noted that the money dispersed through the above three groups does not represent total Arab petrodollar surpluses, which in turn are less than Arab oil revenues. The combined net oil revenues of Saudi Arabia, Kuwait, U.A.E., Qatar, Iraq, and Libya in 1980 are estimated at $190.5 billion, whereas their combined current account surpluses amounted to $100.7 billion, approximately 53 percent of the revenues (see Tables 2 and 3). Approximately half of Arab petromoney surpluses are invested in the United States, mainly in Treasury bills, short-term investments, and deposits in American banks. Almost three-quarters of the surpluses, however, are denominated in dollars. In 1980, some 5 percent of the combined petromoney surpluses of Saudi Arabia, Kuwait, Iraq, U.A.E., Libya, and Qatar were allocated for development assistance purposes; out of this, about 40 percent was channelled through the Arab Funds. In other words, the total amount of loans and grants extended to Third World countries in 1980 by the eight Funds was $1.9 billion, representing a little less than 2 percent of the petromoney surpluses of the above six Arab oil-exporting countries for the same year. Only a small part of the surpluses was channelled through the investment banks or the international financial organizations.

The Arab Funds have extended development loans and grants to more than 50 countries, of which some 30 are in Africa. The only one of the eight Funds that is exclusively devoted to developmental programs within the Arab world is the Arab Fund for Economic and Social Development. The geographical mandate of the Abu Dhabi Fund for Arab Economic Development covers all developing countries outside of Latin America, while that of the Arab Bank for Economic Development in Africa covers all non-Arab developing African countries. The Islamic Development Bank extends developmental loans and grants to all of its member countries. The geographical mandates of the Kuwait Fund for Arab Economic Development, the Saudi Fund for Development, and the Iraqi Fund for External Development cover all developing countries, while the OPEC Special Fund aids the poorest of the developing nations. In 1980, the Arab world was the recipient of only 39 percent of total Funds disbursements,

TABLE 2

NET OIL REVENUES
(In billions of U.S. dollars)

	Saudi Arabia	Kuwait	U.A.E.	Qatar	Iraq	Libya
1974	27.9	---	---	---	6.8	6.8
1975	25.7	7.8	6.4	1.7	8.2	5.0
1976	34.3	8.7	7.8	2.0	9.5	7.5
1977	38.9	8.7	8.6	1.9	10.7	9.0
1978	36.0	9.2	8.1	2.1	23.6	8.8
1979	56.5	16.9	12.5	3.6	23.6	15.0
1980	93.0	18.6	18.7	5.4	34.6	20.2
TOTAL	312.3	69.9	62.1	16.7	117.0	72.3

TABLE 3

CURRENT ACCOUNT SURPLUSES
(In billions of U.S. dollars)

	Saudi Arabia	Kuwait	U.A.E.	Qatar	Iraq	Libya
1974	23.0	---	---	---	2.6	1.8
1975	13.9	5.9	3.2	.9	2.7	-.7
1976	13.8	7.0	3.8	.9	3.6	2.4
1977	12.8	4.8	2.9	.3	4.6	2.9
1978	.8	6.2	2.6	.9	4.0	1.8
1979	15.3	14.2	6.7	2.0	13.1	6.0
1980	40.4	16.1	12.2	3.3	19.6	9.1
TOTAL	120.0	54.2	31.4	8.3	50.2	23.3

Source: John Law, *Arab Investors, Vol. I,* Chase World Information Corporation, New York, 1980, pp. 223, 225.

while Asian countries received 32 percent and other developing nations received 29 percent. Over the period since the creation of the eight agencies, non-Arab developing nations have received more in loans and grants than their Arab counterparts.

Loan disbursements by the eight Funds have gone up; according to figures released by the Coordinating Secretariat of the Arab Fund for Economic and Social Development, they rose from $1.3 billion in 1979 to $1.9 billion in 1980, an increase of over 40 percent. As was true in 1979, the largest lender in 1980 was the Jeddah-based Islamic Development Bank ($422 million). It was followed by the Saudi Fund for Development ($331 million) and the Kuwait Fund for Arab Economic Development ($266 million). This last institution is the oldest, largest, and most diversified of the eight Funds. Its capital was doubled on February 22, 1981 to an amount equivalent to $7.4 billion; its lending capability is approximately $21 billion.

Almost two-thirds of 1980 Funds loans and grants were allocated to transportation projects (31 percent) and financing foreign trade of the recipient countries (31 percent), whereas power projects represented 18 percent of the total, followed by industrial projects (9 percent) and agriculture (7 percent). This reflects the emphasis of these development agencies on the improvement of infrastructure in the aid-receiving countries (see Table 4).

The major problems facing the Funds can be summarized as follows: the excessive duration of the project approval process, the lack of coordination among the different Funds, the failure of the Funds to take the initiative in conceiving new projects of potential benefit to Third World countries, and the low priority given to agricultural development. In spite of all these problems, the record of the Arab Funds has been impressive. The developing world still has many unmet needs, however, and in the future the Funds will undoubtedly play an even more significant role in financing development projects, given the fact that their lending capabilities amount to nearly $40 billion.

One way in which the ability of the Funds to help the Third World could be enhanced would be for them to act collectively or individually to establish advanced research institutions along the

TABLE 4

THE ACTIVITIES OF THE EIGHT ARAB FUNDS DURING 1980

(In millions of U.S. dollars)

Developing Institutions	Amount of Loans/ Grants	No. of Loans/ Grants	Beneficiary Countries	SECTORAL DISTRIBUTION						REGIONAL DISTRIBUTION			
				Transport	Power	Agriculture	Industry	Financing of Foreign Trade	Others	Arab World	Asia	Africa	Other Regions
All Institutions													
I. Loans													
- First Quarter 1980	403.52	47	--	129.20	47.44	43.75	73.14	96.46	13.53	162.17	127.00	113.60	0.75
- Second "	498.21	57	--	148.38	109.01	16.78	31.27	161.53	31.24	239.30	117.35	117.24	24.32
- Third Quarter "	481.49	36	--	142.03	41.37	19.95	5.24	261.71	11.19	125.87	172.71	177.91	5.00
- Fourth "	528.52	45	--	178.48	140.61	58.99	64.88	72.16	13.40	219.64	185.34	110.04	13.50
GRAND TOTAL	1911.74	185	--	598.09	338.43	139.47	174.53	591.86	69.36	746.98	602.40	518.79	43.57
II. Grants													
- First Quarter 1980	0.25	1	1	--	--	0.25	--	--	--	0.25	--	--	--
- Second "	5.43	7	7	0.82	0.29	1.12	--	--	3.20	1.29	1.00	3.14	--
- Third Quarter "	0.37	1	1	--	--	--	--	--	0.37	0.37	--	--	--
- Fourth "	4.76	2	2	3.93	--	--	--	--	0.83	0.83	3.93	--	--
GRAND TOTAL	10.81	11	--	4.75	0.29	1.37	--	--	4.40	2.74	4.93	3.14	--

Source: Coordinating Secretariat for the Arab Funds.

lines of Western "think tanks." Their purpose would be to conduct and finance technical feasibility studies of developmental
projects, and to provide fresh recommendations for new projects.
For example, they could investigate the merits of introducing
desert plantations in the extensive empty areas of the Arab world.
Two particularly promising possibilities here are the growing of
guayule, a desert rubber plant, and jojoba, another desert plant
whose seeds contain a liquid wax that has a potential for use in
lubricants, paper coatings, polishes, electrical insulation, carbon
paper, textiles, leather, precision castings, and pharmaceuticals.[3]
The proposed research institutions could not only cooperate with
other similar existing institutions but also coordinate research
activities among them. This initiative would enable the Arab
Funds to achieve much more in terms of Third World development with the finite lending resources at their disposal.

NOTES

[1] Robert S. McNamara, *Address to the Board of Governors,* The World Bank,
September 30, 1980, Washington, D.C., p. 13.

[2] *Ibid.,* p. 46.

[3] Ibrahim M. Oweiss, "Strategies for Arab Economic Development," *The Journal of Energy and Development,* Vol. III, No. 1, Autumn 1977, pp. 110-113.

ARAB INSTITUTIONS OF HIGHER LEARNING AND THEIR OWN MANPOWER DEVELOPMENT
Samir N. Anabtawi

Of all the institutions that have been engaged in the task of high-level manpower resource development, perhaps none has had a more significant, enduring, or pervasive role than the university. Indeed, no other social unit can rival in sheer numbers the plethora of talent it has produced, nor is there any other agency on which society so much depends for setting so many standards and certifying so many competencies in so many fields.

Curiously enough, however, universities were not, in their inception, designed to fulfill such a utilitarian role. They were loose, and in some instances somewhat informal, collegial associations designed to afford a stimulating intellectual haven for the privileged to reflect upon the verities of existence and the enduring issues of being with which man has been seized since the dawn of recorded time. There were no laboratories or research institutes; there were no credit hours or quality points; there were no comprehensives or qualifying examinations. Education was broadly conceived as the training that a person obtained for the development of his analytical faculties, the crystallization of his belief categories, the sharpening of his civic responsibilities, and the cultivation of his aesthetic sensibilities. In fact there are a great many academics today who still harken to those days of old and who lament what they deem to be the alteration of a university's fundamental mission as the noble custodian of the rational process to that of a plebeian processor of specialized cadres to perform specific tasks.

Samir N. Anabtawi holds a PhD in Political Science from Yale University. Dr. Anabtawi has an extensive background in teaching political science at several universities, including Dartmouth, the American University of Beirut, and the Fletcher School of Law and Diplomacy. He has also conducted research at Princeton, Harvard, and Tufts universities and served as advisor to the Vice Rector for Academic Affairs at Kuwait University. He has written several articles on politics in the Middle East. Dr. Anabtawi is currently Professor of Political Science at Vanderbilt University and has recently conducted research as a Visiting Scholar at the Center for Contemporary Arab Studies, Georgetown University.

125

Lamentable or not, however, for the past century or more universities have come to be viewed not as self-contained units detached from the frenzied concerns of daily life, but as indispensable and conscious agents of change toward socially targeted goals. Particularly since World War II, universities' spheres of activities have transcended those of instruction and training to encompass a search for the cures of social ills and even for the bolstering of security and national defense.

While Arab institutions of higher education have made significant strides in becoming more socially relevant, most would concede that they still lag far behind their western counterparts. Their tardiness in this regard has not been due to an innate diffidence about venturing into hitherto untested domains, nor has it been due to a visceral bias against indulging in what are deemed to be academically inappropriate concerns. Rather, it has been the result of a debilitating immobilism brought on by some fundamental features endemic to present-day Arab institutions of higher learning and by a lack of clear sets of aggregated national objectives which have been consensually integrated as highly valued norms. In fact, far from there being stable, operational, and unambiguous ideological tenors from which institutions of higher learning could take their cue, there exists a cacophony of pronouncements from which it is virtually impossible to discern a harmony of goals. It is difficult for academic institutions to plan effectively for manpower development within a context of chameleon-like objectives subsumed under such nebulous headings as Arab socialism, Islamic capitalism, or within the framework of the *jamahiriyyah* social order envisaged in Qaddafi's *Green Book*.

Compounding this malady is the absence of a distinctively Arab university legacy peculiarly suited to Arab society and from which institutions of higher learning could derive a guiding inspiration or a reassuring link with the past. Instead, what exists is an array of competing, and sometimes incongruous, traditions that have been imported from abroad and transplanted to what in some instances is infertile soil. The result is a curious diversity of institutions and academic subcultures with each leading a solitary existence and looking to its progenitor culture for nourishment and growth. Indeed, it is not uncommon to find different educational traditions operating not only within a single country but also within the framework of a single university, wherein hostile academic citadels have been erected in separate departments, colleges, and schools. Even when a particular academic mode is imported by one Arab country from another, one frequently discovers that it, too, is not entirely in tune with local aspirations or goals.

It would be hopeful if one could confer that this absence of an inherited or highly integrated university academic culture currently represents a transitory phase on the road to the development of endogenous and creative educational patterns and norms. All indications, however, point to a perpetuation and increased dependency on exogenous institutions, traditions, structures, and forms. What is happening in the Arab university community does not represent a systematic process of gestation which will ultimately give issue to an intellectual specie distinct from others around the globe. It is not at all anything akin to what preceded, say, the impressive strides made by Japan at the turn of the century.[1]

To begin with, the development of higher education, and particularly scientific and technical education, in Japan a century ago did not proceed sporadically, saltatorily, haltingly, or along segmented idiosyncratic lines. It was part and parcel of a well-orchestrated drive to catapult Japan to the forefront of the industrialized powers of the day. Nor was it merely a case of promoting knowledge for its own sake, but of acquiring the requisite analytical and scientific skills essential to place Japan along an inwardly generating and increasingly self-sustaining pace. The object was not the transfer of knowledge from abroad, but the manufacturing of it in Japan.

Secondly, the effort to transform the educational system, especially at the higher levels, for the provision of essential manpower was expended within the context of a well-conceived political program that had a fairly clear vision of the role which the Japanese leadership felt their country was destined to play. It was not a contrived agenda grafted onto the authority patterns of old, but a carefully designed part of a set of newly forged social, economic, and political linkages which aimed at recasting the entire social order along substantially different lines. There was, as it were, a constitutional settlement, epitomized in the Meiji Constitution, that facilitated the entry of new forms and afforded them a hospitable environment in which to prosper and grow.

It does not require any great measure of expertise to realize that what prevails in the Arab world today is vastly at variance with what has just been described. Far from there being any single or shared fundamental configuration within which manpower resource development at the university level can play a role, there are instead fragmented, incoherent, and blurred perceptions of the type of future polity with which institutions of higher learning must be enmeshed. In other words, instead of there being a communion of goals, what we are witness to is an array of apostasies, each pursuing its own objectives in an environment of discontinuities whose components cannot even be fused into a symbiotic form. The result is that institutions of higher learning find themselves functioning in a setting within which they have not been assigned, or cannot perceive for themselves, a specified role.

Clearly, in terms of high-level manpower resources, the number of universities, the size of the research and development pool, and the number of PhDs, the Arab world today is at a considerably greater advantage than modern Japan was in its early years. Indeed, it has been estimated that there are at present more than 27,000 Arab holders of the PhD, 50 percent of them in science and engineering, and that their number is increasing by more than 10 percent every year. This figure is "comparable . . . to that of either the USA, Germany, or the U.K. during the period from 1939 to 1945."[2] Furthermore, the "Arab world boasts 30,000 to 40,000 research workers, a number that is equivalent to a third of the world population of R&D workers in 1940."[3] Moreover, 42 percent of all university graduates in the Arab world have specialized in the physical, medical, agricultural, and engineering sciences in recent years.[4]

But if these figures are a source of pride, there are some powerfully jarring counterparts as well. Nearly half of all Arab science and engineering PhDs have left the Arab world. Despite the fact that there are nigh onto sixty universities in the Arab world, the majority of Arab doctoral education continues to take place in Europe, the United States, and the Soviet Union, with very few doctorates outside of medicine and Arab Letters being earned within the Arab world. Only two out of every five Arab researchers actually work in the Arab world. In terms of scientific activity and technical innovation the level of discovery in the Arab world of the 1980s does not even come close to the gains made in a number of western countries half a century or more ago. Measured on a per capita basis, Arab scientific output represents approximately half of one percent of that of advanced countries. To bring matters closer to home, this output is equivalent to only one percent of that of Israel. Zahlan estimates that "the average productivity of an Arab scientist, measured in scientific publications, is less than 10 percent of his counterparts elsewhere."[5]

Given these indices it is easy to see how difficult it is for institutions of higher learning to provide the necessary manpower resources for the herculean and urgent tasks which several Arab states have launched. Indeed, Arab institutions of higher learning themselves are experiencing great difficulties in satisfying their own needs and demands. Nearly every day there appear numerous advertisements in various newspapers inviting applications to fill thousands of academic posts, all the way from the Atlantic to the Gulf, and many a university administrator finds himself at wit's end trying to assemble the necessary staff to educate the growing influx of students in each freshman class.

Much of the effort at recruitment has been, naturally enough, aimed at enticing those Arabs abroad to return. Some Arab governments have even gone so far as to provide considerable incentives to encourage a homeward flow. Others have sharply increased their salary scales in a bid to attract those who might be lured primarily by the prospect of pecuniary gain.

Despite some limited successes, however, these efforts have by and large fallen short of their mark. It soon became apparent that while academics are, like others, sometimes susceptible to considerations of finance, other factors weigh more heavily in their value systems and scales. Living conditions, work facilities, hospitality of the environment to innovation, degree of academic freedom and tolerance, availability of research funding, job security, opportunities for advancement, political stability, systems of administration, the prevailing academic subculture, and many other matters have proven themselves crucial variables in the decisions of those contemplating a return.

It would be fair to say that in none of the Arab countries are all, or most, of these elements provided in ideal or tempting combinations, dosages, or forms. In fact, the accounts and experiences of those who have ventured back suggest that conditions are nowhere near those that are necessary to attract. They tell of a system of university administration that regards a faculty member not as a precious resource, but as a civil servant, a daily wage earner, or even a hired hand. They describe a pattern of evaluation that determines academic performance not by intellectual objectives attained, but by time spent. They portray an intimidating environment of subtle and crass pressures designed to breed a caution that stultifies experimentation, initiative, and creative thought. In certain instances, we are told that academic tenure is based on citizenship, and that professional rewards are determined by membership in a political party, tribe, or clan. They depict a fairly widespread system of incentives that caters to instant rather than delayed gratification — something which psychologists have long regarded as signifying a deep-seated immaturity in personality structures, relationships, and social norms.[6]

It is to be expected, of course, that institutions of higher learning, like other units within a social order, would reflect the prevailing norms in the culture of which they are a part. But there is also the expectation that a university would be somewhat different, that it would somehow transcend the evolutionary cycle of ontogeny recapitulating phylogeny.

Given the aforementioned, it is not difficult to realize why Arab institutions of higher learning do not offer an irresistible magnetism to Arab intellectuals abroad, nor is it too difficult to appreciate why the level of intellectual creativity generated by Arab academic institutions is far below what one would have expected or hoped, given the impressive pool of talent from which the Arab world theoretically can draw. In fact, one of the most disturbing features that currently characterizes Arab higher education is not so much what has been described as the brain drain, but the brain erosion that seems to be afflicting institutions of higher learning in the Arab world. I refer here to the increasing intellectual lethargy, apathy, indolence, cynicism, and resignation that one frequently encounters among academics of varying ranks. It is particularly alarming to find these debilitating maladies among the younger elements so soon after being awarded their terminal degrees. They express themselves in the paucity of research output, meagerness of serious publications, and even in the lack of familiarity with recent developments in their respective fields. In point of fact, there are very few internationally recognized and respected refereed journals or major publishing houses in the Arab world that can serve as worthy conduits for scholarly communications or merely to keep pace.

But if the Arab world is to be castigated for not fostering a truly vibrant intellectual community, then the western world must also be accorded a hefty portion of the blame. All too often one encounters young Arabs armed with degrees, some even from prestigious western institutions, who not only show little or no commitment to their callings, but who also can hardly demonstrate a reasonable grasp of their specialized fields. What these foreign universities do not seem to realize is that far from aiding the Arab world in its developmental aspirations and launching it on the path of self-sustained growth, they are in reality accentuating its academic subservience and perpetuating its dependence on outside educational centers and consultants from abroad. For in their certification of competence they instill in certain Arab circles a false self-confidence and an illusion of self-sufficiency which cause them to embark on a variety of projects and programs for which they are in fact ill-prepared.

It is worth noting in this regard that this educational and socioeconomic dependence is considerably more sinister than meets the eye. It triggers certain ideological mechanisms which not only idealize the characteristics associated with western talent, but which also place a correspondingly low valuation on indigenous capabilities and their capacity to measure up to the rigorous standards that are perceived to be inherent in western skills and thought.[7] In other words, it produces an almost chronic psychological dependence whose ultimate consequence is a self-degradation that commits the entire culture to a denigrating form of self-deprecation and inward distrust. Manifestations of this self-doubt are apparent in the fairly prevalent disposition to employ westerners, sometimes mediocre ones, to proffer expertise and advice, over equally or more qualified Arabs, and at a considerably higher price. In academic circles we even find the curious spectacle of Arab students going to western universities to learn about Islamic institutions, history, and thought.

These psychological elements do not cohere independently, however, but are reinforced by structural relationships between the Arabs and the outside world, which isolates the former's institutions of higher learning and keeps them at best on the periphery of the huge and costly undertakings that are changing the entire character of Arab life. I refer here to the hundreds of billions of dollars' worth of projects that dot the Arab landscape which are supposed to create new economic vistas for the rank and file. It would be fair to say that rarely are Arab institutions of higher learning enmeshed in these gigantic tasks. There is nothing akin to the complex web of relationships which exists between universities, governments, and industries as we know it in the West. Nor is there anything resembling the applied research activity carried on by western universities under the sponsorship of a government or a firm. Most of the major contracts are awarded to foreign enterprises which, when in need of expertise, turn to their research units and academic institutions back home. Some of these contracts are what are termed "turnkey" deals —agreements whereby a company assumes charge of an entire project and is only obligated to present the "keys of ownership" to the sponsoring agency at a specified time. The company is free to subcontract, hire, manage, organize, and pay in any manner it sees fit. Indeed, in some instances it even takes charge of staffing and running the enterprise long after the project is complete. Given the disposition of foreign companies to give preference to their own nationals and to fellow national corporations with which they have previously dealt, it is easy to see how little of an educational, managerial, scientific, or technical legacy accrues to the local population once the foreigners have left. And even when local Arab subcontractors are afforded a role, it quickly becomes apparent that there is an inherent division of labor which assigns them the relatively low-level technical activity, while the patron company arrogates for itself the complex tasks.[8]

All these structural and other factors, however, cannot serve as effective and convincing apologia for all that ails Arab institutions of higher learning and their failure to measure up to the demands of a highly expectant Arab world. True enough, there are certain impediments that arise from a political and social order that sometimes views having a university not as an effective, or indeed, vital element of constructive social change, but as part and parcel of the tangible and innocuous trappings of sovereignty, such as a national anthem or a flag. Nor is there any appreciation that a university is a defenseless and fragile institution that can be easily demoralized and wrecked. It does not require an army to throttle it or to sap it of all intellectual creativity and strength. But it does require considerable latitude and protection to prosper and thrive.

Still, even within the social and political parameters that circumscribe them, there is much that Arab institutions of higher learning can do for themselves. Tightening of academic requirements, more rigorous standards for evaluation and accreditation, reduction in the output of graduates in already overcrowded specializations, and cultivation of a faculty subculture entirely at variance with what currently prevails would go a long way toward alleviating the rampant mood of ennui that one seems to encounter at every turn. None of these, however, can be attained within the current system of university management which seems to be widespread in the Arab world. Indeed, the term "management" is an inappropriate description of the controlling mechanisms which are, in reality, employed. For what we have is a cumbersome and unwieldy pattern of administration whose central features are the scribe and clerk, and whose overriding ethic is based on suspicion and mistrust. It found a splendidly appropriate and hospitable culture in Egypt, where it underwent innumerable mutations over thousands of years on the way to perfecting itself. Anyone who has been ensnared by it can fully appreciate the enervating sense of despair it can instill. It is tragic that one finds it already entrenched in new and fledgling institutions of higher learning, particularly in the Gulf, even though Egypt itself is desperately struggling to break these same administrative shackles that have bound it to its present state.

Unless these and other measures are adopted, there is little that institutions of higher learning can do to improve their lot, or the lot of others, or indeed to keep academic pace. They will remain removed from the frontiers of knowledge and relegated to being intellectual and scientific centers that are not worthy of the name. In fact, there are already Arab colleges and universities that are nothing more than glorified high schools, or even adult day care centers, aimed at occupying and pacifying the youth. The incalculable harm they can generate is something which many Arabs seem to refuse to fathom or to confront. But unless these issues are squarely faced, Arab developmental and educational aspirations shall remain only a distant and fanciful hope.

NOTES

[1] See UNCTAD, *Case Studies in the Transfer of Technology: Policies for Transfer and Development of Technology in Pre-War Japan (1868-1937)*, U.N., 1978. See also Tsuku Hori, "The Brain Gain in the Modernization of Japan," paper presented at an Economic Commission for Western Asia Seminar on the Arab Brain Drain, February 4-8, 1980, Beirut, Lebanon.

[2] Zahlan, A.B., "The Problematique of the Arab Brain Drain," paper presented at an Economic Commission for Western Asia Seminar on the Arab Brain Drain, February 4-8, 1980, Beirut, Lebanon.

[3] *Ibid.*

[4] *Ibid.*

[5] All of the figures provided are from Zahlan, *Ibid.* See also his *Science and Science Policy in the Arab World,* London, 1980.

[6] Mischel, W., "Preference for Delayed Reinforcement and Social Responsibility," *Journal of Abnormal Social Psychology,* 1961, 62, pp. 1-7. Mischel, W.,

"Delay of Gratification, Need for Achievement, and Acquiescence in Another Culture," *Journal of Abnormal Social Psychology,* 1961, 62, pp. 543-552.

[7] Salazar, José Miguel, "Beliefs about Notions and their Relationship to Nationalistic Behaviour," paper presented at the 22nd International Congress of Psychology, July 1980, Leipzig.

[8] For a thought-provoking analysis of the relationship between developed and developing countries, see Galtung, Johan, "A Structural Theory of Imperialism," *Journal of Peace Research,* No. 2, 1971, pp. 81-98.

THE POLITICAL ECONOMY OF DEVELOPMENT

THE POLITICAL ENVIRONMENT FOR DEVELOPMENT *Roger Owen*

To begin with the obvious: the precise nature of the links that exist between the economic and the political spheres is one of the most difficult and elusive topics in modern social analysis. That such links are important few would now deny. But how they work, how they ought properly to be conceptualized and examined, is something that has always evaded a satisfactory answer.

If the point also needs to be made in terms of writings about the Middle East it can easily be done by means of a brief recital of the failures of various attempts to capture the essence of this elusive relationship, including that of Marxists using the concept of "class" to bridge the gap between the two domains and that of the exponents of some form of modernization theory who have posited either a benign link between economic and political change (e.g., Lerner) or a relationship in which the problems of rapid development are so disruptive as to require an almost impossible level of institutionalization (e.g., Huntington).

Nevertheless, the subject is too important to ignore simply on the grounds of its methodological or other complexity, and it might be useful to try to approach it in a more pragmatic way by looking at some of the salient features of the economic and political developments that took place in the 1970s and then attempting to show how they pose particular problems for the future growth of the Arab economies in the 1980s. The natural starting point would seem to be the fact that, unlike the 1960s, the 1970s were a decade of great regime stability as far as the major Arab states were concerned with the most serious political upheavals being confined to such non-Arab neighbors as Ethiopia, Iran, and Tur-

Roger Owen holds a PhD from St. Antony's College, Oxford University. At present, Dr. Owen is Director of the Middle East Center of St. Antony's College where he is also a Faculty Lecturer in the recent economic history of the Middle East. Dr. Owen has lived in both Egypt and Lebanon, and has written a number of works on Middle Eastern economic history, including *The Middle East in the World Economy 1800-1914,* and *Studies in the Theory of Imperialism,* which he co-edited.

key. This is especially remarkable in light of the same decade's unprecedented economic and political pressures at both the intra-Arab and international levels. Events like the Arab-Israeli war of 1973, the Lebanese civil war, and the Iranian revolution as well as processes like the huge increase in labor migration, the lurches in the prices of imports and exports, and the dangerous growth in "food dependency," produced changes of such a magnitude as to make the problems of planning and control exceptionally difficult. As a result, many regimes were driven to quite radical changes of policy—such as Algeria's prohibition on migration to France or Egypt's abrupt move from a close alliance with Russia to an even closer one with America—but most of them survived.

There are five lessons to be learned from all this; they relate to the national (or state) and intra-Arab levels:

1. The stability experienced by the Arab regimes in the 1970s was largely the result of the enormous increase in the power and pervasiveness of the state machinery that had begun to take place from the 1960s onward as a result of the growth of the bureaucracies, of the armed forces, and of state participation in important sectors of the economy. The extent of this can be seen in various indices such as the increase in the proportion of the workforce employed directly by the state, the proportion of real national resources controlled by the state expressed as a proportion of GDP, and so on. A second factor was the ability of most regimes to insulate themselves from the destabilizing effects of intra-Arab conflicts and competition for influence. One obvious feature of this situation was that the major exponents of Arab nationalism and the drive for greater Arab unity were now the various Arab regimes themselves, so that there was little scope for party or popular activity of an Arab nationalist kind. As a result, the way in which schemes for unity and cooperation were presented could be carefully controlled so as to protect regime interests.

2. The regime stability of the 1970s had much to do with the economic progress enjoyed by most Arab states for most of the decade and with the fact that the economic effect of certain disruptive influences such as the closure of borders or the loss of Beirut as a major financial center were kept within reasonable

limits. As indices of this type of progress one might take the growth of national income as well as others like the increase in the proportion of achieved government expenditure to what was actually planned or the growth in the proportion of GDP contributed by industry.

3. However, regime stability (and the related economic progress) involved costs, most notably (1) the stifling of political dissent via the state's ability to exercise control over any group or institution that might act as a vehicle for opposition, and (2) the misappropriation of public funds which was a feature of a situation in which a rapidly growing public sector coexisted with a still active private sector, on the one hand, and with multinational companies avid for contracts, on the other. In these circumstances it was not surprising that such opposition as did exist in an organized and vocal manner usually took a largely religious form and tended to concentrate on the twin concerns of tyranny and corruption, although political pressure from professional people like lawyers, doctors, and journalists and from workers was also significant.

4. At the intra-Arab level, the price paid for regime stability was the way in which each state attempted to control intra-Arab political relations so as to prevent what its regime believed to be potentially dangerous and disruptive movements of men and ideas across its borders and to inhibit other regimes from seeking to influence, and perhaps to encourage, movements of opposition within the country. That such policies have been largely successful goes without saying. But they have contributed to the present atmosphere of mutual mistrust among the Arab states, and they have also flown in the face of the powerful economic and social currents making for greater Arab interaction and interrelationship, such as the flow of labor from poorer to richer states and the reverse flow of remittances and capital investment. Political considerations and the facts of economic life are thus very much at odds. To take only one example, Egypt's regional connections are being maintained, in spite of Camp David, by the continued presence of three million Egyptian workers in Iraq, the Gulf states, and Libya.

5. The Arab regimes are presently facing a range of enormously difficult problems, some of which stem from movements in the international political economy and some from their own attempts to preserve their stability in ways that both provoke domestic opposition and encourage a climate of mistrust in which the many ties that link Arabs across national borders are easily put to harmful or disruptive purposes.

If this analysis is correct, it might be useful to look at the prospects for the 1980s in terms of those policy options which might promote regime stability on a more positive and, in some cases, a less counterproductive basis. Let us begin by examining ways in which the leading role of the state might be tempered by promoting a greater degree of political participation and of freedom of expression.

Perhaps the first point to be made is that all the Arab regimes have paid some attention to these matters in the last few years. There are constitutions that attempt to define how power should be exercised in a regular fashion; there are codes of law. There have also been a large number of experiments in encouraging a somewhat greater degree of popular participation in government through the creation of national assemblies and the use of government parties as forums for discussion as well as through attempts to set up regional administrations (such as in Kurdistan or parts of Sudan) or to establish new forms of local participation (as in Algeria, both through the system of local government and peasant management of the land reform cooperatives). The point here is that the Arab world has quite a wide range of experience to call upon when it comes to the creation of institutional forms designed to encourage greater participation, whatever their success, and that these might well serve as a basis for something more positive.

Second, it is very important to understand how such experiments and innovations ought to be justified and what their aims ought properly to be. It is all very well for people from the West to extoll the virtues of western democracy in general terms, but this has to be done in a way that makes sense under present-day Middle Eastern conditions, the more so as the concept of democracy itself, whether in its western form or in terms of its Middle

Eastern practice in the early independence period, has received such bad press in the region. It would be more useful to try to demonstrate the merits of greater participation and freedom of expression, in particular when it comes to the promotion of economic and social progress. There are obviously a variety of arguments that might be put forward. These include the following:

1. There is an important distinction to be made between the type of economic development that simply relies on an imitation of western methods or western experience and one that places greater emphasis on local innovation and adaptability. As Hoffer has noted in his *The Ordeal of Change,* the former strategy may well actually benefit from an authoritarian political structure making for "local compactness, regimentation and concerted action," while the latter can only flourish in a much freer political climate. For example, while industrialization via import substitution can be carried out reasonably satisfactorily by administrative fiat, industrialization via export promotion is greatly facilitated by the more subtle process of trial and error, requires constant adaptability, and calls for a willingness to listen and learn.

2. The continued promotion of agricultural progress requires not only the substantial reorganization of landholdings and the creation of new institutions like cooperatives—which it has received in most Arab countries—but also a mechanism by which the original structures can be constantly examined and modified as new experience is gained and new problems appear. For instance, the original Egyptian land reform of 1952, though vital in itself, was not subject to a process of constant emendation and review, whereas it would seem that, so far, the Algerian land reform of the early 1970s is open to a process of ongoing criticism both inside and outside the administration.

3. The establishment of a set of clear guidelines demarking the public from the private sector is a problem for almost every Arab country. This is partly the result of a situation in which, while the concept of a "public interest" is as yet underdeveloped, the scope, character, and dynamic of private economic activity is more or less self-evident. The only way in which this problem can be attacked is via the active involvement of a wide variety of

interested organizations, including the press, the universities, and the members of national assemblies.

4. There are at least some Arab countries where the proper protection of national resources—notably oil and gas—has been helped a great deal by the existence of an active public interest. This is certainly true of Kuwait, where the parliament played a very positive role in the early 1970s in trying to find the right balance between the exploitation and conservation of such resources. It could also be argued that, in a monarchical form of government, an assembly acts as a useful buffer between the royal family and the western consumers, making it much easier for the rulers to manage production without being accused of trying to hold the West to ransom.

5. Finally, it is difficult to see how the Arab world can solve many of the most important questions connected with the transfer of technology—the proper choice of what to import, the establishment of efficient programs of research and development—without relaxing the present degree of political supervision and allowing economists and technocrats a great deal more freedom in their professional life. And without such freedom it is extremely unlikely that the huge revenue from oil will be properly used before the wells themselves run dry.

Third, and lastly, let us consider ways in which a greater degree of participation and public involvement might be obtained. On the strength of Arab experience in the 1970s it would seem that President Boumedienne's method of building popular institutions from the local level upward (though useful in itself) will not be of much assistance in meeting problems that surface at a national level. The same criticism can be made of various experiments in "regionalism" which, if they do anything at all other than causing the duplication of costly administrative structures, simply transfer power from a central to a local elite. Another lesson of many Middle Eastern experiments is that freedoms cannot just be "given" by rulers; they have to be needed and wanted by particular groups within the society that are able to organize themselves in such a way as to use and to protect them. For this reason, and because of the drawbacks of the regional approach, it would seem essential to begin the process of encouraging greater participation at the center of national affairs and in such a way that existing interest groups are given some regular means of political expression.

Having looked at the situation as it exists at the national level, let us go on to examine the different set of problems that exists at the intra-Arab level. Here, it is essential to find ways of encouraging the existing trends toward greater Arab economic integration, either directly or via mechanisms to reduce the irregular and unpredictable interference caused by purely national political considerations. One can reasonably argue that stability in the intra-Arab environment is just as important to Arab economic development as stability in the local national environment. One way to move ahead is to strengthen and to rationalize those pan-Arab institutions that already exist, notably the various banks and development agencies devoted to investing Arab capital in Arab lands. A second approach, discussed at the recent Arab summit by Yusif Sayigh and others, is to examine the possibility of drawing up sets of good practices governing the movement of goods, money, and people between Arab countries in such a way as to facilitate such flows, to reduce the possibility of harmful disruptions, and to provide the guarantees that their future development requires. An example of this would be the drawing up of rules to provide legal protection for Arab workers outside their own countries and the establishment of institutional arrangements to ensure that at least part of the earnings and skills acquired by workers abroad are made available for the purposes of development in their home countries. Third, national development plans should pay particular attention to the intra-Arab economic sphere by indicating, for example, those projects which might be funded on a regional basis or which require labor from elsewhere in the Arab world.

My conclusion is neither original nor profound: it is simply that while economic progress obviously requires a considerable degree of political stability, such stability cannot be founded for long just on order and the suppression of dissent or on policies that seek to regulate intra-Arab relations in terms of purely national interests. Stability itself is a dynamic concept and requires constant adjustment to changing circumstances. In today's Arab world, the regime stability of the 1970s is being challenged internally by groups activated by political and economic discontent and externally by forces from the Arab environment that can be contained only at great cost. The purpose of this paper has been both to pose the problem and to suggest some ways of dealing with it.

A NEW FRAMEWORK FOR COMPLEMENTARITY AMONG THE ARAB ECONOMIES *Yusif A. Sayigh*

Introduction

The 11th Arab Summit (Council of Heads of State) held in Amman toward the end of November 1980 was almost wholly devoted to the consideration of the economic affairs of the Arab world and the approval of a new framework for complementarity among the Arab economies. It should be pointed out that Arab economic coordination was a major concern of those Mashreq[1] countries that were participants in the League of Arab States when the Alexandria Protocol was drawn up in 1944 and the League was formally established in March 1945. It has remained a major interest down to the present.

Between 1944 and 1980 a number of ways to promote "economic togetherness" were considered. These ranged from mere (unspecified) "cooperation" to "economic unity" (i.e. a comprehensive relationship between nations having far-reaching legal, institutional, and economic ramifications and providing for a high degree of policy coordination). Since unity by definition requires one framework binding all the countries that opt for it, it subjects the participants to a single "economic sovereignty." The rigor of these conditions is why only a limited number of countries have signed the Agreement for Arab Economic Unity of 1957 and joined the Council for Arab Economic Unity, which was formed in 1962 with the object of setting the drive for unity in motion.

Yusif A. Sayigh holds a PhD in Economics from The Johns Hopkins University. For over 20 years Dr. Sayigh taught economics at the American University of Beirut, where he also served as Director of the Economic Research Institute. He has been affiliated with Harvard and Princeton universities through research and teaching positions. Currently an economic consultant in Beirut, Dr. Sayigh also serves as advisor to OPEC and the Arab Fund for Economic and Social Development. His publications include *Entrepreneurs of Lebanon: The Role of the Business Leader in a Developing Economy, The Economies of the Arab World,* and *The Determinants of Arab Development.*

The opinions expressed in this paper are those of the writer personally.

Between loose "cooperation" and binding "unity" there is a whole spectrum of possible approaches to Arab economic coordination. The actual choices made in this area over the decades were affected by the pressures of current events, the political mood of the time, and what had been learned from earlier experience. Speaking broadly, during the 1950s there was a drive for full economic unity, whereas the 1960s saw a shift of focus toward the more modest goal of increased economic complementarity. During the 1970s, the drive for complementarity continued, but under the more ambivalent label of "joint Arab economic action" and with different areas of emphasis. Concurrently, the 1970s, particularly since the adjustment of oil prices in late 1973 and early 1974, witnessed the gestation of a qualitatively-new framework for complementarity among the Arab economies, a framework which formally emerged at the highest political level in the Arab Summit of November 1980.

Backdrop to the Summit: The Old Framework

To bring out the new features of complementarity as conceived during the late 1970s and formalized at the Summit, it is necessary first to survey the experience of the past 35 years with respect to cooperation and complementarity. In reviewing this period, one must distinguish between (1) pronouncements and even written agreements and published statements and (2) concrete and measurable steps actually taken. Action is the acid test for the seriousness of intentions and the meaningfulness of verbal or written undertakings.

Bearing this precautionary remark in mind, we find that, other concerns notwithstanding, the main interest in the 1950s and through much of the 1960s was in the facilitation of trade among the Arab countries; in second place was the provision of facilities for the reduction of balance-of-payments strains that might accompany intraregional[2] trade in the case of certain countries suffering shortages in foreign exchange. Even though trade across national borders continued to meet with certain administrative and legal problems that reduced its volume, more success was achieved in this area than in that of balance-of-payments facilities. But the slimness of the success, exemplified by the failure of intraregional trade to constitute more than, say, one-tenth of total Arab trade, was mainly attributable first to the inadequacy of the agreements relating to the promotion of trade and second to the insufficient earnestness of implementation.

The emphasis shifted in the late 1960s; from that time until the late 1970s, the focus was increasingly on the establishment of joint Arab projects and companies. The shift was occasioned by two convictions: first, that the formation of projects and companies through the joint effort of two or more Arab countries would lead to greater complementarity among the Arab economies, and second, that the volume of production in the Arab economies, being extremely meager, needed to be (and would be) enlarged through the new projects. Thus, the projects would serve as a major factor in the desired expansion of intraregional trade.

The above convictions notwithstanding, probably the most potent factor behind the remarkable intensification of the process of establishing joint projects came into existence in the 1970s; this was the inflow into the Arab region of substantially increased oil revenues. Another relevant factor should also be noted, namely the dynamism and devotion of the then Secretary-General of the Council for Arab Economic Unity, Dr. Abdul-Aal al-Sakban, who put great effort into promoting the formation of joint projects. In the view of the Council, the acceleration was a practical response to the Agreement for Arab Economic Unity's call for programs conducive to the formation of joint projects, in the service of complementarity.

Some joint projects were agreed upon as early as 1949, and some were actively underway in 1956. Hundreds of joint projects have been established over the past three decades, but the vast majority of these can be ignored for the purposes of this account, since many were formed by two parties and had little or no integrative value, or else they were entered into by Arab and non-Arab parties, thus probably serving complementarity with certain advanced industrial economies more than they did with the rest of the Arab region. To be exact, a recent enumeration found 427 joint projects, 237 purely Arab and 190 Arab/non-Arab. Yet even this long list excludes training institutes, the Arab Fund for Economic and Social Development (AFESD), and the Arab Monetary Fund (AMF), the last two being autonomous regional financial organizations.[3]

A few observations are in order at this point. First, some credit for the formation of a number of projects or institutions must go to the Economic Council (now the Economic and Social Council of the Arab League — not to be confused with the Council for Arab Economic Unity), and some to private initiatives by institutions or citizens in different countries. Second, only a tiny proportion of the total number of projects established are active and contributive to complementarity or cooperation; the rest are either somnolent or continue to exist only on paper. Finally, the most active institutions (projects, regional organizations, companies) such as the Arab Fund for Economic and Social Development, the Arab Monetary Fund, and the companies established by the Organization of Arab Petroleum Exporting Countries (OAPEC) — to list a limited number only — owe most of their creditable performance to the fact that they are autonomous bodies and have enjoyed capable and imaginative leadership. (However, success is not always an unmixed blessing for the regional organization, as we shall see later.)

In descending order of numbers of projects included, the sectors in which the 427 projects fall are finance, manufacturing industry, tourism and related services, construction, agriculture, extractive industry, and transport and communications. 164 projects are bilateral Arab, with an aggregate capital of $8.85 billion, 73 multilateral Arab ($9.91 billion), 91 bilateral Arab-foreign ($7.5 billion), and 99 multilateral Arab-foreign ($5.28 billion). The purely Arab projects have an aggregate capital of $18.76 billion, out of a total of $31.54 billion for all projects. If to the capital of the purely Arab joint projects we add that of three regional financial institutions (AFESD, AMF, and the Arab Authority for Agricultural Investment and Development or AAAID), the total reaches about $22 billion.[4]

In spite of the formation of many joint projects and holding companies, the Council for Arab Economic Unity, which was very instrumental in the joint-project process, has had little success in promoting full economic unity. To date, only thirteen Arab governments have signed the Unity Agreement, and only four have approved *and* ratified the Arab Common Market (ACM) agreement promulgated in August 1964 under the aegis of the Council for Arab Economic Unity. (The ACM became a Free Trade Area in 1971.) Concrete achievements in this field are even more modest; virtually nothing has been done to implement real unity, and even the common market is still nebulous, while complementarity has been only marginally served by most of the joint projects formed thus far.

Other significant institutional developments were taking place along with the spread of joint projects. One of these, the formation of federations or unions of professional bodies, started in the early 1950s with the establishment of the General Union of Chambers of Commerce, Industry, and Agriculture in the Arab Countries. It was followed, mainly in the 1960s, by other federations (engineers, economists, etc.). But these groups were not formed by and under the League of Arab States, though they were to contribute in practical terms to its drive for economic cooperation and complementarity.

Another significant institutional development owed its unfolding to the efforts of the Economic and Social Council. This was the establishment of several specialized regional organizations or agencies, whose main functions were research, advisory work, and some planning, as well as the coordination of efforts of individual countries in the fields of specialization of the respective organizations. These fields include, among others, industry; agriculture; public administration; specifications and measurements; education, culture, and science; tourism; arid areas; telecommunications; and labor.

Special mention must be made here of three categories of institutions that deserve singling out. The first is OAPEC, which was established in 1968 with the object of serving the Arab oil-producing countries. OAPEC later became very active in organizing and conducting studies relevant to its area of interest, holding conferences and seminars, publishing, and forming large joint companies in areas of activity relating to hydrocarbon resources. Five of these have so far been formally set up, with an aggregate capital of about $3 billion. In addition, OAPEC has established a training institute. The second category consists of the three regional financial institutions already referred to — AFESD, AMF, and AAAID; their aggregate capital is about $3 billion. Finally, there are national development funds in Kuwait, Abu Dhabi, Iraq, and Saudi Arabia, whose capital at the time of writing is about $17 billion. Although these funds are owned, financed, and operated by individual countries, their scope of activity is regional *and* international (the latter through assistance extended to non-Arab Third World countries).

It should be added that the above three categories of institutions were established outside the fold of the League of Arab States; the first two, though autonomous, are loosely associated with the League, and considered members of the League "family" of organizations. Indeed, their representatives are invited to the meetings of the Coordination Committee of the League to minimize duplication of work by the various organizations and maximize cooperation.

Finally, the first seven years of the new oil era, 1974-80, have witnessed a new and significant development closely related to the adjustment of oil prices and the substantially raised revenues of the oil-exporting Arab economies. This is, first, the movement of substantial flows of manpower from certain Arab countries (mainly non-oil-producing, but also oil-producing in the cases of Egypt and Syria) toward the oil-exporting countries.[5] The flow is reliably estimated to have well exceeded 3 million men and women who have significantly supplemented the national manpower in the countries concerned (except in Iraq, where the national labor force is of considerable size, and Algeria, where the inflow is negligible). A second flow, that of funds, has moved in the opposite direction, mainly to the labor-supplying countries, but also to other capital-short countries. The flows of Official Development Assistance, which average some $4 billion annually, are substantial in comparison with the region's earlier experience, but fall considerably short of the financial capabilities of the donors, the needs of the recipients, and the volume of capital which the latter are capable of putting to good use for investment. Another $3 billion per year flows as remittances from the Arab expatriate labor force to the home countries.

The Shortcomings of Past Performance

Numerous agreements have been signed, resolutions approved, institutions established, and measures adopted under the umbrellas of the Economic and Social Council and the Council for Arab Economic Unity, as well as under other auspices, both within the structure of the Arab League and outside it. The avowed purpose of all this activity has been to promote economic cooperation and complementarity. In evaluating the degree of success achieved over the years 1945-80, one should bear in mind three vital points that somewhat counterbalance the seeming lack of firm, substantial results during this period.

The first point is that right at the establishment of the League, economic cooperation ranked high among the concerns of the members, and, together with the development it was expected to bring, was (rightly) considered essential for Arab National security. Indeed, an agreement of central significance drawn up in 1950 was called "The Treaty of Economic Cooperation and Mutual Defense." The linkage between Arab National (i.e. regional) development and Arab National security or defense has continued to be understood and appreciated down to the 11th Summit of November 1980, when it received its clearest definition and justification ever, and its most compelling and convincing expression and translation into strategic guidelines, sectoral priorities, and action programs.

The second point that needs to be made is that the continued focus on cooperation and complementarity has been possible only because there is a popular, grass-roots concern with them. Given the growth of centrifugal, separatist tendencies among most if not all of the ruling elites (despite their avowed attachment to complementarity and integration), these elites would not have moved even the present modest distance along the path of complementarity had there not been strong popular feeling supportive of such movement. (At the same time, it is an undeniable fact that this popular feeling and the pressure it generates have in practice been largely shunted aside; we will return to this point later.)

The third observation is that, notwithstanding the vicissitudes, discontinuities, and constraints that have necessarily limited the achievement of a large measure of economic complementarity among the Arab economies, a substantial sector of joint Arab economic action has emerged, as was seen in the preceding section of this paper.[6] That this sector still falls considerably short of what is needed for effective complementarity, let alone integration, qualifies but does not deny its importance.

The evaluation that follows these preliminary remarks will have two parts. In the first, certain shortcomings of performance, or clinical symptoms of its limitations, will be identified, and in the second the deeper causes of failure will be sought.

The *first* symptom of difficulty in the drive for economic coordination is the prematurity of the emphasis on the promotion and expansion of intraregional trade that characterized the efforts of the Arab countries in the 1950s. This emphasis suffered from two flaws. The first is that the productive capacity of the region's countries was (and still is, though to a lesser extent) weak and narrowly based; consequently, it did not put at the disposal of the economies a large volume of goods and services. Naturally, therefore, it could only put into the stream of trade an even smaller volume. To make matters worse, the economies without exception turned out a very narrow range of products, and, in the absence of an advanced division of labor, these products were characterized by a marked similarity which limited exchange and trade. The second flaw was the inherited, and lingering, pattern of strong dependence on the advanced industrial economies of the West, created over centuries of western political and economic domination. This control created a tight network of relationships which dictated (and continues to dictate) the inflow of a large mass of manufactured goods and advanced services into the Arab region, and an outflow limited to raw materials or at best semifinished products to the West.

The *second* symptom of the present inadequacy of coordination is related, paradoxically, to the reasoning that was advanced in favor of shifting emphasis toward complementarity, as a correction to the premature emphasis on intraregional trade promotion. Here it must be noted that this idea was basically sound, as was the choice of the instrumentality adopted for the strengthening of complementarity, namely the establishment of a large number of joint projects and companies. But two flaws in the instrumentality as it now exists reduce its effectiveness. The first is that these projects are joint only with respect to finance. Joint labor force participation is extremely rare in them, except perhaps at the board of directors level. More significantly, the complementarity-promoting aspect remains very weak, because the projects do not lead to the dovetailing or meshing of Arab productive capacity through vertical or even horizontal integration. Building structural interconnections that will have integrative effects requires that joint projects be planned in the context of well-thought-out long-term priorities and objectives. The absence until November 1980 of such a policy framework is the second serious flaw; the result has been a haphazard choice of projects.

The *third* symptom is closely associated with the second. It is the narrowness of the scope of joint projects; that is, the failure so far of Arabs to formulate a broader range of joint programs or to plan for the development of whole economic sectors with complementarity as a central objective.[7] Education and research, technology, food security, communications — just to give a few illustrations — are fields eminently suited for the pursuit of complementarity at the program and sector levels.

The *fourth* symptom can be encountered in the body of institutions that were either formed under the very broad umbrella of the Arab League or, subsequently came to be considered as falling under this umbrella. We refer here to the many regional organizations formed over the years for coordinative, advisory, and generally professional purposes. It would not be unfair to say that many of these institutions are of low productivity and limited effectiveness. Two external reasons must take a good part of the blame. The first is the insufficient attention, financing, and support given by the Arab governments to these organizations, and the tendency of some governments, at times, to slow down the pace of those institutions which prove energetic and effective, particularly if they press the governments to take integrative measures that are too strong for their liking. The second reason is the subordination of the selection of the directors-general of these institutions to political pressures and bargaining, which has the result that the wrong choice is not infrequently made. This spells failure for the institutions concerned right from the start. Faulty leadership, which is to be blamed on the governments at first, ends by becoming an internal weakness as well. Moreover, the region's numerous institutions, unions, and other organizations suffer from proliferation, insufficient control by the governing body (whether the Economic and Social Council or the Council of Arab Economic Unity), and merely nominal, ineffectual coordination. Apart from the inefficiency, sluggishness, and frustration that this situation creates, there is rivalry in certain instances, particularly when some organizations prove efficient and motivated to produce high-quality work. The rivalry that is set in motion is frequently not of the creative but of the wasteful type, which takes the form of feuding and politicking for advantage. Finally, excessive bureaucracy slows down virtually all the institutions under discussion.

The *fifth* and final symptom of the inadequacy of the drive for complementarity lies in the field of finance and emerged essentially during the period 1974-80. This is the fact that the directing of oil revenues toward the poorer Arab countries has taken place in a modest, indeed almost grudging, way. Admittedly, the flow of investment aid to needy economies has become much more considerable than it was before 1974, and the aid record of the Arab oil-exporting countries — themselves developing countries with a vast need for investment and effort — is highly creditable in comparison with that of some much richer and more advanced industrial countries. All the same, the oil-exporting countries could well afford to direct substantially more resources to their sister countries, given the size of their fast-growing reserves in the western money and capital markets (and considering the hazards to which these reserves are exposed). At the same time, the poorer Arab countries could make good use of more funds than they actually receive, especially in view of the fact that absorptive capacity grows as development work proceeds. Finally, aid can combine good business with brotherly sentiment.

The five symptoms just discussed indicate the shortcomings of the 35-year drive for complementarity by intellectuals and large segments of the informed public. We now turn to a discussion of six fundamental causes behind this malaise:

1. *Narrow vested interests in the various countries and their igno-rance or underestimation of the net positive benefits that com-plementarity could bring in the long run.* Even when these benefits are visible, some of the vested interests discount them heavily, since they are concerned with a very short time-horizon. Those economists, opinion-makers, and politicians and civil servants who are firm believers in the benefits of complementarity share a substantial measure of blame for not having exerted enough effort to make a clear, strong, and compelling argument for complemen-tarity as against isolationism. (One should also note the lukewarm attitude that advocates of complementarity of-ten take once they leave their professional posts to be-come ministers. The corridors of power have a remarkable capacity for deflecting personal convictions.)

2. *At the political (and ideological) level, the strong hold of pro-vincialism* (qutriyya) *on significant elements of the political leaderships in power.* Many close observers share the con-viction that provincialism is spreading and becoming more deeply entrenched, at the expense of identification with Arab Nationalism. While there is greater community of life among the Arab peoples, manifested by intraregional flows of manpower and funds, growing economic rela-tions, intensified cultural linkages, and more regional meetings and conferences, this community stops short of close, effective, and binding complementarity with what this implies in *structural* economic, as well as politico-

legal-institutional, ties. It is as though the *outward* signs of community are promoted to make up for the basic hesitation and reluctance in the face of *deeper* community.

3. *Mutual mistrust and fear between the various existing socioeconomic (and political) systems.* This is often suggested as the real reason why complementarity cannot be tightened. However, many analysts believe that while much of the mistrust and fear is genuine, a substantial part of it is feigned; it is used as an alibi to justify the avoidance of firm, sincere measures to promote complementarity. This belief is strengthened by the fact that neither the "capitalism" nor the "socialism" professed in various Arab countries is of a pure type; in Arab practice, each system borrows elements from the other. The so-called socialism of some Arab countries is mostly state capitalism, and the free enterprise of the professedly capitalist Arab countries is heavily mixed with public sector ownership and activity, and with substantial welfare services.

4. *The sharp fluctuations and the temperamental quality of political life, which affect economic relations and weaken the drive for cooperation and complementarity.*

5. *The severe limitations on democracy and freedom of expression, which in no small measure inhibit the believers in cooperation and complementarity from exerting pressure on the ruling elites.*

6. *Finally, the direct and indirect pressures and manipulations resorted to by external (imperialist) forces to strengthen the centrifugal forces in the Arab region and weaken the unitary forces.* Israel is a handy agent for promoting division.

The "New Framework" for Complementarity

The considerations outlined thus far have produced considerable disenchantment among Arab Nationalists — mostly but not exclusively outside the official Arab establishments — with the "old framework" of complementarity, and have encouraged the search for a new framework. The next part of this paper will describe this new framework as it developed over the better part of the 1970s and came to be formalized in November 1980 at the 11th Arab Summit. Because not much is known of the 1980 New Framework outside a rather narrow circle, the approach will be largely historical and descriptive. This will be followed by an assessment of the outlook for the New Framework. It is a mistake to believe that merely because a new set of documents have been drawn up, the drive for complementarity will inevitably be more forceful, more earnest, and more successful in the years to come. Obviously, it could turn out that way if the Arabs — political leaders, popular organizations, the business community, the trade unions, the intellectuals — decide to translate the blueprints of the New Framework into concrete action through joint effort and sacrifice.

The motivation behind the search for a new approach was not merely a recognition of the shortcomings and failings of the old framework, but concern over the dangers — economic, social, political — that the Arab Nation as a whole faces if it does not act as one body to defend itself and to promote its interests and well-being. The documents that constitute the intellectual underpinnings of the New Framework underline these dangers and cite evidence of their enormity.

The centerpiece of the New Framework is the Strategy for Joint Arab Economic Action (the Strategy for short). The need for the formulation of such a Strategy had been felt as early as 1973, and serious work on it began in 1976, largely due to the initiative and relentless efforts of the Assistant Secretary-General for Economic Affairs of the Arab League, Dr. Abdul-Hassan Zalzala, who formed the Experts' Committee for the Strategy for Joint Arab Economic Action (referred to as the Committee of 20, after the size of its membership)[8] and asked it to formulate a Strategy that would serve as the guideline for future action toward complementarity and help planners avoid the shortcomings and failings of previous decades. The complementarity to be sought was to take into account the new economic realities of the Arab region, to create new structural ties among the productive capacities of the Arab economies and strengthen those that already existed, to promote national (country) development through a regional (National) frontal attack on underdevelopment and through regional cooperation, to promote development at the regional level in certain sectors and program areas, and to bolster — directly and indirectly — the National security of the Arab region.

A working group of three[9] was formed to prepare a Strategy document for the consideration of the Committee of 20. The document in question was prepared and submitted early in 1978, and a National Conference (sponsored jointly by the Arab League Secretariat and the Federation of Arab Economists) was convened in May 1978 in Baghdad to examine the document. The examination resulted in the drawing of a number of guidelines to be used in an acceptable Strategy, and the Secretariat of the Arab League asked a member of the Committee of 20 to undertake the formulation of a new document that would take into account the work of the conference.[10] The new document was duly prepared and submitted in the summer of 1979, and in January 1980 a meeting of government experts approved it after compressing it considerably and introducing a few changes. One of these was significant: it stipulated that the plan for joint Arab economic action proposed in the document should be mandatory rather than merely indicative. The new, shorter document was later approved by the Economic and Social Council, by the joint conference of ministers of finance and foreign affairs held in July in preparation for the Summit of November 1980, and finally by the Summit itself. Very minor alterations were introduced in this long process.

It was stated earlier that the Strategy was the centerpiece of the New Framework. Some thirty studies associated with the Strategy were submitted with it to the Summit. This input was necessitated by the fact that the 10th Summit, held in November 1979, had asked the Secretariat of the League to prepare studies around three themes. The first was the intensification of inter-Arab economic relations and cooperation; the second was the use of Arab-foreign economic relations in the service of Arab economic and National interests; and the third was the economic implications of the peace treaty between Egypt and Israel and how they could be faced. There were principal papers on each of the themes, as well as a large number of supportive papers on specific subjects. The first paper in the series presented a general overview and it was designed to submit the case for joint Arab economic action within the context of the New Framework for complementarity, in the pursuit of two overall objectives — development and security.[11]

Two principal papers are of special significance and must be singled out for separate mention before we proceed to survey the central ideas of the New Framework and the body of papers that incorporate it. The first is the "Charter of Arab National Economic Action," which sets out to define the guidelines and principles that should govern inter-Arab economic relations if true and meaningful cooperation and complementarity are to be achieved. The second is the "Draft Framework of the National Plan for Joint Arab Economic Action." This document calls for a significant innovation, namely regional planning, albeit restricted to the joint sector only. Between them, these two papers present principles of conduct and discipline in the activities of the joint sector that, if adhered to, would be a major landmark in Arab economic relations.

The ideas in the New Framework start with a number of basic premises used as points of departure. These include the importance and potential effectiveness, as well as the feasibility, of joint Arab economic action. The credibility of these premises derives from the historical, cultural, and economic ties that bind the Arab peoples together and from the common dangers that they face and the expectations, aspirations, and interests that they share. The objectives set forth center around National development and National security, and these are shown to be closely related, since development provides a solid economic base for security, and security provides protection for economic interests and achievements. Likewise, it is argued that national (country) and National (regional) actions in the areas of development and security also interact, supporting and strengthening each other, provided that there is a deliberate attempt to achieve harmony in country and regional planning and action.

After the points of departure are stated and examined, the performance of the Arab economies in the period 1945-80 is assessed. The basic criteria used are the success of the countries in achieving profound, comprehensive, and self-reliant development (at the regional level); the extent to which development has created employment and reduced unemployment; the speed and quality of industrialization; the sectoral, geographical, and social balances aimed at and reached; the extent to which the development and income gaps inside and between countries have been central concerns of development authorities and other participants in policy decisions and execution; the amount of attention paid to the matter of excessive dependence on the large industrial countries and the earnestness of efforts to drastically reduce this dependence; and the seriousness and effectiveness of regional cooperation and complementarity as factors of direct and strong relevance to development. The assessment finds gaping shortcomings, apathy, and poor performance with respect to the various criteria used. On the basis of this finding, the New Framework presents a strong argument for joint Arab action, through earnest and close complementarity, as the only means of correction, assuming always the basic prerequisite of appropriate political orientation and the will and determination of the Arab countries to work together.

To work together effectively, these countries have to follow a clear strategy of action, according to a system of sector priorities (defined and defended in the documents) that are to be translated into programs also governed by a system of priorities. The whole process would be guided by a plan for the joint sector. The principle of planning *joint* Arab action had never been accepted before; at best coordination was tolerated. The introduction of the instrumentality of planning into the Strategy, and the formulation of a plan framework, are in themselves a significant step forward, even if the plan is not adhered to strictly for a few years.

The papers next turn to the question of machinery, and they suggest a special council to govern joint economic policy. In order to assure the council's authority over individual ministers (for whom rivalry for seniority within each country is often a serious handicap to performance), it is proposed that the council be at the prime ministerial level and that it have a technical secretariat of the highest competence available. Finally, the New Framework calls for appropriate financing, requesting resources totalling $15 billion for the five years 1981-85, on the understanding that these resources would be new allocations, in addition to whatever other contributions Arab governments are already making for joint economic action. The sum proposed is considered minimal for the basic, urgent needs of joint Arab economic action and the objectives set for it, but probably maximal for the present absorptive capacities of regional organizations and other executing agencies, as well as for the mood of the donor countries themselves.

This is the overall structure of what we have called the New Framework for complementarity. Because it was designed to correct the previously-discussed failings of the existing situation, the New Framework emphasizes expanded and diversified production as a prerequisite for expanded intraregional trade. The expansion in production is to be effected not only within the productive capacity of individual countries, but also within regional productive capacity. This entails structural changes and a much closer integration and harmonization (within regional planning) of the national economies. The three concepts thus emphasized — greater production, structural complementarity, and planning of the joint sector — are the major contributions of the New Framework, with its Strategy and system of priorities, in the service of the twin objectives of development and security.

As was indicated earlier, achieving harmony between country and regional action and planning is absolutely essential. The policies of individual countries and of the community of countries must not be at cross-purposes. This condition can be satisfied only through the firm acceptance by governments and popular organizations of the ideas of the New Framework, which are based on the concept of the commonality of Arab interests and destiny. The centerpiece of the New Framework, namely the Strategy for Joint Arab Economic Action, embodies these principles and their applications. Consequently, when it was approved by all the ministers of finance and of foreign affairs in July 1980, and subsequently by the Arab Summit in November 1980, the New Framework could be presumed to have been accepted and approved, along with its constituent parts and documents.

However, the resolutions of the Summit contained three setbacks to the expectations expressed in the documents of the New Framework. First, instead of the $15 billion requested for five years, the Summit approved only $5 billion for ten years —meaning an average annual contribution only one-sixth of the minimum called for in the New Framework. Second, this smaller sum was not earmarked for *joint programs* within the context of the drive for complementarity according to the priorities stipulated in the Strategy (itself approved unanimously); instead, it was to be directed to the six less-developed Arab countries, with preference for joint projects. (In practice, it is extremely difficult to find appropriate joint projects, since only two of the six countries are contiguous.) The third setback related to machinery. The Economic and Social Council was appointed by the Summit as the appropriate, competent authority to lay down policy and provide overall control of the activity stemming from the stipulations of the Strategy, instead of the council of prime ministers proposed and defended in the documents submitted.

If the last setback were the only disquieting issue with respect to machinery, it would have been tolerable, although it meant the choice of an inappropriate level of authority. However, a new factor introduced into the New Framework led to the adoption of an institutional arrangement that, in the opinion of the present writer, sets a worrisome precedent. The new factor was the decision to consider the 1980s the "Decade of Development" (DOD). This carried with it a shift of emphasis from joint action designed to bring about complementarity to mere financial aid for the less-developed countries. It is equally serious that the authority that was set up for policy formulation and overall control relating to the $500 million assigned for aid annually was a board consisting of the finance ministers of the *donor countries only*. Even the cosmetic step of including one minister from the recipient countries was not taken. Although the Arab Fund for Economic and Social Development was designated as the executive agency for allocation of funds for development purposes, its Board of Governors, which includes the ministers of finance of all the members of the Arab League, was not entrusted with the task of overall control of the funds of the DOD. This undisguised polarization, with the "financial haves" setting themselves apart from the "financial have-nots," ought to have been firmly and totally avoided, in the interest of the "haves" themselves as well as Arab cooperation as a whole.

It would not be an overstatement to say that the three setbacks in effect reduced the value of the New Framework considerably. This they did both by creating serious distortions in the orientation of the New Framework as originally designed and approved (through the Strategy, the Charter, and the other papers centering around the Strategy), and by considerably reducing the resources and weakening the instrumentalities available for the proposed drive for development plus security. Serious reflection on the implications of the choices made at the Summit must necessarily lead to anxious questioning, if not considerable frustration. The logic of the core propositions and arguments of the Strategy and the other documents submitted to the Summit is compelling, and it was accepted through the approval of the Strategy. Why, then, did the Summit approve resolutions at variance with the tenets of the Strategy with respect to the central idea of pursuing complementarity to achieve development and security? Is there a deliberate shift in orientation away from complementarity toward mere cooperation, albeit gilded cooperation? If there is, then it must be at the decision-making level, with intensifying provincialism (*qutriyya*) acting as the solvent that diluted the modality of complementarity and turned it into the much less potent modality of financial cooperation. The cynic might conclude that the popular desire for complementarity could be satisfied by the formal approval of the Strategy and all that it means and implies, while, in practice, actions were channeled in ways more desirable to the political decision-makers.

However, the present writer would like to end this paper on a slightly less gloomy though still pessimistic note. The pressure of reality will eventually move the Arab world toward complementarity in the service of development and security. The compelling aspects of this reality include: the disparate and superficial development that is presently taking place; the growing dependence on the advanced industrial world along with the growing financial wealth of an important part of the Arab region, and the exorbitant price that the region is paying for its dependence in terms of technology, arms, and food; the approach of oil depletion at the same time as Arab financial reserves abroad become increasingly a hostage in the hands of their keepers; and, above all, the increasing threat that Israel and the imperialism that bolsters it constitute to the well-being and very existence of the region's true independence. These danger signals are too serious and too glaring to go unheeded for long. But how soon, and how effectively, will they be heeded? In this writer's view, an appropriate response that satisfies Arab interests and is consistent with the legitimate rights of the Arabs is possible. But it will come only when the Arab peoples enjoy a large measure of political freedom. This would make it possible for them to be more aware of the dangers that their individual countries and the region as a whole face, and of the vital interests that complementarity can serve, and enable them to participate politically and thus be instrumental in shaping the policies and actions of their leaderships. That the achievement of this political freedom will require sacrifices does not make it any less critical and urgent; the potential returns are too valuable for the issue to be neglected or ignored. That this conclusion is more an act of reasoning than an act of faith is as far as this author's hope can reach at the present moment.

NOTES

[1] The Mashreq includes Egypt and the Asian Arab countries further east.
[2] The term "regional" here means Arab National (i.e. it refers to the whole Arab world or much of it), while "provincial" will refer to one country (it will stand for "national" with a small "n").
[3] See a monograph by Dr. Samih Mas'oud, *Joint Arab Projects: Between Actuality and Prospects* (Organization of Arab Petroleum Exporting Countries, Kuwait, 1981; Arabic).
[4] Mas'oud, *op. cit.*

[5] In fact, all oil-producing Arab countries are also oil-exporting, but the latter term is usually reserved for those producers who are relatively large exporters and who are members of OPEC, namely Iraq, Kuwait, Qatar, U.A.E., Saudi Arabia, Libya, and Algeria. OAPEC includes these as well as Syria, Egypt, and Bahrain. Oman and Tunisia, though producers and exporters, fall in neither grouping.

[6] See League of Arab States, Department of Economic Affairs, *Working Paper of the Three-Man Committee Formed by the Experts' Committee for the Strategy for Joint Arab Economic Action* (Cairo, 1978; Monograph in Arabic).

[7] There are a few outstanding cases of success, but this does not invalidate the general validity of the observation.

[8] The writer draws on his familiarity with the work of the Committee as one of its members.

[9] The group consisted of Mr. Burhan Dajani (chairman), Dr. Sayyid Jaballah, and Dr. Antoine Zahlan. The first two were members of the Committee of 20.

[10] The present writer undertook the assignment, assisted by Dr. George Corm and Dr. Mahmoud Abdul-Fadeel.

[11] Twenty-five Arab economists formed the team that prepared the studies. The present writer wrote the general overview paper, and served as coordinator of the project and editor.

IDEOLOGICAL DETERMINANTS OF ARAB
DEVELOPMENT *Halim Barakat*

The thesis of this paper is that conceptions of, and attitudes about, development tend to be deeply embedded in a more comprehensive ideology which in turn tends to be a direct product of one's position in the prevailing socioeconomic structure and political order. Specifically, it will be argued that the three basic alternative models of development (namely, the evolutionary, the reformist, and the revolutionary models) correspond rather closely to the three opposed ideologies (i.e. the rightist, the centrist, and the leftist ideologies), which themselves correspond rather neatly to the existing class divisions (the upper, the middle, and the lower classes).

Of course, the above relationship is not something mechanical and absolute. There are many exceptions to the rule, and instances of false consciousness or betrayal of one's class are not that unusual. However, these exceptions and instances as well as other conceptions of development and of ideological orientations merely lead to modifications of the thesis just stated; they do not negate its essence. The privileged classes and those who are affiliated and/or identify with them and aspire after their status are more likely than other classes to subscribe to a rightist ideology and, consequently, to prefer an evolutionary model of development. The middle classes, on the other hand, are more likely than others to subscribe to a centrist or liberal ideology and to find the reformist model of development more in tune with their interests and aspirations. Finally, the impoverished and deprived classes and those who identify with them are more likely than the rest to

Halim Barakat received a PhD in Social Psychology at the University of Michigan. Currently a Research Professor at the Center for Contemporary Arab Studies, Georgetown University, Dr. Barakat has also taught at the American University of Beirut, the University of Michigan, and the University of Texas at Austin. A novelist as well as a social scientist, his works include *River Without Bridges: A Study of the Exodus of the 1967 Palestinian Arab Refugees, Lebanon in Strife: Student Preludes to the Civil War* and *Days of Dust.*

169

subscribe to a radical or leftist ideology and, consequently, to opt for a revolutionary model of development, particularly once they perceive the other models as having failed to achieve the goals of the lower classes, to satisfy their urgent needs, or to meet trying challenges.

In applying the preceding argument to the Arab situation and seeking to validate it through empirical research, it is useful to think of ideology as an intervening variable between the prevailing order together with its socioeconomic structures and conditions (which will be taken here as independent variables) and preferences with regard to development models (treated here as dependent variables). These interrelationships and their directions may be illustrated as follows:

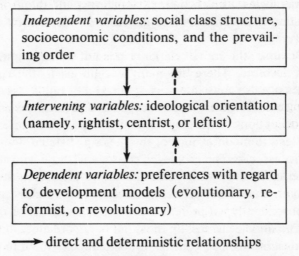

Independent variables: social class structure, socioeconomic conditions, and the prevailing order

Intervening variables: ideological orientation (namely, rightist, centrist, or leftist)

Dependent variables: preferences with regard to development models (evolutionary, reformist, or revolutionary)

⟶ direct and deterministic relationships

--→ indirect and legitimizing relationships

Arab thought during the last century and a half has focused mostly on themes of change arising from (a) the internal dynamics of the Arab society, (b) encounters with the West, and (c) the onslaught of various challenges. A wide variety of concepts such as an-nahḍa *(awakening),* at-taṭawwor wan-noushou' wal-irtiqā' *(evolution),* at-taqaddom *(progress),* at-tajdīd wal-ḥadātha *(renewal* and *modernity),* al-ouṣoul wal-mou'āṣara *(authenticity* and *contemporane-*

ity), al-iṣlāḥ *(reform)*, al-ba'th *(renaissance)*, al-iḥyā' *(revival)*, at-taḥrīr wat-taḥarror *(liberation* and *liberalization)*, at-taghyīr wal-ibdā' *(change* and *creativity)*, at-tanmia or al-inmā' *(growth* and *development)*, at-taḥawwol *(transformation)*, ath-thawra *(revolution)*, and several others have been proposed and reproposed, defined and redefined, and ardently argued and reargued.

Contemporary Arab thought can be understood most clearly in the context of the ongoing confrontations between forces of change and forces maintaining the established order, between classes, and between forces of liberation and forces of domination. It cannot be characterized as unitary but is instead divided into contending currents deeply embedded in these ongoing confrontations. Given this situation, it is naive to claim that Arab thought is always critical of the existing order and that Arab intellectuals constitute a group or even a class in themselves and for themselves.

The contending orientations in contemporary Arab thought may be classified as traditional, liberal, and progressive, corresponding respectively to the ideologies of the ruling classes, the emerging middle classes, and the deprived classes and segments of the society:

I.

The ruling classes (i.e. the aristocracy and big traditional bourgeoisie) and those who are affiliated or identify with them have subscribed to a rightist ideology and have preferred a slow, selective, partial, and evolutionary process of change. Since the beginning of the Nahḍa a century and a half ago, the intellectuals who articulated such a rightist ideology and conception of change have based their thinking on traditions. Their most sophisticated expressions have appeared in connection with conservative thought legitimizing the established order and with the salafia (espousal of ancestral values or earlier forms of Islam) or ouṣoulia and other past-oriented movements.

Conservative thought has served the ruling classes and tried to legitimize the existing order by preaching notions of absolute obedience of the ruler on the grounds of divine law and the unity of the umma.[1] For example, the 'ulama *(prominent clergy)* and learned men serving feudal families viewed "man's relationship to God" and ruler-ruled relationships as ra'iyya-ra'i (literally, *flock-shepherd)* or master-slave relationships.[2] As Hisham Sharabi has pointed out, these conservatives had no prominent intellectuals to serve as their spokesmen because of their inability "to express their ideology in a systematic fashion" due to "their belief that there was nothing new to be said. All energy was directed toward reiterating in traditional terms the old tested truths."[3]

The salafia or ouṣoulia movement rejected some of the prevailing traditions and propagated ideas of return to the pure sources of Islam. The leading spokesmen of this movement, such as Jamal ad-Dīn al-Afghāni (1839-1897), Moḥammad 'Abdu (1849-1905), and Muḥammad Rashīd Riḍa (1865-1935) are usually described as reformists. They called for the adoption of certain liberal innovations, including European sciences and constitutional rule, and clashed with the religious establishment. Yet, al-Afghāni died in the service of as-Sultan 'Abdul Ḥamīd, 'Abdu cooperated with the British administration in Egypt, and Riḍa called for the return of the caliphate after the destruction of the Ottoman Empire and engaged in sectarian strife.

The salafia has continuously been used as a mechanism of reconciliation, the muting of contradictions, and legitimization of the established order. Furthermore, it contributed to the emergence of religious fundamentalism. It has also encouraged a tendency toward obsessive preoccupation with the past at the expense of the present and the future.[4] This tendency, according to 'Abdallah Laroui, has succeeded in abolishing the historical dimension because those involved have failed to see the real and have instead lapsed into the psychology of surrender to the past. In this way the Arab is alienated from reality and experiences "a loss of self in the absolutes of language, culture, and the saga of the past."[5]

The Arab aristocracy and big traditional bourgeoisie lost power to the emerging middle classes in several Arab countries, but they continue to prevail in some others (Saudi Arabia, the Gulf states, Jordan, and Morocco). For the upper classes, development means economic growth (with as little emphasis on a fair distribution of wealth as possible), adopting selected items of western technology without ideology, raising the standard of living (without combating disparities), spreading education (elitist and religious), building the necessary infrastructure, aiming for a free economy, following an open door policy with the West and collaborating with its multinational corporations, placing greater priority and higher value on consumption as opposed to production, promoting traditional loyalties, and insisting on religious rather than secular norms.[6]

As the upper classes see it, "appropriate" development does not involve transforming the existing social structures or changing the prevailing mentality and culture. On the contrary, it attempts to contain the effects of transfer of selected western technology. Social, cultural, and political innovations are rejected. Even science is viewed as being beneficial only to the extent that it agrees with religion. This way, the process of development becomes restrictive, selective, adaptive, partial, slow, and compartmentalized. Essentially, this version of development promotes conditions of dependency, social class disparities, repression, elitism, and alienation. The whole society, in fact, is relegated to historical marginality.

In order to contain the process of development, the ruling classes resort to two mechanisms of control. First, the task of development is exclusively entrusted to ahl al-hall wal-'aqd *(the elites)*. Political parties, labor unions, voluntary associations, and other similar organizations are either not allowed, repressed, or at least dismissed as irrelevant. In connection with this last point, one should note the irony that an integral part of the conservative ideology is the rejection of the very notion of ideology; one of the pretexts for this rejection is the conservatives' characterization of "ideology" as foreign rather than genuine [dakhīl vs. asīl] to Arab culture and as a product of a different reality. The second way in which the elites deal with the development process is by living dual lives based on separation of what is public and what is private. Publicly, they adhere to traditions and strictly enforce their observance on the masses. Privately, however, they may enjoy all sorts of taboo pleasures.

II.

The Arab national bourgeoisie (based in the old and the new emerging middle classes) has tended more than other elements of Arab society to subscribe to a reconciliatory centrist ideology and has conceived of development in terms of western liberalism and modernization, or in terms of Arab socialism, or occasionally in terms of salafia.

A. The national bourgeoisie that opted for western liberalism (and prevailed in Tunisia and Lebanon) defined development as a modernizing process involving (1) replacing traditional value orientations with their opposites (e.g., replacing ascription-based social status with achievement-based status, sentimentality with rationality, past-orientedness with future-orientedness [ousoulia with infitāh], the sacred with the secular, and improvisation with planning); (2) socializing individuals and groups into placing loyalty to the nation ahead of the prevailing segmental loyalties; (3) planning for economic growth and making symbolic concessions to the deprived so as to prevent radicalization (rather than minimizing disparities and bridging the gap between the deprived and the privileged); (4) promoting technological transfer and a consumer economy; (5) modernizing the political system through formation of political parties, reforming the administrative hierarchies, replacing traditional authorities with national authorities, and allowing for symbolic mass participation in the political process.

A number of well-known Arab intellectuals contributed to the development of such western-style liberalism throughout the Nahda. Pioneering representatives of this trend included, among others, Naṣif al-Yazji (1800-1871), Bouṭros al-Boustāni (1819-1893), Qassem Amīn (1863-1908), and Aḥmed Lutfi as-Sa'id (1872-1936). Later in the twentieth century, such noted intellectuals as Taha Ḥussein of Egypt, 'Alāl al-Fassi of the Maghrib, and Constantine Zurayk of the Mashriq were preeminent contributors to this movement.

Boutros al-Boustāni insisted on nationalistic ties, rejected sectarianism, and addressed himself to the "children of the home-land" rather than to affiliates of the same religious faith. He also called for secularism, future-orientedness, and revival of the Ara-bic language; he emphasized the importance of using Arabic as a medium of instruction so that "Syria may not become a Babel of languages . . . as it is a Babel of religions."[7] Al-Boustāni con-cerned himself also with women's issues and published a book as early as 1849 on the education of women that preceded by half a century the pioneering works of another liberal, Qassem Amīn, who wrote two books on the subject: *The Emancipation of Women* (1899), and *The New Woman* (1901). This concern shared by al-Boustāni and Amīn was an integral part of their more comprehen-sive liberal thinking on how to achieve the Nahḍa. According to Amīn, persecution of women is only one of several forms of persecution:

> Look at the eastern countries; you will find woman enslaved to man and man to the ruler. Man is an oppressor in his home, oppressed as soon as he leaves it. Then look at the European countries; the govern-ments are based on freedom and respect for personal rights, and the status of women has been raised to a high degree of respect and freedom of thought and action.[8]

Taha Ḥussein concerned himself with issues of cultural mod-ernization and constantly engaged in what is called maʻrakat al-qadīm wal-jadīd *(the battle of the old and the new)*. His aspirations for Egypt were such that he saw it as a western rather than an Eastern country. In a controversial book, *The Future of Culture in Egypt* (1938), he proclaimed that Egypt was "always part of Europe in all aspects of intellectual and cultural life" and that Egyptians have undertaken "a clear and binding obligation" to "follow the path of Europeans so as to be their equals and partners in civilization, in its good and evil, its sweetness and bitterness, what can be loved or hated, what can be praised or blamed."[9]

The Moroccan intellectual ʻAlāl al-Fassi combined salafia,

liberalism, and aristocratic sympathies. He agreed with some of the notions of salafia in that he called for a return to the pure sources of Islam and saw the French invasion of the Maghrib as an attempt at "eliminating Islam and replacing it with Christianity, and not as a mere imperialist invasion pursuing material interests."[10] On the other hand, al-Fassi rejected the prevailing cultural dualism of the Maghrib, namely the coexistence of strict salafia and al-'aṣria *(i.e. eclectic modernity)*. Instead, he called for al-mou'āṣara *(i.e. contemporaneity — reform from within the society's unique framework without transforming its direction or distorting its essence).*[11] The correct way of thought, according to him, is future-oriented, comprehensive, and responsive to the nation's needs. This requires changing "thinking" and "mentality" in such a way as to enable the Maghrib to deal with its problems "in accordance with the requirements of this age in which matter [al-mādda] and machine [al-āla] constitute top priorities [fi al-maqām al-awwal]."[12] To that effect, he suggested specifically that "we change our customs ['adāt], that we train ourselves . . . to think about events prior to their occurrence, and that we give up the custom of improvisation ['ādat al-irtijāl] which threatens us with impotency and dullness."[13] The aristocratic leanings of al-Fassi revealed themselves in his assertion that "the correct thinking . . . is not the thinking of the masses [ash-shari'] . . . but the thinking of the enlightened class [at-ṭabaqa al-moutanawwira]."[14]

Finally, Constantine Zurayk represents the Mashriq's style of liberalism. He, too, emphasizes the importance of changing Arab mentality rather than the prevailing order and its structures. He believes that salvation lies in future-orientedness and "self-capability" [al-qoudra ath-thatia]. For him, development is a product of future-oriented thinking (i.e. rational foresight involving objectivity and realism on the one hand and moral commitment on the other) and of "self-capability" (which is fourfold: the capability of the mind, represented by science; the capability of the soul — morality resulting from deep faith; the capability to repel aggression; and the capability to achieve national solidarity). In giving priority to a change in mentality, Zurayk warns in the following terms against blaming the prevailing order: "It is a great mistake, indeed a grave danger, to attribute all of what underdeveloped people are suffering from today, including deprivation, powerlessness, and corruption, to the prevailing orders."[15]

B. Since the 1950s, the national bourgeoisie that opted for Arab socialism rather than western liberalism has emerged as a strong force in several Arab countries. Starting out from an ardent nationalist point of view, it gradually learned about the necessities of socialist reform and some aspects of class analysis. The Arab bourgeoisie has tended to form such nationalist and socialist convictions in countries where it has been more dependent on the deprived classes in opposition to the aristocracy or the big traditional bourgeoisie and in countries suffering from foreign domination (e.g., Egypt, Algeria, Syria, Palestine, Sudan, Libya, and Iraq). As such, nationalism in the Arab world has meant a greater awareness on the part of the people of their identity and has stimulated in them a yearning for self-determination. The national bourgeoisie and its intellectuals worked toward crystallization of the concept of nationalism and the establishment of nationalist movements.

A distinction needs to be made here between Marxist socialism and Arab socialism. The latter is essentially nationalist in character, but it has borrowed some Marxist concepts and slogans without integrating them into a comprehensive theory. Arab socialism has compromised on class analysis and the elimination of private property, and has rejected materialistic interpretations of history, sticking to its original idealism and confusing the whole issue as a question of spirit and matter in their religious connotations.

Arab socialism reached power through military coups d'état and managed to eliminate the Arab aristocracy and big traditional bourgeoisie in some Arab countries. During less than a quarter century (1949-1970), more than 35 military coups d'état succeeded in Arab countries (Iraq, Syria, Egypt, Sudan, North Yemen, Algeria, and Libya). Military governments tried to establish their legitimacy through land reform, slogans of liberation, nationalization of big business, calls for Arab unity, support for education, strengthening the public sector, restrictions on importing consumer goods, and closing doors (while keeping windows open) to western influence.

Arab socialism is most clearly represented by the teachings and practices of the Ba'th party, Nasserism, and the Algerian revolution. In all three instances, this kind of socialism has served as an annex to nationalism and has proven ineffective and contradictory, to the great disappointment of the Arab masses; words and actions have not rhymed. Calls for, and attempts at, elimination of exploitation have left the system of private property almost intact. "Identification with the masses" has meant in effect depriving them of the right to participate in the making of their future. Proclamations on class struggle have confused issues and have been used to impose consensus. Slogans of people's power have served to disguise one-person authoritarianism. Hence there is widespread disbelief and cynicism about repeatedly stated claims regarding "elimination of exploitation in all its forms," "achievement of social justice," "transformation of all productive processes for the benefit of the people and society," and "liberation of the oppressed."

The extent of Arab socialism's failure is indicated by the following figures. After two decades of Arab socialism in Egypt, official statistics for 1970 (when one Egyptian pound was worth U.S.$2.30) showed that 77.6 percent of Egyptian families (87.8 percent in rural areas) spent annually less than 250 Egyptian pounds (110 pounds on the average). The families that spent annually between 250 and 1,000 Egyptian pounds constituted 21.5 percent of the total population (12.2 percent in rural areas). Those families that spent annually more than 1,000 Egyptian pounds constituted less than 1 percent (0.9 percent) of the total population (virtually none in rural areas). These statistics also showed that above 10 percent of the population accounted for 45 percent of total Egyptian consumption for that year, and a mere 2.5 percent accounted for almost one quarter (23.4 percent) of Egypt's annual consumption.[16]

C. Finally, it should be noted that some segments of the national bourgeoisie, not unlike the big traditional bourgeoisie, have also used salafia. This is exemplified by the Muslim brotherhoods (founded in Egypt in 1928) and other similar fundamental-ist groups and organizations. Some of these started as splinter groups which became disenchanted with nationalism and social-ism. Encouraged by the early success of the Iranian revolution, they attracted alienated youth from the lower middle and working classes seeking salvation in Islamic militancy. This kind of Islamic resurgence has occurred at times of national crises and increasing western presence in the area, and particularly when secular leftist and nationalist groups have been suppressed by the pro-western regimes. Investigating these Islamic militant groups as "social movements," the Egyptian sociologist Sa'ad Eddīn Ibrahīm found that they seek to build a new social order on the basis of Islam. They see the prevailing political system as corrupt, unjust, inept, and externally controlled by the enemies of Islam. In the area of social affairs, they call for the separation of the sexes and the modesty of women. In talking about economic issues, they ex-press empathy with "al-masakīn wal-moustaḍa'fīn fī al-arḍ" *("the wretched and weak on earth")*. They reject both capitalism and communism as well as the current religious establishment.[17]

III.

The Arab masses — particularly the impoverished, the desti-tute, and the uprooted and marginal among them — are extremely alienated from their ruling classes. This deep sense of alienation and marginality, coupled with feelings of national humiliation at the hands of imperialism (of which Zionism is a colonial exten-sion), has led to the emergence of a revolutionary tradition in contemporary Arab society.

The point of departure of this Arab revolutionary tradition was an acute sense of the historical decline of Arab society and its naked exposure to national and class domination and exploitation. What has been called the Arab awakening began in the Arab struggle for liberation from Ottoman rule, and subsequently from imperialism, as well as from underdevelopment, poverty, and authoritarianism. These issues have been at the core of the devel-opment of Arab revolutionary political culture since its inception during the last quarter of the nineteenth century.

In its formative period, progressive revolutionary thought shared with liberal thought its concern with national consciousness, secularism, rationalism, and liberation. What has distinguished revolutionary thought is its leaning toward socialism.

The pioneers of such progressive thought were Shibli Shumayyil (1850-1917), 'Abdul Raḥman al-Kawākibi (1854-1902), and Faraḥ Anṭūn (1874-1922). Shibli Shumayyil was the first Arab intellectual to present socialism as a comprehensive system and ideology, and to follow a scientific materialist approach in his social and historical analysis. His point of departure was the "no life — no death" situation of the umma. To him, salvation lies in science rather than in religion, which he thought of as divisive, a product of primitive imagination, an "echo not a sound," and a hindrance to development. The benefits of religion, according to him, supersede its disadvantages during its early stages, but the opposite becomes true at later stages. Hence the need for permanent transformation of the system. In 1908, Shumayyil formulated the first Arab program for a socialist party, one whose purpose would be to combat extreme injustice.

Al-Kawākibi raised the same kind of questions that intrigued religious reformers, secular liberals, and fellow radicals: What are the sources of the umma's decline, stagnation, and underdevelopment? What is the solution? How can the Arabs achieve Nahḍa?

He rejected the idea of an Islamic caliphate and opted for Arab nationalism, secularism, democracy, and socialism. His treatise on the nature of despotism and its corrupting influence on all aspects of life reflected keen understanding of the prevailing situation. As a substitute system, al-Kawākibi called for democracy based on "socialist philosophy." He believes that class disparities can be preserved only by despotism. "The poor," he says, "does not seek aid from the rich . . . nor charity. What he seeks is justice . . . wealth is the value of work, and no such wealth may accumulate at the hand of the rich except through all kinds of domination and deception. Justice requires . . . achievement of equality . . . in rights and livelihood . . . No wonder, then, that the socialist pattern of living is one of the most marvelous things envisioned by the mind."[18]

Similarly, Faraḥ Anṭūn saw society as existing in a state of contradiction, and he decided that the Nahḍa can be achieved only through socialism, science, and secularism. He expounded many of his basic ideas through the medium of the novel. One of his novels, entitled ad-Dīn wal-'Ilm wal-Māl *(Religion, Science, and Money),* depicts human beings in conflict and presents a lively debate between representatives of workers, businessmen, and scientists. The message is resolving social dilemmas and improving the human condition through socialism and reliance on mind instead of faith.

These pioneering ideas prepared the way for the emergence of Arab progressive revolutionary movements, parties, organizations, groups, programs, and so forth since the turn of the twentieth century. Such developments made it imperative that conservative and liberal movements reexamine their stands and add some socialist notions to, or integrate them into, their own ideologies.

This remains true today. Early in the Nahḍa, much Arab thought occupied itself with problems of decline. Currently, Arab thought explores the realms of al-kāritha *(disaster),* and the same old models continue to compete in shaping Arab consciousness. Retreat and compliance defer rather than resolve the question of overcoming the condition of alienation.

What is the nature of Arab underdevelopment? Where does the process of change start and toward what goals? Who is to carry out the challenging tasks of change? What are the effective mechanisms and instruments of change? Many of the disagreements on these and other questions are due to the different positions in the existing structures held by those involved in the debate, the classes and groups or communities that they affiliate and identify with, and the kinds of goals that they envision for the society and themselves.

The conservatives see the society in a state of harmony, and hope for stability. Their most effective ways of preserving the existing order are mechanisms of repression. The liberals are able to foresee problems and recommend partial and cosmetic reforms, and hope for reconciliation and containment of contradictions. The kind of change that they recommend pertains mostly to value orientations and mentality and would be carried out through socialization and by the educated elites. Their mechanisms are negotiation, convincing the ruling elites of the dangers that they face and consequently of the need for compromise, and appeasement of the deprived through welfare, expressions of compassion, and generation of false hopes.

The revolutionary model of development posits that change must start on the system level and aim at the prevailing political, economic, and social structures. Behind this view is an assumption that development is not a mere state of mind as much as it is a state of the society and its overall order. The transformation of the society from a state of underdevelopment to a state of development must begin with change in the very substructures that give rise to the prevailing mentality.[19] This kind of change is required by the nature of the goals that the progressive movement envisions for the society (many of which are not shared by the conservatives or the liberals): (1) achieving liberation from the condition of dependency (which involves achieving Arab unity, solving the Palestinian problem, ending undue foreign influence, bridging the gap between the Arab world and the developed world, setting in motion dynamic processes of production as opposed to leisurely consumption, and strengthening Arab control over Arab natural resources); (2) overcoming poverty and eliminating class disparities; (3) replacing the existing authoritarian hierarchies with democratic self-government; (4) transcending the condition of alienation.

In addition to requiring basic transformations at the level of society as a whole and of the prevailing order itself, aims such as these also require the active involvement of the deprived and oppressed through popular movements. Because the ruling classes violently resist any such transformations, the oppressed may not be able under certain conditions to avoid revolutionary confrontation.

The prospects of revolutionary change in Arab society are presently dim indeed, but the idea of such change cannot easily be dismissed as the product of utopian thinking. The prevailing conditions are extremely alienating, so much so that a process of polarization between forces of change and forces preserving the status quo is increasingly leaving Arabs with little choice. Sooner or later, Arabs will have to mobilize to put an end to their destitution and historical marginality. For this reason, the progressive nationalist movement urgently needs to recognize and correct its previous mistakes.

NOTES

[1] See Albert Hourani, *Arab Thought in the Liberal Age, 1798-1937,* Oxford: Oxford University Press, 1970, Chapter One.

[2] Hisham Sharabi, *Arab Intellectuals and the West: The Formative Years, 1875-1914,* Baltimore: The Johns Hopkins Press, 1970, pp. 11-12.

[3] *Ibid.,* p. 13.

[4] See Majid Fakhry, "The Arabs and the Lure of the Past," unpublished manuscript, Center for Contemporary Arab Studiês, Georgetown University, 1981.

[5] 'Abdallah Laroui, *The Crisis of the Arab Intellectual,* translated from the French by Diarmid Cammell, Berkeley: University of California Press, 1976, p. 156.

[6] Ministry of Planning, Kingdom of Saudi Arabia, *Second Development Plan,* (1395-1400 A.H./1975-1980 A.D.).

[7] Nasif Nassar, Naḥwa Moujtama' Jadīd *(Towards a New Society),* Beirut: Dar an-Nahar, 1970, p. 28.

[8] Quoted in Albert Hourani, *op. cit.,* p. 168.

[9] *Ibid.,* pp. 329-330.

[10] See the special issue on salafia, Al-Thaqafa Al-Jadīda (Morocco), Vol. 5, No. 22, 1981, p. 113.

[11] 'Alāl al-Fassi, Al-Naqd Al-Zati *(Self Criticism),* Beirut, Cairo, Baghdad: Manshourat Dar al-Kashshaf, 1966, p. 100.

[12] *Ibid.,* p. 20.

[13] *Ibid.,* p. 40.

[14] *Ibid.,* p. 49.

[15] Constantine Zurayk, Naḥnu Wal-Moustaqbal *(We and the Future),* Beirut: Dar al-'Ilm lil-Malaeen, 1977, p. 350.

[16] Adil Hussein, "Khiṭat Mouḍa'afat ad-Dakhl al-Qawmi" *(Plan for Doubling National Income),* At-Talī'a, Cairo, Vol. 8, 1972, pp. 78-88.

[17] See Sa'ad Eddin Ibrahim, "Anatomy of Egypt: Militant Islamic Groups," unpublished manuscript, 1981.

[18] 'Abdul Raḥman al-Kawākibi, Al-A'māl al-Kāmila *(Complete Works),* Beirut: Al-Mou'assasah al-'Arabiyya Lil-Dirasāt Wan-Nashr, 1975, pp. 169-172.

[19] See Halim Barakat, "Socio-economic, Cultural and Personality Forces Determining Development in Arab Society," *Social Praxis* 2 (3-4), 1976, pp. 179-204.

CASE STUDIES IN TECHNOLOGY TRANSFER IN THE ARAB WORLD *Lawrence L. Edwards*

For over four years I have been a program manager in the Division of International Programs (INT) of the U.S. National Science Foundation (NSF). My initial responsibility was the U.S.-Egyptian Cooperative Science Program which had been started in 1972. The funds to support this program came from the sale of U.S. agricultural products (mainly wheat) to Egypt. The Egyptian pounds earned from these sales had to be spent in Egypt; therefore most of the research activity supported by the program was actually carried out in that country. Because of the source of the funds, this program was called the Special Foreign Currency (SFC) Program. It ended in 1981 when the SFC funds were exhausted; during its last few years the funding level was equivalent to about $2 million per year.

What technology or knowledge was transferred in this program? Most of the projects it supported consisted of basic and applied scientific research carried out in Egypt under the supervision of an Egyptian scientist, while a U.S. scientist, usually more senior, visited the project site annually. In many cases the American scientist was the former research director of the Egyptian researcher. In those instances the project amounted to an extension of the graduate training of the Egyptian scientist. In any case, what was transferred by the program was knowledge and research skills in various scientific fields.

How successful was the SFC Program? Certainly research got done under its auspices. Papers were published that would not have been otherwise. Access to new equipment made it possible

Lawrence L. Edwards earned a PhD in Chemical Physics at Harvard University. Presently a Program Manager at the National Science Foundation's Division of International Programs, Dr. Edwards's position has involved extensive work on technical and development projects with Algeria, Egypt, and Saudi Arabia. He has taught chemistry at the University of California at Northridge and at the American University of Beirut. He has published a number of articles on chemical spectroscopy.

185

for participating graduate students to do better research. The researchers were able to travel to international conferences. But each project ended; eventually the program ended. What was left was a number of researchers with new equipment and increased research experience, a number of graduate students with improved research theses, and some other benefits. But no institutions were established and most of the projects did not generate any lasting changes. While it was beneficial, the SFC Program did not succeed in bringing about a permanent transfer of skills or knowledge to Egypt.

It should be noted that some of the SFC Program's projects did not fit the above general description. One of these exceptional projects was designed from its inception to transfer a specific medical technology, diagnostic ultrasound. This acoustical analogy of radar is a powerful, non-invasive tool for observing conditions inside the human body, which is now used in the United States on an almost standard basis in yearly physicals and checkups for pregnant women. The project involved the Cairo University Faculty of Medicine and the U.S. Alliance for Engineering in Medicine and Biology, a professional organization. When the work began five years ago, there were no medical ultrasound units in Egypt, nor were there any people capable of operating them. By 1980 there were over thirteen units in several institutions in Egypt with over a score of trained operators as well as medical doctors trained in interpretation of the results. The project is now supported by its own income plus funds from the Egyptian government. The outcome, then, was a very successful transfer of a sophisticated technology.

Why did the ultrasound project work so well? First, the project center was established as an independent unit (i.e. outside of any bureaucracy), with funding directly from the NSF. Second, the personnel involved were of very high quality. Third, the project had the support and interest of a highly placed Egyptian official, and this freed it from many administrative encumbrances. As a result of the foregoing, the Egyptian project director was completely in charge. To be sure, there were U.S. experts, consultants, and other types of assistance, but the director was clearly the leader. He had the sole authority to make decisions on salaries, hiring, firing, and buying equipment — in short, all the important issues. Furthermore, there was a great need (or market) for the technology. The procedure rapidly became part of Egyptian hospital routine. The equipment was used over 20 hours per day throughout the year. The patient caseload increased dramatically throughout the life of the project. The project center pioneered the use of ultrasound in the investigation of schistosomiasis, a parasitic disease very common in Egypt. In fact, one of the most moving experiences of my professional career occurred during a site visit to this center. A young M.D. was just starting a scan on a very old man from Upper Egypt. In less than two minutes both the presence of both forms of schistosomiasis and the extent of infection were determined. I had a strong reaction to this scene. First I was sad for this old man who had suffered his whole life and had never even known what he was suffering from. He probably contracted the disease as a youngster playing in the Nile and had never known good health. But then I felt the promise represented by the young physician working with a powerful new tool in the fight against a disease that has plagued Egypt, and other parts of the world, for many centuries. To both I could only wish "Allah maakum" (God be with you).

Another technology-transfer-related activity I participated in was a program funded by the U.S. Agency for International Development (USAID) intended to encourage Egyptian scientists to do applied research. The program was carried out in cooperation with Egypt's Academy for Scientific Research and Technology (ASRT). I helped in the planning and was the contract manager for a subproject aimed at setting up maintenance and repair (M&R) facilities for research instrumentation at several Egyptian institutions.

The reasoning behind the design of the project was very simple. Since there is very little M&R of scientific equipment at Egyptian government research institutions, the necessary technology and skills would have to be imported and an institutional base for training developed in Egypt. Therefore, Egyptians were sent to appropriate institutions in the United States to be trained in M&R. The idea was that they would then return to Egypt to repair instruments and train others. U.S. experts went to Egypt to advise on establishment of physical facilities and administrative procedures for M&R.

The foregoing sounds very straightforward. In fact, the plan was doomed from the beginning to a partial success at best. The difficulty lay in the low salaries paid to Egyptian governmental employees. An implicit assumption in the project design was that trained Egyptian personnel working for the project would receive pay commensurate with their skills. This was not the case. Skilled M&R personnel are paid more, often by a factor of 5 to 20, in the Egyptian private sector or in other countries than by the Egyptian government. This was one of the reasons why there was so little M&R in the Egyptian government research institutions in the first place. The effects of this situation on the project were manifold. First, it was difficult to find people to train, since those with skills in M&R were already in well-paying jobs outside the government. Therefore, many of those selected for training had no previous background in M&R. After six months of basic training in the United States, these people had a working knowledge of M&R but were by no means experts. Unfortunately, the Egyptian government's expectations about their capabilities were unrealistically high. Second, about 15 percent of the trainees did not return to Egypt, but chose to go to countries (including the United States) where job opportunities and salaries were better than in Egypt. Third, those who did return acquired second and third jobs, so that they were not focused on using their M&R skills on project equipment. The salary problem is most dramatic in Cairo, where much of the Egyptian and foreign private sector is located and where people are more mobile, more likely to leave the country. The problem also exists in Upper Egypt but is less severe there.

The obvious solution was to raise the salaries of Egyptian project personnel, and we certainly tried to arrange this. Since a few thousand dollars per month used for this purpose would have saved ten times that amount in training costs, it would have been an enormously worthwhile investment. The problem was that the Egyptian government was hearing the same refrain — "an increase in salaries will increase effectiveness" — from virtually all other USAID project personnel (and those of other countries' foreign assistance programs as well). The government's concern was that if all salaries were raised, then inflation would set in and political problems would ensue. Why not raise some salaries and not others? This is being done to a limited extent, but support for science is not a high priority in Egypt. It should be noted that the ultrasound project did not fall into this trap. Because the funding source was an NSF grant, salaries could be (and were) relatively high. Since there were not many SFC grants in Egypt, they were considered special situations, so it was permissible to have high salaries.

Another difficulty besetting the USAID scheme was the interaction of the several bureaucracies involved with the project: ASRT, USAID/Cairo, USAID/Washington, NSF, U.S. National Academy of Sciences, Egypt's National Research Center and Scientific Instrumentation Center, and several Egyptian universities. I am not saying that these institutions performed poorly, but it is a reality that as the number of parties involved in the decision-making process increases, action becomes more difficult. This needs to be understood if expectations are to be realistic. (The ultrasound project, on the other hand, had relatively little bureaucratic involvement.) However, when all is said and done, the USAID project did succeed to some extent.

My final example is a project involving the NSF and the Saudi Arabian National Center for Science and Technology (SANCST). This agreement to assist the Saudi Arabian government in developing its capabilities in science and technology (S&T) is under the auspices of the U.S.-Saudi Arabian Joint Commission on Economic Cooperation, which was established in 1974 and is administered by the Saudi Arabian Ministry of Finance and National Economy and the U.S. Department of the Treasury. NSF's basic role in connection with this agreement is to transfer to SANCST the technology of administering a research funding and S&T policy-making institution.

Since I have been working in this program for only a few months, I am not personally acquainted with all the activities carried out in the last five years. My overall impression is that the process has been slow, primarily because the professional staff at SANCST is very limited. This is not unusual in Saudi Arabia, but the problem is especially acute at SANCST because the requirements for working there are high, i.e. a PhD in science, managerial capability, and Saudi nationality. People meeting these standards are hard to come by. Even so, much has been accomplished. One good example with which I am personally familiar is the Applied Research Grants Program. This program is modeled on NSF grants programs in that proposals are unsolicited and evaluation is by peer mail review, followed by a panel review. In the most recent competition over 100 proposals were received. I participated in the panel review in February 1981. In two days, 30 proposals in various fields of applied science were reviewed by 13 panel members. Each proposal was discussed in detail before a recommendation was made. The whole process ran smoothly and accomplished the job. It is my belief that SANCST will grow slowly but surely into a major research supporter in the world.

I would like to conclude with some generalizations drawn from my experiences with technology transfer in the Middle East.

First, the probability of success varies dramatically depending on country, source of funds, personnel, regulations, size of bureaucracies, and many other factors.

Second, when decision-making authority is diffuse, as in the USAID project, communication among decision-makers takes on the utmost importance. In fact, day-to-day communication is necessary. In effect this means that a representative of each decision-making institution must be on-site.

Third, the other bureaucracy is often perceived as impossibly slow while one's own bureaucracy's efficiency is seen as quite reasonable. This is analogous to an individual's tendency to judge himself by his values but others by their actions.

Fourth, the more flexible the organizations involved, the greater the chances of success of the project.

Fifth, positive personal attitudes are very important in any technology transfer project. The more complex the project, the more important the attitudes are. By a positive attitude I mean a willingness to cooperate with others and work for a common goal.

Finally, a support infrastructure is critical to some technologies (e.g., M&R is impossible unless spare parts can be obtained as needed).

ADMINISTRATION: THE FORGOTTEN ISSUE IN ARAB DEVELOPMENT
Omar El-Fathaly and Richard Chackerian

The Arab countries differ markedly in their responses to the problems of development. This is understandable when one recognizes that the Arab world is divided *inter alia,* between the ultraradical and ultraconservative, between the extreme rich and extreme poor, and between the overpopulated and underpopulated. Unfortunately, most, if not all, of the Arab world shares severe problems of administrative development which block the region's overall progress.

Through their work in connection with the developing and developed world, researchers and scholars have provided some concrete examples of how administrative problems can hinder development.[1] Few serious studies have been done, however, on the subject of administration and its relation to development in the Arab world. Most of the existing material is in the nature of isolated case studies that do not provide a basic and general understanding.[2] Nevertheless, a general consensus exists among leaders in the Arab world concerning the urgent need for administrative reform, since any attempt to initiate development is likely to result in complete failure if the administrative agency responsible for planning, implementing, and following up on the development process is itself ineffective. Slogans such as "Administrative

Omar El-Fathaly holds a PhD in Political Science from the Florida State University, where he is Professor of Political Science and Public Administration. In the past, Dr. Fathaly has officially represented Libya at a number of international forums and conferences. He has written on political and social development in Libya and North Africa; his publications include *Political Development and Social Change in Libya.*

Richard Chackerian earned a PhD in Political Science at the University of Washington (Seattle). He is presently an Associate Professor and Director at the Middle East Administrative Studies Program, Florida State University. Dr. Chackerian has consulted extensively for various local, state, and foreign governments in the fields of public policy and public administration. He has also published numerous articles on such topics as comparative administration and bureaucracy, Libyan society, and American social patterns in the state of Florida.

Revolution," "Administrative Reform," "Administrative Innovation," and "Restructuring of the Public Sector" are heard throughout the region. The problems of administrative development are interrelated and none can be solved on its own; most concerned individuals and groups recognize that meaningful change in this area will have to involve all aspects of the socio-economic, cultural, and political norms of the society.

Given the differences in the constraints, resources, and priorities of the Arab countries, it does not seem possible to provide a single solution that can be generalized to all Arab states. But an examination of case studies does indicate that certain general types of problems manifest themselves in the administrative systems of many Arab countries. We turn now to a review of some of these widespread problems.

Problems of Administration in the Arab World

1. *Governmental Expansion and the Colonial Heritage.* The administrative systems currently in place in the Arab world are relatively new and immature. Most were created after 1945, under conditions far different from current ones. For the most part, they have been unable to respond to the enormous changes since 1945 or to cope with the increasing burdens placed upon them as the role of government in society has expanded. Furthermore, most Arab administrative systems were either created under the supervision of a colonial administration or inherited the colonial forms of governance at independence, and they continue to reflect the values, goals, and structure of the colonial period. For this reason, distinct differences in administrative style still exist between the three regions of the Arab world that were under British, French, and Italian colonial administrations.[3] Fascination with the Weberian model of bureaucracy, unresponsiveness on the part of civil servants to popular concerns, and an inadequate appreciation of the need for change are not uncommon symptoms of the lingering impact of colonialism.

2. *Traditional Arab Culture.* The administrative problems of the Arab world do not arise solely from the retentions of colonial norms; certain aspects of traditional Arab culture also play a part.

The primacy of the family, the low status assigned to manual labor, and the sense of fatalism are seen by many observers as seriously detracting from work motivation and neutrality in the performance of organizational roles. While it would be premature to generalize about the relative importance of the various problems discussed thus far, it is our considered judgment that the cultural influence has been given too much attention and the colonial heritage, along with the governmental expansion, has not been given enough attention. Again, the Arab world is complex and diverse. In some areas, particularly the oil-rich countries, the problems created by governmental expansion seem to be predominant. In other countries, particularly among the "resource-poor" lands, traditional culture may be the major stumbling block. In a third set of countries, the colonial administrative heritage has been an important hindrance. In any event, all three factors are important to some degree in each Arab country and the three interact with one another in complex ways.[4]

3. *Excessive Concentration and Diffusion of Authority.* Both academicians and Arab executives complain bitterly about "red tape," poor coordination, and failures of communication in Arab bureaucracies. Often these conditions are associated with a situation where formal and informal authority is extremely concentrated at the top of an administrative hierarchy, while authority and responsibility are diffuse in the lower reaches of the hierarchy. Job descriptions are likely to be vague or nonexistent, and overlapping duties, functions, and jurisdictions are common.[5] As one might expect, where authority and responsibility are diffuse, strategic program objectives are difficult to formulate and planning becomes an impossibility.

4. *Data Bases and Planning.* The problems of poor coordination, communication, and program planning are due not simply to structural defects but also to the newness of most Arab bureaucracies. There simply has not been enough time to develop the data bases required for planning purposes. One of the most pressing problems facing Arab administrations is the lack of reliable and consistent information about such matters as population, housing, and industry. When data is accumulated, it is usually done

with a temporary surge of interest over a short period of time, the gathered information then being tucked away in its raw form without further analysis or updating to make it useful. The outcome of planning based on little or no information can be seen all over the Arab world, but especially in those countries where sudden oil wealth has induced public spending for development. In most of the oil-producing countries, the ministries in charge of planning and development of projects relating to housing, communication, education, health, transportation, and other community-oriented services know that their plans do not reflect the real priorities, needs, and resources of the society. Privately, executives in these states insist that their societies neither need nor are able to absorb such large development plans and projects, and that smaller plans and budgets would be more consistent with their current administrative capability. This point leads us to another problem facing Arab administrations, namely vulnerability to excessive political intervention and influence.

5. *Political Interference.* The interference usually comes from the political leadership or influential socioeconomic power centers. Such powers interfere to safeguard their own activities or to manipulate public programs to serve their own immediate and long-term interests. Political leadership in most Arab countries follows one of several patterns. Traditional Islamic leadership is mainly concerned with the maintenance of its own power and uses the administration to serve this end. A modernizing autocratic leadership, which exercises considerable authority over the mass public, uses governmental bureaucracies to distribute rewards or inflict punishment for supporting or opposing the regime. Such leadership may be either military or charismatic. In the case of military leadership, conflict often arises between the military and the bureaucrats, which handicaps the development of the society. Often neither has much respect or trust in the objectives or capabilities of the other. Under charismatic leadership, the leadership may object to the restrictions imposed by administrative regulations and laws. When a charismatic leader is prevented or limited by the administration from functioning freely, he either ignores or bypasses regulations by claiming that the administra-

tion is not functioning correctly.[6] When a political party dominates the political scene, the administration usually finds itself
restricted by the party's ideological commitments.[7] Any administrator who tries to act on his own initiative often ends up being
thrown out of office, or worse. Whatever the particular form of
government, the leadership is likely to interfere with administration either directly through its political organizations or indirectly
by using the influence of closely allied socioeconomic groups.
Such interference results in confused plans and program strategies
because developmental priorities are overridden by the concern of
interest groups outside of the administrative structure.

6. *Mismatches in Training and Education.* Another serious
problem facing Arab administrations is poor training and the lack
of congruency between the state's needs and available educational
and training programs. A good percentage of trainees from the
Arab world choose to reside where they have been trained (particularly in the case of Egyptians, Syrians, Iraqis, Lebanese, Jordanians, Tunisians, Sudanese, Algerians, and Moroccans). Of those
who return to their native countries, a large percentage seek employment in the private sector, sometimes with multinational corporations working in the Arab world (as in Saudi Arabia, Kuwait,
Qatar, U.A.E., Libya, Bahrain, and Oman). Such external and
internal migration is due in part to the often inadequate material
incentives and working conditions at home in the public sector. A
related problem is that a large number of people trained either
abroad or locally are assigned jobs unrelated to their training. The
fact that only a small percentage of the administrative personnel
have gone through training programs makes the mismatch
between skills and job assignments particularly disturbing.[8]

The program emphases of institutions are often poorly
coordinated with the actual needs of the state. For reasons of
culture and tradition, Arab societies tend to neglect the technical
fields of study. This bias, and the absence of governmental policies to do something about it, results in an avoidance by Arab
students of technical fields and a surplus of graduates in fields like
law, literature, philosophy, and the social sciences. Egypt provides
a good example of this problem and Saudi Arabia, with half a

dozen universities and scores of colleges and other educational institutions, faces a similar situation.

7. *Public Participation and Involvement.* Undoubtedly, successful development requires public participation and involvement. Such participation means a strong and positive relationship between the general public and the administrative structure of state institutions. Unfortunately, in the Arab world the public's relationship to administration tends to be very weak. The situation is almost one in which the public plays the role of a passive recipient and the state administration acts as an agency that provides and distributes what it chooses.[9] The citizen in the Arab world (as well as in most other developing countries) often has no say in who gets what and how. He receives public services more as a matter of favor than as a right. He plays no role in formulating or implementing socioeconomic development plans. Consequently, citizens tend to see themselves as nonparticipants who are neither responsible for nor involved in the developmental process of their community, society, or state. Without a responsible and participating citizenry, it is difficult to envision how the Arab world can develop and progress in any sector.[10] If the citizen is to play a positive role, efforts are needed to educate, motivate, politicize, and commit him. Only when adequate and acceptable institutions that function as channels of communication, dialogue, and participation are developed can citizens be responsible, participating agents of change and development.[11]

8. *Bedoucracy.* Though some are able to acquire technology and products from the modern world, Arab society is on balance still closer to traditionalism and underdevelopment. Arab administrators, being a product of that society, are unable to break away from traditional norms even though they deal daily with questions and problems typical of modern societies. The Arab administrator tends to approach concepts like "time," "productivity," "technology," "work," "public services," "civic responsibilities," and so on with the mentality, understanding, and methods of a bedouin. Professor M. Al-Rumaihi of the University of Kuwait calls this situation "Bedoucracy."[12]

9. *Corruption.* The Arab administrator, like his counterparts

in many other places, is burdened with corruption, which is a persistent feature of bureaucracies nearly everywhere in the Arab world. The reasons for this include the absence or weakness of key institutions, inadequate financial compensation, the perspective and values of administrators in relation to public services, the considerable distance between the masses and the administration, and the administrators' weak feelings of attachment and belonging to the state. All of these, in addition to other socioeconomic and political factors, encourage the spread of corruption within Arab administrations.[13] Indeed, corruption has become so widespread as to be acceptable as a legitimate means of "getting up there." Individuals who have "made it" are respected in their communities, even if the means they used were clearly questionable. They are described as smart and knowing how to get ahead. These practices will become part of the value system of the younger generation unless severe measures to stop them are implemented.

10. *Staffing.* Arab world administrations can be divided into two groups, one facing the problem of being overstaffed and the other of being understaffed. In the first group (e.g., Egypt, Morocco, and Sudan), the administration has more employees than jobs, which results in a confused and poorly coordinated bureaucracy. Here public service employment becomes a way to disguise unemployment and a means of absorbing the young into the labor market. Productivity and efficiency are not the main considerations in such administrations, nor is employee satisfaction. These objectives are outweighed by a concern for political stability, general public welfare, and survival.

In the second group (e.g., Kuwait, Libya, Saudi Arabia, Qatar, and U.A.E.), the administration is extremely understaffed and many of its employees are underqualified. The only available alternative in this situation is to depend on foreign personnel in almost every field. In some cases, native workers are a small minority, particularly in the skilled and semiskilled categories of employment. A consequence of this heavy dependence on foreigners is lack of continuity and consistency on the part of the administration. The diverse cultural backgrounds of the foreign workers also contribute to poor communication. Beyond administrative issues, national security and sociocultural stability may be threatened in such situations.[14]

It should be mentioned that the expatriates in these countries, though they fill administrative vacancies, are often not fully utilized because a workable plan for doing so has not been developed. Many executive expatriates complain bitterly about their lack of understanding of their role and responsibilities. Their native superiors often avoid answering their questions or pass them to underqualified native administrators. It will be years before such countries can develop their own skilled and specialized labor forces. Until then, the foreign labor force must be utilized to the maximum by being assigned well-defined roles and responsibilities; this will also permit numbers to be minimized.

A Typology of Administrative Systems and Their Problems

Clearly, each Arab country does not face the problems outlined above in equal proportion. Indeed, each administrative subsystem within a single country is faced with a different combination of conditions and problems. Because of this complexity, attempts have been made to develop typologies of administrative systems as a means of facilitating consideration of the range of problems faced and of the most appropriate administrative solutions.

Morstein Marx classifies administrative systems into guardian, caste, patronage, and merit bureaucracies.[15] More useful is Fainsod's categorization of them as representative, party state, ruler dominated, military dominated, and ruling.[16] Ruler dominated systems are typified by traditional autocratic regimes in which the bureaucracy tends to be subservient to a traditional elite whose skills and orientation are quite different from those of the bureaucracy (or at least of the ideal Weberian bureaucracy where expertise rather than religion, tradition, or family position is the primary basis of authority). Ruler dominated administrative systems (e.g., Saudi Arabia, Morocco, Jordan, and Oman) tend to be heavily centralized, with real power and authority vested in the hands of those at the very top of the hierarchy, people in these positions often being members of the ruling family. This results in a tendency to avoid responsibility on the part of lower-level bureaucrats. Procrastination, ambiguous committee decisions, and endless consultation ("red tape") are not unusual. The desire to avoid responsibility renders the Western emphasis on specialization in training and job classification meaningless, political elite interference normal, and popular participation and involvement impossible. When pressures arise for economic development, the solution chosen is often "turnkey" projects, but of course this alternative is possible only where there is oil wealth. A somewhat different situation holds with respect to ruler dominated administrations in small countries that have an extremely high per capita income (e.g., Bahrain, Kuwait, Qatar, and U.A.E.). Under these circumstances the smallness of the bureaucracy means that the concentration of authority and the tendency toward group decision-making at the bottom does not necessarily preclude reasonably efficient functioning. Additionally, the enormous wealth of the system allows a great deal of redundancy in training, planning, and programming.

In a ruling system, bureaucratic elites are also the political elites, the bureaucrats themselves being the ruling authorities. The Tunisian regime comes closest to a bureaucratic ruling system and to the Weberian machine bureaucracy which is characteristic of this administrative style. These administrative systems tend to be hierarchical, but unlike ruler dominated systems, they have fairly well-defined departmentalization and specialization at the lower levels, with personnel of considerable expertise and professionalism. Political influence and nepotism are less visible because of the lack of a distinction between political and bureaucratic elites. Because of the emphasis on hierarchy and expertise, however, these systems tend to provide few opportunities for involvement by the mass public.

In party state systems, a ruling party directly and through mobilization of the citizenry controls the bureaucratic apparatus. Although party state systems depend more on party ideology than traditional values, the potential gap in values and perceptions between political and administrative elites is as great here as in the case of ruler dominated systems. The instrumental, technical orientation of bureaucrats is likely to conflict with the policy orientation of party members and elites, particularly if the party is committed to mobilization and involvement of a mass public that is relatively uneducated. While a mobilizing party system provides opportunities for popular participation in administrative affairs, it also creates problems of internal bureaucratic coordination, control, and communication because the power environment is potentially diverse and decentralized. Certainly there are signs of this in Algeria and Libya. In these environments the neat departmentalization and specialization of Weberian bureaucracies gives way to constant mismatches between competence and position, and there is little serious interest in long-term planning. Political interference is seen as being normal, appropriate popular involvement.

Military dominated administrative systems sometime involve a partial merger of political and bureaucratic authority because the military may directly perform certain civil functions and may be the major source of technical expertise in the country. It is for this reason that the relations between military political elites and bureaucracies are somewhat unpredictable.

Representative systems are those which have liberal democratic institutions including competitive parties and popular elections. The competitive process and the consensus that arises out of it sets the bounds for the exercise of administrative discretion in representative systems.

The Weberian "Machine Bureaucracy": Is It A Solution?

The Fainsod typology discussed above elucidates the relationship of administrative systems to their political environments as well as their characteristic styles and problems. It is not very helpful for understanding how bureaucracies ought to be designed to overcome some of these problems. The approach that has generally been followed, particularly in the West, has been to advocate versions of the Weberian "machine bureaucracy" model of organization. The essential elements of the Weberian model include monocratic hierarchical authority, complex and fixed departmentalization, and the maintenance of administrative impersonality through specialized training, professionalization, and protection of tenure.[17] The questions that must be asked about Weberian administrative designs are "What are they designed to do?" and "Do the design assumptions fit the conditions found in the Arab world?" These questions are central because an unquestioning commitment to the Weberian model of administration has blinded many Arab scholars and practitioners to alternatives, some of which will be discussed later in this paper.

It is now well established that machine bureaucracies are best suited to perform specialized routine functions.[18] Moreover, to be successful they need an environment in which policies and problems are well defined and fairly stable, and in which there is relatively little conflict among political authorities. It is also necessary that program solutions to problems be clear and well understood in principle. Finally, to function well machine models of administration require considerable certainty about when decisions will be made and who has the authority to make them. Whether these conditions exist is dependent, of course, on the broader social, political, and technical environment of the society.

A common theme in Arab states, in spite of the differences among them, is a commitment to development and change. The reality of and aspirations for development are of unprecedented proportions in the oil states, but are also significant in other Arab countries. Experience has shown that machine bureaucracies are not appropriate devices for pursuing these objectives because they are simply too inflexible to deal with the uncertainty and complexity of developmental processes. Why, then, do so many of the Arab states find the Weberian model appealing? Certainly one reason is that colonial administrations, which were more concerned with control than with development, found this hierarchical and rigid structure suited to their needs and consistent with their own experience.

A more important question than that of why the machine model has been so attractive is the one of how to design systems that meet the particular needs of a given state. One of our major premises is that no single model of administration can fit the wide variety of regimes and environments in the Arab world; at the same time, each approach used must be capable of dealing with change and development.

Power and Coordination: Basic Elements of Administrative Design

The design of administrative systems requires consideration of two major questions: "What is the proper distribution of power and authority?" and "What is the most appropriate vehicle for coordination?"[19] For the purposes of this discussion, a given configuration of administrative power can be described in terms of the relative influence of the operating line, middle managers, the hierarchical apex, program staff, and administrative staff. The operating line, middle managers, and apex are somewhat arbitrary divisions of the administrative hierarchy from the bottom (operating line) to the top (apex). The staff units are formally *advisory* to those in the structure of hierarchical authority but they deal with different issues and provide different types of expertise. The program staff are experts in the substance of the programs being administered, while the administrative staff are experts in providing support services such as budgeting, auditing, personnel, information systems, purchasing, etc.

The primary methods of coordination are standardization of work processes, standardization of skills, specification of criteria for judging the output from organizational subunits, cross unit liaison teams, and direct supervision. A full consideration of each of these methods of coordination is beyond the scope of this paper, but it is important to note that the focal point of coordination differs in each case. When work processes are standardized, the focal point is the impersonally and formally defined position and its relationship to other positions. Standardization of skills focuses on the individual worker and the expertise of the worker. Professionalization is one way to standardize skills, whereas on-the-job training would be more consistent with standardization of work processes. Specification of criteria for judging output focuses on the production unit rather than the individual position or position occupant. In large administrative systems, analyzing the quality of output from subunits may be the only way in which coordination is possible because of the complexity of the organization. From the perspective of those in the organization's apex, specification of output criteria allows system-wide coordination of subunits while subunit internal coordination is left to the subunits themselves. The use of teams constituted of members from several interacting units and direct supervision of subordinates focus respectively on interunit coordination and interindividual coordination but here objective criteria for judging coordination are not specified; many of the details of coordination are left to group and individual discretion.

Administrative Design and Environment

The desirability of a given combination of power distribution and coordination methods depends on the nature of the environment within which the administrative system functions. More particularly, it depends on the degree of complexity of demands, the degree of change, and the degree of hostility of the environment vis-à-vis the organization.

For example, it was noted earlier that in ruler dominated administrative systems there is a tendency toward heavy concentration of authority at the top of administrative hierarchies and diffusion of authority below. Coordination is achieved by direct supervision and intervention by those at the top in the day-to-day affairs of those at the lowest levels; in short, coordination is achieved by direct supervision of operating line workers. Authority is not readily delegated nor is individual responsibility readily accepted. There is little standardization of skills or work processes; this is accompanied by a tendency toward a careless mismatching of job requirements and skills. Planning takes a back seat to crisis management. This style of administration may not seem effective from a Western perspective, but it is predictable given the environmental conditions that exist in many Arab states. In environments that change rapidly and that are perceived to be hostile, errors in the exercise of administrative discretion can be very serious, indeed threatening to the survival of the organization and the individual decision-maker. Close supervision can be understood as a way to avoid these potentially fatal errors. Dynamic environments make it very difficult to develop standard rules and procedures; each case is special and requires fresh consideration. There is a striking similarity between what some authors have called "simple structures" and this administrative style which is often found in the Arab world.[20]

The effectiveness of these simple structures in dealing with development and change depends, however, on the size and age of the administration. Relatively small and young organizations should be coordinated using simple structures if change is a major feature of the environment. Small size allows top-level administrators to give effective direction to subordinates. In addition, if the structures are new the necessary discretionary judgment, experience, and training may not be sufficiently developed at the bottom of the organization.

It may happen that a particular pattern of administration is the product not simply of environmental pressures, but also of the style developed during the founding of the administrative system.[21] The oil states, for example, started out as relatively small systems that were perhaps adequately administered by simple structures. Now, however, the size and complexity of administrative commitments have made obsolete the simple structures, but these all too often persist nevertheless.

The simple structure is probably the dominant form of actual administrative practice in the Arab world, but as we have seen, it is the "machine bureaucracy" that seems most often to provide the ideal model. In these systems power is highly centralized in the apex as in simple structures, but coordination is achieved primarily through the standardization of work processes rather than through direct supervision. We have already suggested that it is inappropriate to rely on this method of coordination (namely, one involving standardization of work processes) in situations where the environment is changing. Indeed, because it is inappropriate, this method, though formally in place, may be ignored or used only when politically convenient.

Part of the superficial attractiveness of machine bureaucracies is that they do quite well in coping with hostile political environments. Power is centralized in the administrative apex, and this arrangement provides clear responsibility for administrative action and quick response to *political* threats. The highly specialized task structure, on the other hand, divides the middle management and operating line so that they cannot develop opposing coalitions. A large, older administrative system must decentralize if it is to deal with change effectively, but this will not happen unless it has legitimacy and acceptance (i.e. unless the political environment is sufficiently benign that the just-mentioned political defensive advantages of Weberian systems are not perceived by the organization as vital to its security). Thus a prerequisite for the development of an administrative system that can cope with and direct change is reasonably good relations between the organization and those who are important for its survival.

One form of decentralization, "professional bureaucracy," gives more power to the operating line and coordinates the activities of professionals through the use of liaison groups. Because authority and expertise are placed lower in the administrative hierarchy, this kind of system is much better suited than a machine bureaucracy to coping with a diverse and changing environment.

Another form of decentralization, the "divisionalized bureaucracy," delegates power to subunits and uses output criteria for each subunit as the vehicle for coordination. This approach to decentralization is appropriate for very large systems concerned with change and facing a great diversity in needs. Certain subunits, for example, given their environment, may require a structure akin to the simple structure noted above, whereas others with different needs and environments might more appropriately be patterned along the lines of the professional bureaucracy or classic (i.e. machine) bureaucracy.

As was noted earlier, no single administrative strategy can be applied across all Arab states because of the substantial differences between them. Additionally, within a single state there are substantially different sub-environments with their own distinctive technical, political, economic, and educational conditions. In each case there must be a careful diagnosis of the sub-environment, a prescription of the appropriate administrative design, an understanding of existing administrative arrangements, and finally development of a strategy to make the required changes. These steps will enable the Arab world to take full advantage of its current opportunities for development.

NOTES

[1] See, for example, Robert P. Clarke, *Development and Instability,* Hinsdale, Illinois: Dryden Press, 1974; Morroe Berger, *Bureaucracy and Society in Modern Egypt,* Princeton: Princeton University Press, 1957; Elie Salem, "The Role of Public Administration in Development," in *The State and Development* (in Arabic), Beirut: Development Studies Association, 1966; Fred Riggs, *Administration in Developing Countries,* Boston: Houghton Mifflin, 1964; J. Montgomery & W. Siffin (eds.), *Approaches to Development, Politics, Administration and Change,* New York: McGraw-Hill Book Company, 1966; Myron Weiner (ed.), *Modernization: The Dynamics of Growth,* New York: Basic Books, Inc., 1966.

[2] Ibrahim Mohamed Al-Awaji, *Bureaucracy and Society in Saudi Arabia,* PhD dissertation, University of Virginia, 1971; Gay Roland Daniel, *Public Bureaucracy, Political Processes and Modernization in South Asia and the Middle East,* PhD dissertation, University of Pittsburgh, 1970; Nakib Khalil Adib, *Bureaucracy and Development: A Study of the Lebanese Civil Service,* PhD dissertation, Florida State University, 1973; Al-Kubaisy K. Amer, *Theory and Practice of Administrative Development in New Nations — The Case of Iraq,* PhD dissertation, The University of Texas at Austin, 1971; Abu-Hilal Ahmed Khader, *Jordanian Administration — The Relationship Between Their Subcultural Backgrounds and Professional Attitudes and Behavior,* PhD dissertation, Stanford University, 1970; Omar El-Fathaly *et al., Political Development and Bureaucracy in Libya,* Lexington, Massachusetts: D.C. Heath, Lexington Books, 1977.

[3] For examples, see Clement Henry Moore, *North Africa,* Boston: Little, Brown and Company, 1970; John P. Entelis, *Comparative Politics of North Africa,* Syracuse: Syracuse University Press, 1980; and John Wright, *Libya,* New York: Praeger, 1969.

[4] For further discussion of this interaction, see Monte Palmer, *Dilemmas of Political Development,* 2nd ed., Itasca, Illinois: F.E. Peacock, 1980.

[5] Nazih N. El-Ayoubi, *The Administrative Revolution,* Cairo: Strategic and Political Studies Center, (*Al Ahram*), 1977.

[6] See Omar El-Fathaly and M. Palmer, *Political Development and Social Change in Libya,* Lexington, Massachusetts: D.C. Heath, Lexington Books, 1980; and Charles M. Micaud, "Leadership and Development: The Case of Tunisia," *Comparative Politics,* July 1969.

[7] See Micaud, *op. cit.;* and William H. Lewis, "The Decline of Algeria's FLN," *The Middle East Journal,* Spring 1966.

8 See Nazih El-Ayoubi, *op. cit.;* Adnan Iskandar, *The Civil Service of Lebanon,* PhD dissertation, The American University, 1964; and Shuster James Robert, *Recruitment and Training in the Moroccan Civil Service,* PhD dissertation, Princeton University, 1969.

9 Morroe Berger, *The Arab World Today,* Garden City, New York: Doubleday and Company, 1962. See also Myron Weiner, *The Politics of Scarcity: Public Pressure and Political Response in India,* Chicago: University of Chicago Press, 1962; Samuel Eldersveld, *The Citizen and the Administrator in Developing Democracy,* Glenview, Illinois: Scott, Foresman and Co., 1968; and Charles Anderson, *Political and Economic Change in Latin America,* Princeton: D. Van Nostrand Co., 1967.

10 Omar El-Fathaly, *Public Participation and Political Development in Libya,* PhD dissertation, Florida State University, 1975.

11 Samuel Huntington, *Political Order in Changing Societies,* New Haven, Connecticut: Yale University Press, 1968.

12 See Muhammad Al-Rumaihi, *The Social Roots of Democracy in the Contemporary Arab Gulf Societies* (in Arabic), Kuwait: Kathema Press, 1977.

13 John Waterbury, "Endemic and Planned Corruption in Monarchical Regimes," *World Politics,* Vol. 24, 1973; J. Waterbury, "Corruption, Political Stability and Development: Comparative Evidence From Egypt and Morocco," *Government and Opposition,* Vol. 11, No. 4, 1976; and Marun Yusef Kisirwan, *Attitudes and Behavior of Lebanese Bureaucrats: A Study in Administrative Corruption,* PhD dissertation, Indiana University, 1971.

14 See Henry Azam, Nader Ferjanni, and Muhammed Al-Rumaihi, "Labor Movement," in *New Arab Problems* (in Arabic), three specialized papers published in *Al-Mustaqbal Al-Arabi (The Arab Future),* Vol. 23, 1981, Beirut: Center for Arab Unity Studies. See also J.S. Birks and C.A. Sinclair, *Arab Manpower,* London: Croom Helm, 1980.

15 Fritz Morstein Marx, *The Administrative State,* Chicago: University of Chicago Press, 1957, Chapter 4, pp. 54-72. Other typologies can be found in Gabriel A. Almond and G. Bingham Powell, *Comparative Politics,* Boston: Little, Brown & Co., 1978, 2nd edition, pp. 372-90 and James A. Bill and Carl Leiden, *Politics in the Middle East,* Boston: Little Brown & Co., 1979, pp. 24-37.

16 Merle Fainsod, "Bureaucracy and Modernization: The Russian and Soviet Case," in Joseph La Palombara (ed.), *Bureaucracy and Political Development,* Princeton: Princeton University Press, 1963, pp. 233-67.

17 See *From Max Weber: Essays in Sociology,* H.H. Gerth and C. Wright Mills (eds. and trans.), Oxford: Oxford University Press, 1946, pp. 196-198.

18 For example, see Paul R. Lawrence and Jay W. Lorsch, *Developing Organizations,* Reading, Massachusetts: Addison-Wesley, 1969.

19 Our discussion of organizational designs is heavily influenced by Henry Mintzberg, *The Structuring of Organizations,* Englewood Cliffs, New Jersey: Prentice-Hall, 1979.

20 *Ibid.,* pp. 365-400.

21 John R. Kimberly, Robert H. Miles, and Associates, *The Organizational Life Cycle,* San Francisco: Jossey-Bass, 1980, pp. 1-14.

ASPECTS OF ARAB TRANSFORMATION

ISLAMIC REVIVALISM AND THE CRISIS OF THE SECULAR STATE IN THE ARAB WORLD: AN HISTORICAL APPRAISAL *Philip S. Khoury*

Introduction

In recent years the countries of the Middle East have been experiencing a phenomenon known in western academic and media circles as "Islamic Revivalism."[1] This revivalism has manifested itself in a variety of ways and in varying degrees of intensity, depending on the country and society under investigation. Islam has come to play an increasingly active role in a number of critical areas, including law, education and culture, and politics.

In the area of law, especially criminal law, Islam has been regaining ground in Middle Eastern legal systems. In the realm of education and culture, the number of religious teachers is rising while religion receives greater stress in school curricula. The number of books on religious subjects is growing rapidly, inundating bookstalls in major cities throughout the region. On the social level, there is a noticeable change in the dress code for non-elite women, who are reverting to traditional garments in an effort to protect their dignity in the workplace and as an expression of opposition to western cultural hegemony. Connected to this, campaigns against gambling, alcohol, drugs, and prostitution are being fiercely waged, in the name of Islamic morality. Finally, in politics

Philip S. Khoury holds a PhD in History and Middle Eastern Studies from Harvard University. Dr. Khoury is presently Assistant Professor of History at the Massachusetts Institute of Technology. He served as a Research and Teaching Associate at Harvard University's Center for Middle Eastern Studies, where he completed his doctoral thesis on "The Politics of Nationalism: Syria and the French Mandate, 1920-1936." A member of the editorial board of *MERIP Reports,* he has published a number of articles on the Syrian Arab nationalist movement, and has contributed several entries to *Collier's Encyclopedia* and the *Merit Students Encyclopedia.*

This article has benefited from the suggestions and criticisms of three friends in Cambridge: Mary Christina Wilson, Feroz Ahmad, and Luis Baracaldo. Although I cannot hold them responsible for my conclusions, I believe that we are in agreement on many points.

213

Muslim organizations are gaining strength all over the Middle East, becoming more conspicuous actors in the political arena and even engaging in armed struggle against the state. Meanwhile secular political parties have become increasingly conscious of the need to emphasize religious matters in their programs. Political leaders find it necessary to stress their religiosity and piety more than ever to counter religious opposition and to reassert legitimacy. On the regional and international levels, Islam is being used as an instrument of diplomacy and political influence alongside petrodollars.[2]

The purpose of this article is to construct a framework for explaining the phenomenon of Islamic revivalism. This framework is not intended to be all-encompassing; rather, it is meant to apply to certain societies in the Arab Middle East that have encountered and tried to accommodate the twin forces of modernization and secularization over the last 100 years. And though references to specific countries will generally be avoided, no attempt will be made to disguise the fact that this framework is of particular value for understanding developments in Egypt and Syria, countries which have enjoyed a considerable degree of state formation without the overwhelming assistance of petroleum profits. In particular it would be desirable for this framework to help provide answers to three related questions: What is the historical context out of which Islamic revivalism emerges? What are some of the major social and political forces engaged in revivalist movements? What does Islamic revivalism mean in a wider political and social context? But before offering answers to these questions, let us state our major argument.

The Central Argument

In the societies and countries we have singled out, Islamic revivalism can best be understood as a reaction to a crisis in the modern secular state. This crisis may be defined as "state exhaustion." The reaction is to the state's inability to bring the whole of society into modernity. More specifically, it is a reaction of certain classes in Arab society to the failure of the modern secular state to live up to its professed goal: to mobilize and assimilate these classes to a new socioeconomic order. These classes are most closely attached to the traditional social and moral value system commonly identified with Islam. But they are also classes that in recent years have been drawn into the modernization process but have not been assimilated by it. Consequently, these classes have been disfigured and disoriented by the overall process and this, in turn, has invited their response.

Four additional points will help to round out our argument:

1) On one level the state's exhaustion is a result of regional and especially international pressures on it to accept its role and fate as a weak economic and political entity — a dependency — in a new world order managed by the West. Islamic revivalism is, in its broadest expression, a reaction to these pressures.

2) On another level, however, the general crisis of the state is directly linked to the way the classes and elites supporting and running the state have consolidated their power, defined their interests, and made their choices for society. Islamic revivalism is a response to the inability of these classes and elites to close the gap in wealth and opportunity between themselves and the rest of society, a gap which has been growing wider in recent years.

3) More specifically, Islamic revivalism is a direct response to the state's inability to solve several long-term problems and short-term crises that combined in the 1970s to produce a major crisis of confidence in the state, one which brings into question its very legitimacy.

4) For the classes sponsoring revivalism, Islam must be seen as the vehicle for political and economic demands, rather than as being itself the "impulse" behind these demands.[3] Given the positions of these classes in the social hierarchy and their continued attachment to the traditional sectors, Islam is their most convenient, readily available ideological instrument.

The Historical Context

The emergence of the modern secular state was one of the most important corollaries of the integration of the Middle East into a world economic, technological, and political order dominated first by Europe and, after World War II, by the United States and the Soviet Union (with Europe and Japan playing the role of junior partners). Two comments can be made about this process of integration. First, it was rapid in some regions and more gradual in others; but even within a particular region it tended to unfold unevenly, increasingly differentiating society and creating tensions between its component parts. Second, the managers of this new world order have never intended to iron out the disparities in power and wealth that emerged from this process of integration. In any case, all major events and developments connected with the growth of the modern secular state must be interpreted in relationship to this emerging world order and the changes taking place in its structure.

The growth of the modern state in the Middle East was itself a defensive reaction to a dramatic and seemingly decisive shift of the international balance of power in Europe's favor in the nineteenth century. The primary goal of the ruling elites in the Ottoman Empire (and in Egypt) was to redress the adverse balance by carrying out a major reformation of central institutions and a reorganization of government, focusing first on military reform. While reform from above did not correct the balance, it did introduce large rationalized bureaucracies supported by secular legal, educational, and financial institutions manned by new civilian and military elites imbued with secular liberal ideas. Of equal importance for our argument, "defensive modernization" steadily reduced the influence of religious institutions and religious experts to the point where the state intervened in various social arrangements whose traditional arbiters or mediators had been the religious institutions and the "class" of scholars directing them. Indeed, in the twentieth century, the state went so far as to seize control of these institutions.

The religious establishment reacted to the internal erosion of religious institutions and the loss of monopoly over the law, education, and other areas of social activity. In the late nineteenth century a small but influential group of religious experts sought to revive Islam as a "religious system" in an effort to reassert their influence. To be able to do so, however, they had to accept that

Islam could be adapted to the new demands of modern life. Acceptance of rationalism as the dominant idea animating the emerging order, and of science and technology as the key to the universe, ran against the grain of the two main religious orders in Muslim society: the legal hierarchy of religious experts and the mystical (*Sufi*) orders. Indeed, in seeking to revive Islam, these religious reformers sought to shake the religious establishment to which they belonged out of its conservatism and at the same time to weaken the hold of the mystical orders, which they viewed as a seat of intellectual stagnation and political quietism. However, their efforts actually weakened the foundations on which the influence of the religious establishment rested. By attacking the mystical orders these reformers destroyed many of them, cutting the link between educated Muslims like themselves and the general populace, much of which was tied to these orders. And though they justified change through reason, Islamic modernists were unable to provide an adequate framework of principles through which they could control change. Their failure opened the doors even wider to secular liberal ideas coming from the West.[4]

Modern Secular Nationalism

Secular nationalism was certainly the single most important idea and movement to emerge out of the nineteenth century search for renewal and reformation in the Ottoman Empire. The destruction of the Empire and the imposition of direct European control in the Arab Middle East after World War I made nationalism the most useful and topical political idea of the times.

Two types of nationalism emerged — one territorial, the other ethno-cultural — and both types coexisted in all nationalist movements in the region. Although nationalism was not a thoroughly secular idea, because no interpretation of Arab history and culture, on which nationalism rested, could deny the contribution of Islam, it nevertheless possessed strong secular foundations.[5] Indeed, the classes that translated nationalism into a political movement in the early twentieth century rejected the idea, propounded by Islamic modernist ideologues and activists, that Islam could provide the principles for governing the modern nation state. For them, Islamic law was too outmoded as a governing system. This attitude reflected the position of these classes in the social hierarchy; these classes provided the secularized elites who were educated in modern schools, often had experience in the new secular branches of government, maintained no strong attachment to the weakened religious institutions, and were composed of the great urban absentee landowning and merchant families, ex-Ottoman army officers, the provincial bureaucratic elite, and an emerging group of middle-class intellectuals.[6]

These elements steered the national independence movements in the Arab Middle East between the two world wars. Naturally, they first sought independence from European rule. Beyond this, however, their political concepts and aims incorporated liberalism. They pressed for constitutional government, parliamentary forms, and personal freedoms. Their brand of nationalism and their political style and behavior were clear reflections of their class backgrounds. Their ideology was a version of bourgeois nationalism tailored to fit their historical circumstances. Not surprisingly, they placed little or no emphasis on socioeconomic reforms that might disturb their ultimate aim: to seize state power once Britain and France withdrew from the region.

For these classes and forces, nationalism was first and foremost an instrument with which to consolidate local power. Foreign occupation in the interwar period obviously contributed to their success, but so did the reality that the forces in control of nationalism did not face any serious challenges to their position from classes further down the social scale. The rather chaotic struggles and petty rivalries between different factions and parties in Syria, Palestine, Iraq, and even Egypt, which characterized Arab political life in the 1920s and 1930s, were not for the most part between elements from rival classes but rather between members of a single class. These conflicts could go on ad nauseam largely because the politically active elements of this upper and upper-middle class felt no particular need to close ranks and define their common interests as a class on crucial political and economic issues.

Meanwhile, the power and influence of the religious establishment in these countries continued to decrease. For one thing, the secularized and westernized Arab elites were much better qualified to engage in the politics of diplomatic accommodation and compromise which featured so prominently in the strategies of the national independence movements. Furthermore, the European authorities had no respect for the Muslim religious establishment, which they viewed as reactionary and sterile, an obstacle to progress.[7]

The Challenge of Radical Arab Nationalism

The real challenge to the class and elite steering the Arab national independence movements came only after World War II when the ruling elite proved unable to link nationalism to state power. The challenge came from new social classes and forces that had first begun to gain ground in the late 1930s through the acquisition of modern education and the effect of structural changes brought about by the more rapid integration of Arab economies into the world market. The new classes and forces, belonging to a new generation, were armed with new secular ideas about progress and development. Moreover, they had had the opportunity during the nationalist struggle to acquire organizational skills which they translated into modern political parties and national youth organizations. This enabled them to enjoy wider political and social bases in new institutions where the older generation of bourgeois nationalists held less sway.

The new political forces, led by middle-class liberal professionals, indigenous army officers, and an emerging class of small industrialists, sought to redefine relations with one another and with the government. Ultimately, they aimed to seize control of state power from the big landowning and merchant classes which a generation earlier had molded the idea of nationalism to guarantee their own control of the state on independence. Not surprisingly, the challenge posed by these new forces took the form of a struggle for control of the ideology of nationalism. Their assault was threefold.[8] First, the emphasis on nationalism was shifted to correspond to and accommodate the rapid social and economic changes that had taken place in Arab society. The new reformers stressed socioeconomic justice rather than constitutionalism, liberal parliamentary forms, and personal freedoms. Their vocabulary had socialist undertones: mass education, national welfare programs, rapid industrialization through the agency of the state. Second, these new forces rekindled the flame of Arab unity which they accused the old guard of forsaking. They refused to accept the artificial state frontiers imposed by the colonial powers which ran against the very grain of Arab nationalist ideology, and they blamed their rulers for willfully contributing to the loss of Palestine in 1948. Third, they advocated political neutralism in international affairs, accusing those in control of government of retaining too strong political and commercial ties to Europe and to America.

As for the role of Islam in the new concept of the Arab nation, these ascendant forces made the most systematic effort yet to refine the idea of Arab nationalism. But they no longer had to face as high a degree of tension and conflict between religion and secularism on the political level.[9]

During the 1950s and early 1960s these struggles and ambitions were played out in Egypt, Syria, and Iraq, and new elites — civilian and military, radical nationalist and socialist — replaced the bourgeois nationalists, in the process wedding their brand of nationalism to state power. Their stated goals: to bring their societies into the modern world and to forge a new basis of loyalty in society, one superseding all others — that of loyalty to the nation.

The Character of the Modern Secular State

With the new elites' assumption of rule, the modern secular state began to assume its present shape. The state seized control of the national economy through forced nationalizations. The public sector grew dramatically and with it the state bureaucracy. Meanwhile, the apparatus for a national welfare system was constructed. Another corollary of this process was the spectacular growth of the repressive apparatus — army, police, intelligence networks — and the increased role of government in the lives of the people. By the 1960s the new elites had blended into a new class which can be labeled, for want of a better term, the "state bourgeoisie." But though this new class rested on a wider social base than had its predecessor, it still stood at a distance from the majority of society. Its members belonged to the modernized sectors and professed beliefs and values that distinguished them from a populace still tied to traditional beliefs and values associated with Islam.

In order to graft a new identity onto society, the new ruling class aimed to shape society, to define its priorities, and to make its critical choices from above for what the state claimed was the highest good of society. The rulers aimed to create an all-encompassing modern class structure, through which modernizing reforms could be pushed with the least resistance from below.

The state enlarged the bureaucracy; it dismantled the power base of the old ruling class through land reforms; it stressed industrialization over agriculture; it expanded its control over national economic resources; it brought education to the masses in the cities and increasingly into the countryside; it weakened the religious institutions and seized control of them; it created a single party system under firm state control, packing the party with bureaucrats; and, if it did not directly promote rapid urbanization, it nevertheless identified rapid urbanization with progress. And the state, in its clear commitment to modernization, contributed greatly to the mobilization of large sections of society that until then had been firmly attached to the traditional order. ("Mobilization" here means the creation of new expectations and a new consciousness with respect to one's role in society.) However, mobilization has not always led to the assimilation of these classes to the new sociocultural and (above all) political patterns drawn by the modern secular state. Assimilation has rarely proceeded at as rapid a pace as mobilization has. Those sections of Arab society which have not yet been assimilated consequently find that their material and psychological conditions do not correspond to their new expectations. This lag between mobilization and assimilation has been especially great in the area of political participation, because the ruling elite, invested with so much power, assures society that the national army will defend the national honor and that the government will promote economic interests. Therefore, the masses are encouraged to remain apart from political action, a separation that the repressive apparatus of the state helps to reinforce.

As was noted earlier, the general unevenness of state-imposed development — itself attributable to the Arab states' vulnerability to international and regional pressures and to the specific interests of the state bourgeoisie—has in recent years created a disturbance in the societal balance evoking different reactions from different sectors of Arab society. Certainly one of the loudest reactions comes from those forces labeled as "Islamic."

State Exhaustion

To return to our central argument, by the early 1970s the secular state began to show signs of strain in its effort to modernize society. At the same time, the state felt growing pressures from the West to make the political and ideological compromises required to attract the hard loans and other forms of foreign capital needed to regenerate a sluggish economy. What were some of the problems and pressures exhausting the state?

1. Agriculture: In general, the agricultural sector was given relatively little attention by the state. Within this sector, cash-cropping continued to spread, making the Arab countries less and less self-sufficient in food and thus requiring them to rely increasingly on foreign earnings to finance food imports. Meanwhile, land reform measures, though allowing the new ruling class to destroy the economic base of the old social classes, did not benefit the mass of peasants. Rather, reforms served the interests of the rural middle stratum from which the new elites came. All this added to the ranks of the dispossessed and landless peasantry.

2. Industry: The state found it increasingly difficult to build a modern industrial base without the assistance of foreign capital. The old landowning class failed to reinvest its compensation from the land reforms in industry, and import-substitution industries had built-in limits on growth. Meanwhile, the political and ideological orientation of the new radical nationalist regimes created automatic barriers to western investment, and the commitment of

material and human resources to a succession of wars with Israel was by its very nature unproductive.

3. Population Growth and Rapid Urbanization: The steady drop in infant mortality rates due to improved medical and hygenic care contributed to dramatic population increases, especially in urban areas. Meanwhile, increasing rural uprootedness forced cities to try to absorb larger and larger numbers of landless peasants seeking new livelihoods. These immigrants quickly discovered that regular and gainful employment was hard to come by. Industrial growth could not keep pace with population growth in the cities and rapid urbanization without rapid industrialization swelled the ranks of the urban unemployed. This process also helped to reinforce the geographic and sociocultural divisions in the city, which generally included, on the one hand, modern districts inhabited by westernized elites and containing new institutions, schools, landscaped parks, government offices, and modern business areas, and, on the other, an old town of ancient quarters, mosques, churches, and bazaars populated by classes engaged in traditional trades and casual labor who were still attached to values associated with Islam. But rapid urbanization also created a third division in the city: the shantytowns and refugee camps on the city outskirts where immigrants from the countryside and refugees from wars and natural disasters lived in conditions of squalor. To the extent that the city provided public works and services, these went first to the modern city, then to the old town, and only rarely to the recently settled poverty belts.

The state also faced several other problems. Although it made significant progress in spreading education to the masses, a factor of immense importance in the mobilization of large sections of the urban population, the state found it increasingly difficult to provide the requisite remuneration expected by the newly educated. The state also encountered difficulty in its drive to enforce a modern national identity on all communities. On the one hand, there was the pull of supranational loyalties (to pan-Arabism, for example) and, on the other, there was the more complicated pull of subnational loyalties, to religious and ethnic communities, especially in the case of compact minorities seeking cultural and political autonomy and sometimes independence. And, of course, the state's continued failure to uphold the national honor after a quarter-century of military defeats by Israel tended to erode the legitimacy of Arab nationalist regimes.

Finally to exacerbate an already deteriorating situation, there were serious indications that certain factions of the state bourgeoisie were growing restive by the late 1960s and early 1970s. Having contributed heavily to the creation of a new state order and having become in the new state order a ruling class, these elements now wanted to enjoy the prerogatives of that status. Throughout the 1960s the state bourgeoisie had been hampered in this by radical nationalist austerity measures and the socialist rhetoric of the progressive wing of the state bourgeoisie. But the built-in shortcomings of the economy enabled the conservative wing and its allies in the private sector to redirect state policy. This wing argued that the regimes were bankrupt and ineffectual at modern organization and development planning and that if they hoped to survive they would have to lift the institutional barriers and political impediments barring the foreign capital needed to regenerate economic life. Behind this argument for economic liberalization, of course, lay the desire of this fraction of the ruling class to enjoy the material benefits of an alliance with foreign capital.

The way was cleared for a shift in direction after the June 1967 war with Israel when Egypt began its retreat into localism. This trend, however, was more firmly established after Jamal 'Abd al-Nasir's death in 1970 and the rise of Anwar al-Sadat, who (a year later) consolidated power by discrediting and defeating the 'Ali Sabri group. The conservative wing of the state bourgeoisie was now in charge in Cairo. In Syria a more gradual and indeed uncomfortable shift took place after Hafiz al-Asad's victory over the Salah Jadid wing of the military-Ba'th alliance, also in 1970. No corresponding shift took place in Iraq until much later, largely because of that state's control of vast oil wealth which freed the Saddam Hussein regime from a heavy reliance on foreign investments and loans. The important point is that the ideals of Arab unity and pan-Arabism embraced so tightly by Nasirist and Ba'thist ideology were weakened and then superseded in the 1970s by the force of regionalism: Egypt-Sudan, Syria-Lebanon-Jordan,and Iraq-Arabian Peninsula and Gulf. The best indication of this economic and political realignment was the 1973 war with Israel, which was launched by Egypt and Syria with limited aims: to clear the ground for a diplomatic solution to the debilitating Arab-Israeli conflict. The October War enabled the Arab regimes to liberalize their economies and expand their private sectors (in Egypt's case, it facilitated an acceleration of the *infitah* or "open door" policy begun in 1971). Though the new institutional arrangements created to attract foreign capital did not always work smoothly, due to various infrastructural deficiencies and to resistance from the progressive wing of the state bourgeoisie and other disaffected elements, those in the accommodationist wing capitalized on the convergences of international and regional pressures with their personal interests to take charge.

In sum, rapid urbanization without dynamic industrialization, the increasing inability of the state to distribute goods and services adequately, the retreat from pan-Arabism, successive defeats at the hands of Israel, and mounting external pressures on the state to liberalize the economic system (liberalization, among other things, contributed directly to escalating inflation in the 1970s) combined to increase polarization in Arab society. One important expression of this polarization has been Islamic revivalism.

The Social and Political Forces of Revivalism

To explain why Islam has become the main vehicle for expressing discontent with the state, we must investigate the nature of forces most actively engaged in revivalism.

Briefly, the leadership and the rank and file of movements in the Arab countries identifiable as Islamic come largely from those sections of the urban populations most closely attached to the traditional order and belief system. These forces are the ones the modern secular state has so far proved unable to assimilate to the new socioeconomic and political infrastructure it has built. Consequently, they have paid a heavy price for the state's efforts to modernize society from above. One should, however, recognize the social and economic distinctions between leadership and rank and file.

Rank and File

The rank and file are recently settled immigrants from the countryside, an uprooted peasantry that has been drawn into the process of rapid urbanization. Many of these immigrants have come directly from the rural sector to the city; others, however, may have stopped in intermediary towns along the way to the big city, where they may have acquired some skills and experience enabling them to adjust more easily to the problems of this massive transition.[10] Some of these uprooted peasants have managed to settle in the ancient popular quarters of the city, though most live in the new mushrooming peripheral districts in temporary and often inadequate housing. Most have had difficulty securing regular employment and have ended up in the vast pool of casual labor or among the unemployed. Although this class has been mobilized, its limited education and lack of opportunities for steady employment have prevented its assimilation to the modern sector.

The problem faced by recent immigrants is not simply one of economic subsistence, however. Forced to settle in the anonymity of the big city in districts with no firm traditions, immigrants have been cut from their roots, stripped of the symbols of their culture and heritage. Alienated and disoriented, they want to preserve their identities by reinforcing traditional culture and values. And though their interpretation of Islam — a mixture of popular religious belief and village customs — may not conform to the highest principles of the religion and law, they frame their search for and defense of identity in what they claim to be Islamic terms. Here the recently settled immigrants from the countryside are given added encouragement by popular leaders, both religious and secular, who belong neither to the religious establishment nor to the urban bourgeoisie.

The Leadership

The main force behind Islamic revivalism that shaped it into a sociopolitical movement seems to be composed of elements from the urban lower-middle class: the shopkeepers, small bazaar merchants, middling bureaucrats, popular preachers, and university students. In general they form a "class caught in between," composed not so much of those who have been completely passed over by the state in its drive to modernize society and thus are angry bystanders, but rather of groups who have been pulled by the interventionist state in the direction of modern society and culture to a certain point where they encounter barriers to advancement due to the state's growing impotence and its economic policy reorientation. Their appetites whetted, they are then prevented from fulfilling their new expectations. This "class caught in between" is largely concentrated in the old city; though its members are not recent immigrants, they often maintain links to the countryside. Furthermore, unlike the rank and file, many of these elements have acquired a relatively high level of modern secular education, enough to draw them into the mobilization process but not enough to provide them with satisfactory employment opportunities or incomes. Perhaps they did not acquire a sufficiently advanced degree to be able to advance to a higher rung on the bureaucratic ladder. Or, perhaps they were unable to acquire foreign language skills that might have given them an entrée into the expanding private sector (especially the service sector) of the last decade with its intimate ties to foreign capital.

Families from this class had hoped to move out of the old city and decaying quarters into wealthier modern districts but soon discovered that they could not afford the transition. Young university-educated men found it impossible to marry and start their own families because they were unable to afford the key money on an apartment or even the rent. Instead, they were obliged to continue living with their parents, grandparents, and siblings with little or no hope of improving their situation as they watched their real incomes decline due to the rapid inflation of the 1970s. Meanwhile, these mobilized and, in some cases, partially assimilated elements grew increasingly jealous and angry as the ruling class began to flaunt its wealth and power publicly, revealing its decadence and corruption.

But, as in the case of the marginalized immigrants from the

countryside, the "class caught in between" did not just face problems of material subsistence. The effects of mass education left men and women disoriented and confused, their values and traditions twisted by the unevenness of modernization. It is thus not surprising to find elements from this class seeking to recapture their traditions and trying to retreat into what they claim is authentic culture, as embodied in Islam.

The power of the "class caught in between" (which provides the leadership of Islamic revivalist movements) can be measured by its ability to establish ties binding it to the truly dispossessed in the city. Indeed, the leadership's main aim is to create a dependency relationship in which it dominates the rank and file, articulates its beliefs and values, channels its frustration, and even protects it from the state in return for the mass support that might enable the lower-middle class to regain position and power in society.

One additional characteristic of the revivalist leadership needs underscoring. In the Arab countries that have experienced a substantial amount of secularization and modernization over time, the leadership of Islamic movements tends to come from outside the Muslim religious establishment. Whereas in Iran the Shi'i Muslim clergy managed to retain a certain degree of independence from the state, in Egypt and Syria the Sunni Muslim religious leadership was long ago co-opted by the state, its members often serving as salaried officials of the government. Indeed, the revivalist leadership, though difficult to define precisely, appears to be a mixture of lay intellectuals and liberal professionals and a sprinkling of popular Muslim preachers supported by bazaar merchants. But the absence of an independent Muslim religious leadership in command of Islamic movements in the Arab countries does make them vulnerable to criticism and even subversion by the state. Arab regimes can rely on government-controlled religious institutions administered by religious officials to counter the challenge of an independent Islamic opposition and even to co-opt it.

At this juncture one may justifiably ask why the social classes involved in revivalism have not been attracted to other ideological movements in the Arab countries such as leftist political organizations which also focus on opposition to the state and to western control? The answer seems to be that in most of these countries left-wing parties have rather bad reputations. Often they are thoroughly discredited in the traditional sectors of society. This is especially true of the communist parties, which are viewed as more extreme secular versions of what already is embodied in the state. Not only do communist parties have difficulty dealing with the question of religion in their programs, but they are also seen as unauthentic, too closely identified with and under the control of the Soviet Union. Also, there is no doubt that communist parties primarily appeal to the modern organized working class, the middle-class intelligentsia, and, in some cases, to religious and ethnic minorities, none of which are closely tied to the social formation from which Islamic revivalism springs. In any case by the 1970s the "Arab Left," and in particular the communists, had been systematically suppressed, purged, or co-opted (depending on the country) and was in no position to rally the forces of opposition to the state.

Islamic Revivalism in its Wider Political and Social Context

Now that we have tried to isolate the different forces and classes behind the recent resurgence of "Islam," we should highlight some of the major issues on which revivalism focuses.

Revivalist movements generally express strong anti-western sentiments on several related levels — political, economic, sociocultural — due to the West's dismal record in the Arab world, with special emphasis on the United States and its many activities in the area. Within this context, revivalists are particularly hostile to the penetration of western capital, whether through loans, joint ventures, or multinationals, because this is perceived as harmful to the material interests of the Arab world. Revivalists also oppose the entry of luxury goods from the West which the "westernized classes" have been importing in much greater quantity with the relaxation of import controls in the 1970s. But even though Muslim revivalists oppose western capital, they should not be classified as anti-capitalist. On the contrary, they appear to be in fundamental agreement with the ideas of capitalism: profit, financial returns on investments involving risk, and, above all, private property.[11] However, their inclination is toward some form of autarky or national economic self-sufficiency in which goods and services will be distributed more equitably throughout society.

Along with their opposition to western capital, revivalists are demonstrating a growing intolerance for the religious minorities. This is particularly true with respect to Christians, who have been historically identified with the West and foreign capital and who have recently become more conspicuous and aggressive in their roles as middlemen, export-import merchants, and leaders in the service sector, all because of economic liberalization.

In the area of politics, revivalists express their hostility both to the United States and to its major ally in the region, Israel, which is perceived as a western implantation occupying Arab-Muslim territory. By adopting a rejectionist line on the question of a peaceful diplomatic resolution of the Arab-Israeli conflict, revivalists also can criticize their governments for their continued failure to liberate "Palestine," calling into the question the very legitimacy of these regimes. At the same time, revivalists attack the state for turning away from the other major goal of nationalism: Arab unity. Some movements may try to compete with the government for control of the ideology of Arab nationalism, though the inclination of most is to stress pan-Islamic principles in order to distinguish themselves clearly from the state which is still in control of nationalist institutions.

It should also be added that revivalists are not particularly enamored of the modern working class and trade unions, which are perceived by the revivalists as relatively privileged and are, in any case, either under firm state control or linked to left-wing political organizations like the communist party. Not surprisingly, revivalism is strongly anti-communist and anti-Soviet. The Soviet Union is seen as an interventionist power in every sense, one that seeks to impose its atheist ideology on Islam.

So far we have discussed what revivalism is a reaction to and what it opposes. It is also important to explain briefly what revivalists are seeking in more positive terms. First one must recognize that wherever revivalism has been translated into political movements, these movements have demonstrated modernist tendencies. Indeed, in their political manifestation, the revivalists are organized into parties with leaderships, political and socioeconomic programs, and propaganda arms such as journals and newspapers (legal and illegal). After all, the leadership of the Islamic revivalist movements has had access to modern education, giving them, as one observer has put it, "the ambience, contacts, and intellectual tools to organize groups and movements. . . ."[12]

Revivalist programs, however, seem to be a mixed bag of traditional and modern ideas, reflecting the position in society of the revivalist elite. At the same time, their programs are rarely systematic or consistent. Indeed, they are often superficial and characterized by contradictory principles. In part this can be explained by the leadership's intermediary position between the traditional and modern orders in society, but it is also due to the fact that Islamic movements in the Arab countries are still fundamentally opposition movements, more concerned at this stage with "practical action" rather than philosophical rigor and consistency.[13]

Islamic movements are concerned with more than a return to and reinforcement of traditional rules of behavior and the reestablishment of the *shari'a* (religious law). Prohibition of alcohol, drugs, prostitution, gambling, and the like are issues around which to rally the masses against the state's failure to uphold traditional norms of morality, the corruption and decadence of the upper classes, and westernization in general, but they are also a way of expressing a growing need to defend a culture and way of life from erosion at a time when nothing positive or suitable has been offered as a replacement. So the contradictions embodied in Islamic revivalism are to be expected. Mobilization without full integration or assimilation into a new modern order is bound to create conflicts and tensions for those classes that have been drawn into the process and are now "caught in between," disoriented and confused. It is not surprising to discover revivalists, as they watch their women being drawn into the public sphere of life, on the one hand stressing the need for women to return to their traditional activities and places in the home and, on the other, beginning to realize how important a second income is to the survival of their families. And women's reversion to traditional dress is not just a way of voicing opposition to the westernized ruling class and to the aggression of the West; it is also a way to help preserve their self-respect and dignity, which are being eroded by the sexual division of labor imposed in the public workplace.

In many ways, Islamic revivalism is fundamentalist in the sense that it seeks remedies to present ills in old truths, by linking current problems to evil, satanic powers and men—local and foreign — and by arguing that recovery requires a rediscovery of traditional ways.[14] Yet revivalists do not reject modernization, industrialization, or even the idea of a powerful interventionist state. On the contrary, they want these and more, but they also want to create their own framework to guide development.[15]

Their aims and aspirations are to be realized through the creation of an Islamic state which revivalists claim will reestablish the moral link between government and society that has been severed by the classes in power. But the contours of such a state are hard to trace. With a pliant religious establishment in the Arab countries, the question of who would form the leadership of an Islamic state would be difficult to resolve. Would the new urban leadership be able to take control of a state based on Islamic law when this leadership itself is not qualified to interpret the law?

Conclusion

Islamic revivalism, in its political manifestation in countries such as Egypt and Syria, is a movement of opposition to the modern secular state. It is peopled by elements from urban classes who are still closely attached to their religious beliefs, traditional values, and culture. Islamic revivalism has great potential for building a base in the traditional sectors of urban society, among the poor immigrants from the countryside and the lower-middle class, and it has capitalized on the failure of the left-wing secular movements to establish a strong foothold in these sectors of society.

Like other Islamic movements of the past, Islamic revivalism's great appeal is that it makes the traditional classes in Arab society feel temporarily better (in a psychological sense) because revivalist leaders are able to provide an explanation for their frustrations and disorientation in acceptable and comprehensible language. These leaders offer solutions and cures that they claim have always been rooted in Islamic culture but have been neglected and need restoration.

Islamic revivalism is initially defensive but it also seeks to be creative. It wants to recreate Arab Muslim society according to the society's own inner dynamics and thus win final cultural and economic independence from the West. In this creative sense Islamic revivalism is potentially attractive to large sections of society. In fact, the more radical elements among revivalists are known to have adopted certain socialist theories and principles and are seeking a massive social and political revolution that would topple the present system of government and transform the economic system.[16] But so far, Islamic revivalists have been unable to strike deep roots in the modern classes in Arab society, which view revivalism as dangerously backward and reactionary and, in the case of the ruling class, as a direct threat to the rulers' security.

Islamic revivalists have managed to force the state to accede to some of their demands to the extent of allowing Islam to creep back into certain institutions and other aspects of social life. The state's accommodation is itself an admission of revivalism's potential for destabilizing current regimes; it is also, however, a way of reasserting a regime's legitimacy.

Yet, in the sense that Islamic revivalism is a tool wielded by a certain class to regain position in society through the domination and manipulation of another class, it is as narrow as were bourgeois and radical nationalism before it. Whether Islamic revivalists succeed in the end in toppling current Arab regimes or in radically redefining them, one thing seems certain: they are not seeking to stem the tide of history and to obstruct development. Rather, through the ideological force of Islam, the traditional social classes seek to redefine their relations with each other and with the state, to their advantage. By doing so they hope to clear the prickly path between tradition and modernity on which they are destined to tread.

NOTES

[1] Both the "academy" and the media failed to predict this revival. For the most systematic explanation of this failure and the bias and misunderstanding in which it is rooted, see Edward W. Said, *Orientalism* (New York: Pantheon, 1978) and Said, *Covering Islam* (New York: Pantheon, 1981). For a select bibliography of recent literature (in English) on different interpretations of Islamic revivalism, see the list at the end of this article.

[2] See "Contemporary Islamic Revivalism, Discussion Group with a Paper by M. E. Yapp," *Asian Affairs* 11 (June 1980), p. 178.

[3] *Ibid.*, p. 189. Here I must concur with the conclusions arrived at by a group of experts in Britain studying the phenomenon of revivalism.

[4] This passage borrows heavily from the analysis of Albert Hourani, "Middle Eastern Nationalism Yesterday and Today," in *The Emergence of the Modern Middle East* (London: The MacMillan Press Ltd., 1981), pp. 183-185.

[5] *Ibid.*, pp. 186-187.

[6] The social foundations of Arab nationalism before World War I are discussed in my unpublished doctoral dissertation: "The Politics of Nationalism: Syria and the French Mandate 1920-1936" (Harvard University, 1980).

[7] This characterization of bourgeois nationalism is derived from "Politics of Nationalism."

[8] This is suggested in Hourani, "Middle Eastern Nationalism," p. 190.

[9] *Ibid.*, p. 188.

[10] "Contemporary Islamic Revivalism," p. 185.

[11] On the subject of Islam and capitalism, see Maxime Rodinson, *Islam and Capitalism* (New York: Pantheon, 1973), and John Thomas Cummings, H. Askari, and A. Mustafa, "Islam and Modern Economic Change," in J. L. Esposito (ed.), *Islam and Development: Religion and Sociopolitical Change* (Syracuse: Syracuse University Press, 1980).

[12] Nikki Keddie, "Iran: Change in Islam; Islam and Change," *International Journal of Middle Eastern Studies* 11 (July 1980), p. 529.

[13] "Contemporary Islamic Revivalism," p. 186.

[14] See Maxime Rodinson, "Islam Resurgent?" *Gazelle Review* 6 (1979), pp. 1-17.

[15] "Contemporary Islamic Revivalism," p. 186.

[16] For one view of the historic role of revolutionary movements in Islam, see Thomas Hodgkin, "The Revolutionary Tradition in Islam," *Race and Class* (1980), pp. 221-237.

SOME RECENT LITERATURE ON ISLAMIC
REVIVALISM AND ON THE CRISIS OF
THE MODERN SECULAR STATE

Ahmad, Eqbal. "From Potato Sack to Potato Mash: On the Contemporary Crisis of the Third World," *Monthly Review* 32 (March 1981), 8-21.

_____ . "Post-Colonial Systems of Power," *Arab Studies Quarterly,* 2 (Fall 1980), 350-363.

Ahmad, Leila. "The Resurgence of Islam: The Return to the Source," *History Today* 30 (February 1980), 23-27.

"Contemporary Islamic Revivalism, Discussion Group with a Paper by M. E. Yapp," *Asian Affairs* 11 (June 1980), 178-195.

Crecelius, Daniel. "The Course of Secularization in Egypt," *Islam and Development: Religion and Sociopolitical Change.* Ed. by John L. Esposito. Syracuse: Syracuse University Press, 1980, 49-70.

Cummings, John Thomas, Hossein Askari, and Ahmad Mustafa. "Islam and Modern Economic Change," *Islam and Development.* Ed. J. L. Esposito. Syracuse, 1980, 25-48.

Enayat, Hamid. "The Resurgence of Islam — The Background," *History Today* 30 (February 1980), 16-22.

Hodgkin, Thomas. "The Revolutionary Tradition in Islam," *Race and Class* (1980), 221-237.

Hourani, Albert. "Middle Eastern Nationalism Yesterday and Today," *The Emergence of the Modern Middle East.* London: The MacMillan Press Ltd., 1981, 179-192.

Hudson, Michael C. "Islam and Political Development," *Islam and Development.* Ed. J. L. Esposito. Syracuse, 1980, 1-24.

Keddie, Nikki. "Iran: Change in Islam; Islam and Change," *International Journal of Middle Eastern Studies* 11 (July 1980), 527-542.

Pipes, Daniel. " 'This World is Political!!' The Islamic Revival of the Seventies," *Orbis* 24 (Spring 1980), 9-41.

Rodinson, Maxime. "Islam Resurgent?" *Gazelle Review* 6 (1979), 1-17.

SOCIAL IMPLICATIONS OF LABOR MIGRATION IN THE ARAB WORLD *Janet Abu-Lughod*

Just as the seventh century saw a massive out-migration from the Arabian Peninsula to what later became known as the Arab world, so the late twentieth century is witnessing the opposite, a significant reflux of population toward the Peninsula. Although today's migration does not match the earlier movement in terms of the proportion of total population taking part, it does involve a considerably greater number of persons. Moreover, the present trend differs from the former in its consequences. Assimilation, the building of a common culture, and the establishment of a polity capable of incorporating new groups were the goals of the first migration; all these are different in the present migration.

How many persons are currently involved in the "new migration" cannot be determined with accuracy. All told, Arab labor migrations to Europe and the Americas (which will not be discussed in this paper), as well as those internal to the Arab world (the focus of our attention here), probably now involve some five to six million persons, including dependents moving with the laborers but not those left behind. If family members left behind are added, the *minimum* number of persons affected doubles. And if one considers all Arabs affected by migrations over the past few decades, the number may again double. Since the Arab world includes a total population of about 160 million, one can estimate that one out of every eight Arabs is affected, directly or indirectly, by international migration. The proportion would be even higher if persons residing in areas of population in-migration, as well as those in areas of out-migration, were included.

Janet Abu-Lughod earned a PhD in Urban Sociology at the University of Massachusetts. Currently Professor of Sociology and Urban Affairs at Northwestern University, Dr. Abu-Lughod has served as Director of the Comparative Urban Studies Program at Northwestern University and has taught at the American University in Cairo. She has written extensively, particularly on Middle Eastern cities, as well as on urban sociology and demography. Her works include *Cairo: 1001 Years of the City Victorious* and *Rabat: Urban Apartheid in Morocco*.

237

Others[1] have concentrated on the difficult task of specifying the exact *(sic)* number of persons migrating for employment in the Arab world, on the economic characteristics of the sending and receiving countries, and on the demands for labor at varying levels of skill and in different economic sectors in the separate countries. For many reasons, even the most careful estimates must be treated with extreme caution.[2] One could dispute almost every important component of such estimates. Here I shall not attempt, except in passing, to evaluate specific figures. Rather, this paper presents an overview of the migration situation in the Arab world and examines the social implications for both sending and receiving societies of such movements. In order to do this it is first necessary to sketch the main outlines of what has been happening.

Premodern Precedents for Migration

Although the premodern Islamic world was noteworthy for its open borders and the free mobility of Muslims, in actual fact migrations were of three types. Most often mentioned in the medieval literature were the wanderings of small numbers of individuals, mostly members of the *'ulamā'* or religious bureaucracy, whose transferable talents as judges, civil servants, educators, or even agents for long-distance trade made them welcome wherever they went. A second conspicuous form of migration was the periodic movement or transfer of armies and tribal groups, a movement related chiefly to military crises or purposes. Finally, there was the less selective, less organized, slow peregrination of pilgrims making their way to and from Mecca, often over periods of many years. A number of these pilgrims resettled, either in the *hajj* centers themselves or at diverse points along the way.

With the introduction of the modern state, this free mobility began to be constricted, although, due to the vast extent of the Ottoman Empire, what would now be considered international migration was treated in legal terms as intranational migration. Furthermore, while centers of settlement were coming to be more closely associated with "nationality," the outlying areas, particularly in cases where "borders" cut across thinly populated deserts, tended to retain an indeterminate status because the traditional routes of nomadic groups often crossed these arbitrary state boundaries.

It was not until the gerrymandering of the Arab world through European colonialism that there was a real decline in population flows, as increasingly-enforced barriers were placed in the path of migrants. But even so, the older ideals of the Islamic *Umma,* plus the common Arabic language and culture, made it possible for Arabs to relocate and be assimilated to their new homes. The exceptions with regard to assimilation and intermarriage were traveling members of minority *millets,* who remained apart from the host society while assimilating to their coreligionists in the new region.

Although mobility, albeit somewhat more restricted, was still possible in the twentieth century, in fact not much was occurring. Nomadic circuits continued between the Egyptian Sinai and Palestine, between Cyrenaica and the western edge of Egypt, and between such nominally distinct centers on the Peninsula as Saudi Arabia, the Yemen, and Oman. And, despite the competing colonial interests that controlled different parts of the Fertile Crescent, modest but steady movements across the frontiers that "separated" Lebanon, Syria, Palestine, Jordan, and Iraq continued to occur. But the Egyptians, who constitute the largest mass of population within the Arab region, were notoriously stable and, as cities and agrarian populations grew elsewhere, the oscillations of population decreased. The most reasonable prediction, if one ignored the possibility of unexpected shocks to the region, would have been one of decreased mobility and gradually hardening frontiers.

Consequences of the 1948 War

It is essential to note that the first *(and discontinuous)* phase of the contemporary migration of Arabs was not labor-linked at all but, rather, had military and political origins. It was set into motion by the sudden expulsion of more than 700,000 Palestinians from the areas Israel occupied in 1948.[3] This traumatic event ushered in a period of mobility during which migratory streams caught up larger and larger numbers of persons. Victims of the first Palestine War sought refuge almost exclusively in the adjacent Arab states that, only a few years earlier, had gained their independence from European colonialism. Despite their independence, however, the legacy of European-style nationalist exclusiveness evidently outweighed centuries of Islamic empire precedent. Among the new states in which Palestinians took refuge, only Jordan extended to them the rights of citizenship, an act related more to its decision to annex what remained of eastern Palestine than to the values of the Islamic *Umma*. Palestinians in the Gaza Strip, administered by Egypt, retained their nationality, a benefit of dubious value. Elsewhere, Palestinians became stateless "guests" of governments from which only a few were able to obtain naturalization. This statement of the refugees as juridical strangers, which deviated so drastically from earlier Islamic-Arab practices, created a legacy which continues to shape the nature of migrant labor absorption in the Gulf and Peninsular states.

While the *causes* of Palestinian migration were certainly not economic, the *consequences* were. Some 70 percent of the exiled Palestinians had been farmers, and yet virtually all settled in or around cities and attempted to join the urban labor force. Over the subsequent 33 years, Palestinians who settled in Syria managed, despite their lack of citizenship, to move into urban occupations, so that their current labor force characteristics now approximate those of urban Syrians.[4] In Lebanon, however, the Palestinian class structure became polarized. Refugees having urban origins, high education, and/or family connections in Lebanon were gradually absorbed into the urban labor force, many obtaining Lebanese citizenship; those less favored remained in refugee camps and were relegated to the marginal fringe of the labor force, engaging mainly in occasional agricultural day work, petty trade, or unskilled occupations.[5] Palestinians who settled in Jordan, primarily in and around the burgeoning capital of Amman, actually helped to create the economy that absorbed them and, assisted by citizenship and propelled through education (which represented their only way to compensate for lost capital), became the backbone of the urban bourgeoisie and labor aristocracy, as well as of the civil service and the professions. But the economy of the East Bank remained too underdeveloped to sustain these upwardly mobile classes at a level commensurate with their expanding skills. Economic developments on the annexed West Bank lagged even farther behind, since refugees from the territories occupied by Israel overtaxed the area's still largely agrarian economy and modest natural resources.

During the 1950s, out-migration began to occur from the so-called West Bank and the Gaza Strip (into which substantial numbers of refugees had crowded despite its even leaner economic base). West Bank residents had the option of going to the East Bank or to the Gulf, where labor migration to Kuwait, the first "oil" state, was already commencing. Residents of the Gaza Strip had few choices because they lacked acceptable "papers." They could join the Egyptian-run militia or seek higher education in Egypt as a passport to emigration, or they could move as clandestine migrants to Gulf/Peninsula countries, although the demand for their relatively unskilled labor remained low. The dominant pattern evidently became one in which younger members of a family were sent out for school or work, leaving the rest of the family behind and partially dependent upon remittances.[6]

Palestinians found their most promising opportunities in Kuwait, where the small local population was insufficient to meet fully the challenge of early oil. By 1957, the date of the first Kuwaiti Census, there were already close to 93,000 foreigners in residence. While most of these were Iranians, some 14,000 were Palestinians. By 1965 this situation had changed drastically. The number of Iranian workers (virtually all male) had risen only slightly from 27,000 to 30,000, while the number of Palestinian/Jordanian residents (about one-third female) had climbed to almost 78,000. Other nationalities contributing to Kuwait's 1965 population included some 26,000 Iraqis (almost exclusively male workers), 21,000 Lebanese (some of them of Palestinian origin), 20,000 chiefly male workers from Muscat and Oman, and close to 17,000 Syrians. Although there were modest infusions of Indians and Pakistanis (about 11,000 each), one notes, ironically, a shift from Asian to Arab labor sources at this time.[7]

Other events of the 1950s were beginning to foreshadow the future, however. The discovery of oil in Libya late in the decade called forth the beginning of a labor migration to that country, largely of Palestinians to man expanding government services. The Egyptianization regulations imposed by Nasser after 1956 led to some out-migration from that country, not only of European and Greek foreigners but also of Egyptian Copts who had often been their partners. But still, out-migration was highly selective and involved an insignificant proportion of the population. The 1958 revolution in Iraq also had repercussions, as some Iraqis associated with the old regime, or fearful of the new, defected. But the scale of migration was small and its linkage to labor demand *per se* remained tenuous.

Consequences of the 1967 War

The above situation changed radically in the aftermath of the 1967 war. That second upheaval shook population stability with even greater force than had the earlier war, increasing the distances travelled by those affected and expanding the ranks of the sending countries. The strongest impact was, of course, felt by the people of Gaza and the West Bank. Between June and October of 1967, approximately 300,000 Palestinians from these areas passed into the East Bank of Jordan[8] and an unknown number moved more clandestinely through Egypt and out to the Gulf/Peninsula. Some of those who went to the East Bank continued their journey, eventually joining pioneer relatives in Kuwait. By 1970, the Palestinian/Jordanian community in Kuwait had grown to almost 150,000 (with a far more normal age and sex structure), far outstripping the Iraqis and Iranians (each with slightly under 40,000, predominantly male, residents) who remained the next most numerous foreign groups in the country. By then, foreign residents constituted a significant majority of Kuwait's population.[9] Palestinians from Gaza evidently found it easier to migrate to Saudi Arabia, which apparently had few Palestinians before the 1967 war. By the Census of 1974, however, there were presumably over 80,000 Palestinians living in the Kingdom of whom more than half were carrying "Palestinian Identity Papers" rather than Jordanian passports.[10] Lesser Palestinian communities were also forming in the recently established oil exporting states along the Gulf, but the numbers there were quite small.

The 1967 war also transformed Egypt into a significant labor exporter. Egyptian teachers and professionals had always worked abroad but on a temporary basis and in modest numbers. The effects of the war added new impetus to their search for foreign employment. Widespread destruction in cities of the Suez Canal Zone dislodged almost a million Egyptians who flocked to Cairo, where not all of them could find new homes or jobs. Once in motion, many of these refugees were willing to move again. Economic difficulties compounded the situation. In the war Egypt lost not only its oil fields that were then beginning to yield, but also its canal, on whose user fees it had become dependent for foreign exchange. The defeat plus these losses took the steam out of the country's faltering industrialization program. Thus, serious out-migration from Egypt began, not only of educators and professionals but of unskilled and semiskilled workers and even of domestic servants. By 1970, there were over 30,000 Egyptians in Kuwait (17,000 males and 13,000 females), and Egyptians were also making their presence felt in Saudi Arabia and in other parts of the Gulf in numbers that, by then, exceeded their representation in Kuwait. An even more important outlet for Egyptian population pressures was Libya, which encouraged the immigration of Egyptian farmers to handle the agricultural sector which Libyans were rapidly abandoning in favor of expanding opportunities in urban and oil-linked areas. Despite altercations that periodically upset Libyan-Egyptian relations, Libya continued to serve as the major locus of employment for Egyptian migrants, although since the 1977 break in diplomatic relations this has taken on a more clandestine character and Tunisians have increasingly been substituted for Egyptians.

The situation in the Peninsula, however, was not greatly affected by the war of 1967. Older patterns tended to continue. Yemenis still moved to and from Saudi Arabia but, because they needed neither visas nor work permits, it is not possible to determine their numbers. And in the small and not yet independent "sheikhdoms" along the Gulf coast, still "protected" by Great Britain, time-honored mixtures of Arab bedouins, Iranian workers, Indo-Pakistani merchants, and others continued their curiously symbiotic coexistence. Thanks to the umbrella provided by Commonwealth status, there were large colonies of ethnically-foreign (i.e. non-Arab) populations who were effectively "at home" in such places as Bahrain, Qatar, Dubai, Oman, and South Yemen. The question of citizenship had not yet come up. Great Britain supervised (and authorized) immigration from its former colonies on the Indian subcontinent, and in fact there was little to be gained by exclusiveness. This was to alter drastically by 1971, when most of the states were given independence and when oil exploitation began to create economic advantages worthy of competition (see Table 1). Citizenship was to become the key to

TABLE 1. Arab Oil States by Dates of Oil Discovery, Large-Scale Extraction, and Political Constitution

Name of Country	Year Oil First Discovered	Year Oil First Extracted in Quantity	Year of Establishment of Current State
Bahrain	1932	1940s[a]	1971
Kuwait	1938	1946	1961
Libya	1958	1961	1969[b]
Oman	1964	1967	1970
Qatar	1939	1971	1971
Saudi Arabia	1933	1958	1932
United Arab Emirates[c]	1960s		1971
(largest components)			
Abu Dhabi		1962	
Dubai		1969	
Others		1970s	

[a] These reserves are close to depletion by now.

[b] Libya independent of Italy in 1951; monarchy overthrown 1969.

[c] Seven "city states" united.

SOURCE: Data compiled from separate entries in H. Haddad and B. Nijim, eds., *The Arab World: A Handbook* (Wilmette: Medina Press, 1978).

preferential access to wealth and privilege, but this change did not fully emerge until after 1973.

Consequences of the 1973 War

The 1973 war ushered in the third and present phase of labor migrations in the Arab world, a phase marked by as much discontinuity in scale and source as the first phase initiated by the Palestine War of 1948. The two factors of greatest significance were the withdrawal of Egypt from the Arab-Israeli conflict and from state-socialist development plans, and the spectacular increase in oil prices. The first led directly to three consequences: (1) the open door policy which released the flood gate on Egyptian emigration, now estimated at two million or more; (2) the virtual loss of hope for an early end to Israeli occupation of Gaza and the West Bank, and subsequent heightened expulsions and emigration of Palestinians who had up to then remained in these places; and (3) the complete military vulnerability of southern Lebanon to invasion by an Israel no longer restrained by fear of a wider war, which contributed to the Lebanese civil war and a resultant restructuring of the economies of neighboring countries as well as to further labor migrations. The second factor, the rapid rise in oil prices, led directly to other consequences: (1) the consolidation of states and statelets in the Gulf, each of which began to focus upon ambitious plans for economic development and diversification, even though citizen populations were too small to carry them out; (2) enormously expanded demands for labor, together with rising wages capable of drawing potential labor forces with irresistible magnetism; and (3) a more prominent geopolitical role for the Gulf region which has drawn foreign interests even more intrusively into the area. All of these factors have led to decisive shifts in the scale and character of population movements in the Arab world.

As was noted above, Egypt's policy changes helped generate a greatly expanded supply of "labor for export." The chief sources remained Egypt and Palestine/Jordan but, after the outbreak of the Lebanese civil war, Syrians and Lebanese also joined this labor pool. Egyptian demobilization in 1974 released a flood of ex-soldiers into the labor market; crackdowns on the West Bank and in Gaza "encouraged" the reunion of families abroad; and Lebanon's fighting and related economic decline drove the middle class out in search of greater security.

Saad Eddin Ibrahim has assembled various estimates of Arab labor migration, as made by Birks and Sinclair, the International Monetary Fund, and M.A. Fadhil.[11] An adaptation of his table appears here as Table 2. From the enormous discrepancies evident in that table it is clear that even the best and most sincere efforts to specify orders of magnitude for post-1973 labor migrations fail to yield reliable or reproducible results. Nevertheless, the figures do permit one to make some general observations.

Most noteworthy is the significant rise in the number of Egyptians participating in labor-related migration, a participation that exceeded half a million by 1977.[12] Considering the facts that in 1972, according to Birks and Sinclair, there were under 45,000 Egyptian workers in Libya,[13] (at that time the country containing the most Egyptian emigrant workers), that in 1970 there were only 30,000 Egyptians (including dependents) in Kuwait,[14] and that, according to the Saudi Census of 1974, only 20,000 workers from Egypt were employed in the Kingdom,[15] the rise is dramatic. It is estimated that the number of Egyptians in Libya peaked at about a quarter of a million by 1976-1977, just prior to the break in relations between the two countries. Although the current number in Libya is considerably lower, there was a compensatory rise in the export of Egyptian labor to the Gulf, to Saudi Arabia, and even to Jordan and Iraq, where unskilled laborers and farmers have been sought to cover growing deficits. The most recent estimates of Egyptians abroad for employment approach one million, although it has been impossible for me to verify any figures. Impressions support these estimates. Certainly no one who has recently traveled by plane in the Arab world would doubt the enormous mobility of the Egyptian peasant work force, and no one who has recently visited schools and government offices in the Gulf and Saudi Arabia would doubt the expanded presence there of Egyptian professionals and white-collar workers.

Palestinian/Jordanian emigration for employment also increased significantly in the 1970s. After 1973 the size of the

**TABLE 2. Various Estimates of Arab Labor Force Migration
1975-1977**
Adapted from Ibrahim (1980)

	Estimates by:		
	A. **ILO-** **Durham Univ.** **(Birks & Sinclair)**	**B.** **International** **Monetary Fund**	**C.** **Arab Sources** **(M.A. Fadhil)**
Countries	**(1975)**	**(1977)**	**(1977)**
A. Major Arab Labor Exporters			
Egypt	398,000	350,000	600,000
Arab Yemen	290,000	500,000	600,000
Democratic Yemen	70,000	300,000	300,000
Palestine/Jordan	265,000	150,000	225,000
Sudan	46,000	50,000	174,000
Syria	70,000	n.a.	70,000 (1975)
Lebanon	50,000	n.a.	50,000 "
Tunisia	39,000	n.a.	39,000 "
Others	68,000	n.a.	68,000 "
TOTAL	1,296,000	1,350,000	2,126,000
B. Major Arab Labor Importers			
Saudi Arabia	700,000	900,000	1,170,000
Libya	310,000	325,000	420,000
Kuwait	143,000	276,000	350,000
n.a.E.	62,000	96,000	115,000
Qatar	15,000	19,000	26,000
Oman	9,000	12,000	16,000
Bahrain	6,000	7,000	9,000
Iraq	15,000	n.a.	100,000
TOTAL	1,260,000	1,635,000	2,206,000

SOURCES: A.: Birks, J.S. & C.A. Sinclair, *International Migration and Development in the Arab Region* (Geneva: ILO, 1980), pp. 134-135.

B.: International Monetary Fund Survey (IMF), Washington, D.C., September 4, 1978, pp. 260-262.

C.: Fadhil, M.A., *Oil and Arab Unity,* in Arabic (Beirut: Center for Arab Unity Studies, 1979), p. 30. Estimates by Ibrahim are based on a wide range of official sources.

Palestinian/Jordanian community in Kuwait went up drastically. By 1975 it exceeded 200,000 and it has continued to rise to a total of 300,000 by 1980.[16] However, some recent changes indicate that this outlet for Palestinian emigration may be drying up. In 1977-78, Kuwait government policy began to make it increasingly difficult for Palestinians to enter as immigrants. At that time, recruitment of labor shifted toward non-Arabs and particularly non-Arab Asians who, for example, received 30,604 (or 63.4 percent) of the 48,270 new work permits granted by the Ministry of Labor and Social Affairs in 1978.[17] It appears that for some time to come increases in the Palestinian/Jordanian community of Kuwait will derive more from the natural increase of persons already resident than from new in-migration.

As indicated in footnote 10 above, there is reason to doubt the accuracy of some estimates of the size of the Palestinian/Jordanian component of the migrant work force in Saudi Arabia. Birks and Sinclair claim that there were 175,000 workers of Palestinian origin in Saudi Arabia in 1974, despite the fact that the Saudi Census of 1974 counted only some 23,000 workers in the Palestinian/Jordanian category. Even if there were a substantial undercount of foreigners in the census, it is impossible to believe the estimate of Birks and Sinclair, which would have placed the total number of Palestinians/Jordanians at over half a million by 1975. Estimates by the International Monetary Fund and Fadhil, both for 1977, probably give a more accurate idea of the total number of Palestinian workers now in the Gulf, Kuwait, and Saudi Arabia. A work force of perhaps 200,000, accompanied by dependents who would increase the total to between half a million and three-quarters of a million, appears to be the absolute maximum that one could expect. In Saudi Arabia, as in Kuwait, there has been a growing reluctance to admit additional numbers of Palestinian-origin migrants. This reluctance was already evident in 1974, at the time of census.[18]

It is virtually impossible to determine the extent of out-migration from Lebanon and Syria during the 1970s, since data on this will not be available until the findings of 1979 and 1980 censuses are made available and until better data become available for Saudi Arabia. We do know that the exodus began in the middle of the decade, making it too recent to show up in any of the estimates or censuses of 1975. As can be seen from Table 2, only Birks and Sinclair have attempted to provide figures on this (Fadhil simply accepts their report). They estimate that 120,000 Lebanese and Syrian workers were abroad in 1975, a number which seems too high.

The Impact of Oil

Regardless of the figures, the outflows of Egyptians, Palestinians/Jordanians, Lebanese, and Syrians are the only ones that can be attributed *directly* to war. The main effects of the 1973 war on labor migrations were indirect rather than direct. Much of the migration was stimulated by the dramatic increase in the demand for labor within the few Arab states that found themselves the sudden recipients of enormously expanded financial resources — resources which were then to be mobilized for the creation of infrastructure, social services, and, hopefully, diversified industrial development. Table 3 summarizes some of the economic changes that occurred during the 1970s, chiefly as a result of higher oil prices.

TABLE 3. Changes in the Gross Domestic Product of Selected Oil States Between 1970 and 1977

Country	Total GDP in 1970 (in Millions of $s)	Total GDP in 1977 (in Millions of 1970 $s)	Percentage Change in GDP (constant $s)
Bahrain	244	354	45
Kuwait	2,691	13,013	384
Libya	3,991	19,360	385
Oman	278	2,527	809
Qatar	302	2,864	848
Saudi Arabia	3,866	43,985	1038
United Arab Emirates	1,470	13,288	804

SOURCE: Table 1, p. 19, of Atif Kubursi, "Arab Economic Prospects in the 1980s," Institute for Palestine Studies, Beirut: 1980.

While the astronomical percentage increases in GDP partially reflect the low levels of the beginning of the decade, they also highlight the suddenness with which wealth came to many states in the Gulf and the urgent need this created for economic planning to absorb and utilize these funds derived from an essentially nonrenewable source. The exceptionally modest GDP shift of Bahrain was viewed by all as a warning sign. Early extraction had already severely depleted Bahraini oil reserves, so that the country could not benefit, except indirectly, from the new conditions of the oil market. Other desert states, if they wished to avoid an eventual "ghost town" fate, had to act quickly to utilize their energy and financial resources to establish a more long-term economic base. Part of the strategy had to be to reduce the rate at which depletion was occurring, in order to buy more time for development. The other part of the strategy had to be rapid reinvestment of the profits.

During the second half of the 1970s the newly expanded resources were earmarked toward ambitious development plans. The Five-Year Plan (1975-80) for Saudi Arabia anticipated an average investment of over $23 billion per year, 14 percent of which was for construction alone. Infrastructure and services, not including communication and transport, absorbed the largest share of investment (over two-thirds). Manufacturing and oil together were allocated less than 10 percent. During the same period, the United Arab Emirates planned average annual investments on the order of $1.5 billion; Oman planned to invest more than $0.75 billion each year; Kuwait anticipated average annual investments of $3.3 billion; and Libya's anticipated annual investment budget was close to $5 billion. (Neither Qatar nor Bahrain had development plans for the period.)[19]

Clearly, capital was available. What was lacking was sufficient manpower to carry out the plans being made. Since 1975, labor imports to the oil countries have increased considerably, and more traditional Arab sources of labor have been supplemented from a broadened base of sending countries, chiefly Asian. While the data are missing that would permit a detailed study of this phenomenon — which constitutes a research subject of highest priority — the main outlines are becoming clearer and can be roughly sketched. It is essential, in the following analysis, to distinguish between those types of labor imports that constitute a mere expansion of already existing patterns and those types involving a sharper break with the past.

The migrations differing more in scale than in kind from the past are those that redistribute population from poorer to wealthier Arab states. Yemeni labor migration, chiefly to Saudi Arabia, is the best example of this. North Yemeni males have always constituted an important component of the Saudi labor force. In fact, according to the Saudi Census, by 1974 there were already a quarter of a million North Yemeni workers in the country, constituting some 14 percent of the total labor force. Another 30,000 (chiefly male) workers hailed from South Yemen. North and South Yemenis together held almost one out of every six jobs in the Kingdom in 1974. As can be seen from Table 2, Yemenis were quick to respond to the heightened demand for labor generated by the new economic plans. By 1977, the number of North Yemeni workers abroad had at least doubled, and there was a remarkable exodus of workers from South Yemen, which hitherto had not been a significant supplier of labor to the oil-rich countries. Egyptians and Sudanese also apparently responded elastically to the new demand for labor in Saudi Arabia and the Gulf, if the figures in Table 2 are any indication.

The relative decline in the proportion of labor migrants from the area of Greater Syria (Palestine, Lebanon, Jordan, Syria) also represented a shift in scale rather than a change in kind. Professional and technical workers, white-collar employees, and skilled workers continued to be recruited from these sources, but, in comparison to the expansions of migration from other sources, people from this area became less significant in overall labor migration. Birks and Sinclair argue that the recent shift toward non-Arab Asian countries, as the pool from which new workers are increasingly being drawn, can be explained primarily by the depletion of the pool of available Arab workers. They stress the growing labor shortages being experienced in (East Bank) Jordan, for example, due to "excessive" labor export to the Gulf, and suggest that inadequate supply rather than shifting demand explains recent changes. My own view is that the explanation is more to be found in changes in demand.

First, having greater resources, the oil states have begun to substitute European and American labor at the technical and professional levels for the lower-paid Syrian, Palestinian, and Lebanese workers they previously depended upon; and from the other direction they have now begun to substitute their own trained nationals for foreign Arabs in more sensitive posts. Second, the majoi quantitative expansion in labor demand has been in construction, unskilled and semiskilled labor, and services (domestic, hotels, hospitals, etc.). In these areas of employment, the issues of low cost and labor discipline are central. It appears that governmental policies are being changed to minimize both economic cost and the potential tensions that could arise from the existence of a permanent expatriate community with moral claims on the state but without political rights. Given the ancient values of the Islamic *Umma* and the more recent values of Arab unity, it has become increasingly anomalous to withhold equal opportunities and citizenship from members of permanently-settled Muslim Arab communities. To minimize this contradiction, as well as to economize on labor costs, there has been a conscious shift to the vast labor pools of Asia for the new workers required by the development schemes.

One must not confuse the new influx of Asians into Saudi Arabia and Kuwait with the earlier labor force participation of Asian residents in the smaller Gulf countries. The Gulf, along which most of the oil states are arrayed, is inhabited by Arabs on its western side and by non-Arabs on its eastern side. Indeed, prior to the modern development of the Arab countries along the Gulf, resident non-nationals were drawn from the closest countries — whether these were Arab (e.g., Iraq) or non-Arab (Iran, Pakistan, India). Although temporary workers were chiefly from Iraq or Iran, there were also, as was noted earlier, resident communities from the Indian subcontinent at many points along the Gulf. Increases in the number of laborers drawn to such countries as Bahrain, Qatar, Oman, and the United Arab Emirates from these traditional sources therefore do not represent a break with the past. Qatar is a case in point. According to that country's 1970 census, almost 60 percent of the total population were not citizens. The largest "foreign" group was Iranian; they constituted some 20 percent of the total population and a third of the foreign population. Next in importance were Pakistanis, who constituted some 15 percent of the total and a fourth of the foreign population.[20] While I have not been able to locate similar data for the pre-oil period in the other small Gulf states, it is well-known that similar situations existed in Dubai, Bahrain, and, to a lesser extent, Oman, which, at the time, was also a labor exporter.

After 1973 these small states, suddenly faced with larger labor requirements, continued to recruit new workers from traditional sources. But by that time Iranian migrants were less available, since Iran too was experiencing the same oil-boom-related need for labor. The logical remaining sources were the overpopulated Asian countries nearby. Birks and Sinclair present a table that clearly demonstrates the shift in labor supply sources for Bahrain, Kuwait, Qatar, and the United Arab Emirates between 1970 and 1975.[21] According to this table, the non-national labor forces in these countries expanded by over 55 percent during the period in question. However, expansion was much slower in the non-national Arab labor force than in the non-national Asian labor force. Whereas Asians (not including Iranians) constituted only about a quarter of the foreign labor force in 1970, by 1975 they constituted over 45 percent. I do not have individual country data for such changes, but Birks and Sinclair do provide 1975 estimates for Oman and the United Arab Emirates that are suggestive. By that year 83 percent of the foreign workers in Oman were Indians or Pakistanis,[22] and in the United Arab Emirates in the same year some 64 percent of all foreign workers were drawn from those two sending countries.[23]

Unfortunately, in generating their key table, Birks and Sinclair grouped Kuwait with the other small states, which seems inappropriate, given the fact that Asian labor had previously played only a minor role in the Kuwaiti labor force. For Kuwait, the recent increase in the use of such labor represents a real discontinuity with the past. The full dimensions of the change are not apparent from the 1975 data, as can be seen from Table 4 which is based on Table 34 of Birks and Sinclair. According to Al-Moosa, the major shift began in 1977-78, which means that its full impact is not yet known. But the trend cannot be ignored, given projections that by the year 2000, such non-Arab workers may constitute one-third of the total labor force in the country.[24] Thus far, non-Arab migrant workers in Kuwait have been drawn almost exclusively from Iran, India, and Pakistan, with the first of these being of declining importance and the latter two of growing significance. Recently, sources of Asian migration have come to include less traditional suppliers such as Korea, Sri Lanka, Thailand, and the Philippines.

A similar move toward diversification is taking place in a much more organized way in Saudi Arabia, which, because of its comparative size and heavy investments, is the single most important employer of migrant labor in the Arab world. Saudi policies will be the major determinant of labor migration trends in the region for the next few decades. For this reason, it is particularly distressing that data on Saudi Arabia's role in labor migration are very poor and are likely to remain so for some time. What we have available are estimates and guesstimates, together with impressionistic observations. All statements, then, must be made with caution. First, we have no firm idea of the total population of Saudi Arabia, much less of the exact number of foreign nationals or foreign workers in that country. If we accept the findings of the 1974 Census, there were under 400,000 non-national workers in the country at that time, of whom 280,000 were from the Yemens. On the other hand, Birks and Sinclair estimated that 773,400 workers of foreign nationality were present in 1975, a figure we have questioned as too high (see discussion in note 10 below). The International Monetary Fund estimated that 900,000 foreign workers were in the Kingdom in 1977, a figure raised to 1,170,000 by Saad Eddin Ibrahim in his (1980) paper. A *New York Times* article (February 23, 1981, p. 4) placed the number of foreign workers in Saudi Arabia at over two million, out of an estimated total population of 7.5 million. Given the wide discrep-

TABLE 4. Kuwait: Migrant Population by Country or Area of Origin, 1965, 1970, and 1975

Country or area of origin	1965		1970		1975	
	No.	%	No.	%	No.	%
Jordan and Palestine	77,710	31.4	147,700	37.7	204,180	39.0
Egypt	11,020	4.4	30,420	7.8	60,530	11.6
Iraq	25,900	10.5	39,070	10.0	45,070	8.6
Syrian Arab Republic	16,850	6.8	27,220	6.9	40,960	7.8
Lebanon	20,880	8.4	25,390	6.5	24,780	4.7
Saudi Arabia	4,630	1.9	10,900	2.8	12,530	2.4
Democratic Yemen	2,640	1.1	8,600	2.2	12,330	2.4
Oman	19,580	7.9	14,670	3.7	7,310	1.4
Yemen	140	0.1	2,360	0.6	4,830	0.9
Arab Gulf	2,010	0.8	5,520	1.4	4,060	0.8
Sudan	420	0.2	770	0.2	1,550	0.3
Other	6,140	2.5	230	0.1	1,060	0.2
Arab countries	187,920	76.0	312,850	79.9	419,190	80.1
Iran	30,790	12.4	39,130	10.0	40,840	7.8
India	11,700	4.7	17,340	4.4	32,100	6.1
Pakistan	11,740	4.7	14,710	3.8	23,020	4.4
Other	5,130	2.1	7,240	1.8	7,600	1.4
Non-Arab countries	59,360	24.0	78,420	20.0	103,560	19.8
TOTAL	247,280	100.0	391,270	100.0	522,750	100.0

SOURCE: Birks and Sinclair, *International Migration and Development in the Arab Region* (Geneva: ILO, 1980), p. 149.

ancies among the various figures (which cannot be attributed only
to the fact that the figures are not all for the same years) and given
the margins of error for each of the estimates, it is clearly not
possible to make any even quasi-scientific statements about labor
migrations to Saudi Arabia (or therefore, to make any even
approximately correct estimates concerning total migrations to the
Peninsula and Gulf). One can, however, make certain generalizations about the geographic distribution of foreign workers in Saudi
Arabia and some (unquantified) statements about changes in the
sources of labor for that country due to the impact of recent
economic plans.

Foreign workers are still to be found chiefly in a relatively
concentrated belt of settlements in the Kingdom. This was true in
1974 and is undoubtedly still true today. In general, it is the more
populous and developed regions of Saudi Arabia that contain the
highest proportions of foreigners. These developed regions lie in a
belt in the center of the country connecting the oil-producing
zone on the Gulf (the Eastern Province) with the urban centers of
the west (Medina, Mecca, Jiddah) and passing through the growing "connecting node" of the capital, Riyadh. Even as early as
1974, 21 percent of Mecca Province, 15 percent of Jezzan Province, almost 12 percent of the Eastern Province, 9 percent of
Riyadh Province, and 8 percent of Medina Province residents
were foreign nationals. Most of the other provinces contained
considerably lower proportions of foreigners. The distribution of
non-Arab foreigners was even more skewed, since they were to be
found almost exclusively in the Eastern Province or in cities on
the western coast.

Since 1974, foreign workers have chiefly clustered in these
same regions. Consideration of the Saudi Arabia 1975 Five-Year
Plan, from the standpoint of spatial implications, reveals that
development continues to be concentrated in the central belt connecting Dhahran-Dammam with Riyadh and then Jiddah.[25] In
addition to the already existing centers, the plan envisaged the
development of two major port-industrial complexes, one at
Jubail on the east coast to the north of Dhahran-Dammam, and
the second at Yanbu on the west coast to the north of Jiddah. By

1980, the Jubail port complex was well on its way to completion, with imported ex-soldiers from Korea as the chief labor force. Intensive efforts are now being made to further the second major complex at Yanbu, using American technical and professional personnel and primarily Asian laborers. These two developments reveal much about the changing nature of labor migration to Saudi Arabia, how labor is being recruited, and how the foreign workers are being kept isolated from Saudi society.

Construction contracts have increasingly become a Korean monopoly in Saudi Arabia. According to a working paper by Richards and Martin based in part upon U.S. intelligence sources, Korean firms won all of the new construction contracts in Saudi Arabia in 1979 and now have a corner on one-fourth of the Middle Eastern construction market. "Since such firms provide most of their own laborers, who work very long hours and who live in isolation from the local population, their increasing popularity in the politically jittery Kingdom is not surprising," the paper notes.[26] Birks and Sinclair point to the obvious "practical" advantages of the turnkey labor contracts Asian firms are able to provide,[27] but Saad Eddin Ibrahim brings out the deeper economic and sociological significance of this trend when he suggests that, through this system, the Saudi elite seeks to "have its cake and eat it too"; that is, to benefit from the fruits of an inexpensive and disciplined labor force while being "protected" from any social service demands or cultural "contamination."[28]

Not only Korean firms but some from the Philippines, Thailand, and Malaysia have begun to provide turnkey labor to Saudi Arabia. Other countries in the Gulf area, impressed with the ease and trouble-free character of contract labor from Asia, have also begun to turn their backs on the more expensive and "demanding" Arab labor in favor of this solution. Precedents set by the Ruweis project in Abu Dhabi, the Jabal Ali project in Dubai, and the Umm Said scheme in Qatar — precedents that are now being followed more and more throughout the Gulf region — are changing the nature of labor migration, with far-reaching consequences for the future.

This paper has hinted throughout at some of the social consequences of the labor migrations that have been occurring in the Arab region during the past 30 years. It is now appropriate to try to summarize some of the more important consequences and to raise some basic questions. These can be organized in terms of (1) consequences for countries providing the migrants, and (2) consequences for countries attracting the migrants.

Sending Countries

Palestinian migration. Of the four million Palestinians in the world today, only 1.8 million still live within the territory of Palestine. While East Bank Jordan contains the next largest number (about one million), an increasing proportion of Palestinians are now living along the Gulf and in Saudi Arabia. The fact that they have been denied citizenship (except in Jordan), and that in other Arab states even those with many years of residence have not been naturalized, creates an anomalous (and morally uncomfortable) situation that grows increasingly sensitive. Many host countries are evidently uneasy about this and have recently been seeking alternative sources of labor, not only because it costs less (no dependents are allowed) but because it is unlikely to pose moral dilemmas comparable to those associated with the presence in large numbers of fellow Muslims and Arabs. Emigration from Palestine and from areas settled by Palestinians immediately after 1948 is likely to continue, since East Bank Jordan has a weak economic base, Israeli expulsions may well intensify, and Lebanon remains in deep distress. Whether the Gulf countries and Saudi Arabia will continue to serve as hospitable recipients of this migration is currently in question. One must also look at the second generation, i.e. Palestinians born in Kuwait and Saudi Arabia who consider those countries as much a home as they have ever had. Can they continue to be considered "foreigners"? And finally, one must ask how this dispersion is affecting Palestinian identity.

Egyptian migration. There is no doubt that recent emigration has served a useful function for the Egyptian economy, at least in the short run. Habitually overpopulated rural areas have benefited from the exodus, and remittances flowing from the Gulf countries have apparently helped to reduce Egypt's foreign debt.[29] The Egyptian government has welcomed the migration-related opportunities with alacrity and is indeed beginning to "contract" with Gulf governments to provide the labor they need. One good consequence of out-migration is that large numbers of males in their prime are temporarily absent, which has undoubtedly contributed to recent declines in the Egyptian birth rate. Against this must be weighed the strains placed on families by prolonged separations. Another positive consequence of out-migration is that it is likely to make the Egyptian social structure a little more fluid. Work abroad equips the lucky few with the resources to improve their economic and social position when they return. In a society which has suffered in the past from too rigid a class structure, this new opportunity for mobility is certainly good. On the other hand, one must consider the possible deleterious effects on Egypt in the long run. To what extent are the most competent workers more likely to emigrate? And what is the eventual effect on the psychology of a people of knowing that the "chance" to get ahead lies not within their own society but elsewhere?

Yemeni migration. Yemeni migration is characterized by periodic circular flows of young males. The number of participants in this process has now reached astronomical proportions — a million workers out of a combined Northern and Southern population of only some seven million. What are the implications for economic development in the Yemens, for the nature of Yemeni family life, and for the future relations between the Yemens and Saudi Arabia of such total dependence upon work outside the country? This issue warrants careful study. What would be the effect, for example, of a political break between Saudi Arabia and either one of the Yemens, if it closed off the frontier? What are the implications for future prospects of independence or merger?

Asian migration. While the subject is outside the scope of this paper, it seems that there are important aspects of Asian migration to the Arab region that have not been adequately studied so far.

Receiving Countries

While a country-by-country discussion of the labor importers will not be attempted here, there are major differences among them concerning the extent to which they are dependent upon imported labor and the extent to which they have been substituting Asian for Arab labor. Despite these differences, however, all the receiving countries will increasingly be confronted with a basic contradiction arising from labor importation. The shift to Asian labor may postpone but cannot prevent an eventual encounter with the ultimate dilemma.

Other societies have been built by the efforts of immigrants, but most granted newcomers the right of eventual citizenship. Other societies in the contemporary period have utilized "guest" workers on a temporary basis, but such workers never constituted a sizeable minority, much less a majority, of the total residents of the host countries. Other societies, even when they have restricted immigration and naturalization, have tended to give preferential treatment to migrants who shared basic cultural affinities.

Societies of the Gulf and the Peninsula are the first to attempt to maintain a monopoly on citizenship privileges while being so heavily dependent upon migrants for their labor forces. Initially, they accepted long-term residents who formed normal communities of workers and dependents; these communities, sharing Islam and Arab culture, had a moral call on services, on juridical rights, and on eventual assimilation, given the basic values of the Arab Islamic world. Instead of evolving in a natural way in this direction, however, the countries of the Gulf/Peninsula are evidently retreating from this natural consequence by moving more and more toward a system that deals with labor as a rented commodity and treats laborers in the same impersonal way that one might treat a machine. One must ask what the effects of such a choice will be on the character of the host society. Can a culture that dehumanizes workers in this manner and that bases its own privilege on a caste system of this type endure, and can it train citizens who practice the ideals of Islam?

NOTES

[1] Most noteworthy are the numerous, lengthy, and detailed country-by-country studies done by Birks and Sinclair, conducted over a period of many years with full funding, international cooperation, and preferential access to data. Successive simplifications and the omission of detailed methods were inevitable when the summary results were recently published (ILO, 1980). Unfortunately, due to a sudden and pressing demand for such data, their results have been reified and are being uncautiously quoted by many scholars, without sufficient caveats and reservations.

[2] The two most important caveats concern the uncertain accuracy of the Saudi Arabian Census of 1974 and the fact that since 1975, the benchmark year selected by Birks and Sinclair, labor migration to the Gulf is rumored to have doubled in magnitude and has certainly changed in character.

[3] See my "The Demographic Transformation of Palestine," in *The Transformation of Palestine,* edited by Ibrahim Abu-Lughod (Evanston: Northwestern University Press, 1971).

[4] These developments are treated in considerably greater detail in my "Demographic Characteristics of the Palestinian Population," Special Technical Report prepared for the UNESCO Palestine Open University Feasibility Study, February 1980. Syrian labor force data are found in Table XVII, p. 65.

[5] *Ibid.,* Table XXII, p. 72, based on a sample study of population in Lebanese camps in 1971.

[6] Our data come from a slightly later time. According to a census taken by Israeli military authorities just after their conquest of the West Bank and Gaza in 1967, many families had sons or daughters abroad and about 15 percent of all families were receiving remittances from children working outside. See Israel Defense Forces, Census of Population 1967 Conducted by the Central Bureau of Statistics, *The Administered Territories: Additional Data from the Sample Enumeration,* Publication No. 5 (Jerusalem, 1970), Tables 17-62.

[7] For nationality figures, see Kuwait, Ministry of Planning, Central Statistical Office, *Annual Statistical Abstract 1978,* pp. 23-24, which compares 1965, 1970, and 1975 census findings on foreign nationals.

[8] See J. Abu-Lughod, "Demographic Characteristics . . .," Table V, p. 23, plus associated discussion in the text. The estimates are based upon net school transfers as well as before-and-after population figures derived from Jordanian, Egyptian, and Israeli sources.

[9] The same source as note 7 *supra.*

[10] These totals are derived from the nationality breakdowns presented in the 14 separate provincial volumes of the Saudi Census of 1974. The census distinction is between Jordanians (most of whom are presumed to be of Palestinian origin and primarily of West Bank residence) and Palestinians (presumably chiefly from Gaza). Despite the arguments of Birks and Sinclair in their "The Kingdom of Saudi Arabia and the Libyan Arab Jamahiriya: The Key Countries of Employment" (International Labor Office, Geneva, Working Paper dated May 1979) that the Saudi Census was merely a sample survey and therefore unreliable, I cannot agree with their decision to reduce the figure given for native Saudis while doubling the estimate of foreign residents. The Saudi

Census gave a resident foreign population of 761,100 (of whom 528,000 were males). Birks and Sinclair raised this estimate to over 1.5 million, of whom they estimate 773,400 were in the labor force alone by 1975. I have not been able to check the exterior-generated figures they claimed to be cumulating in order to reach this total, but I do have major reservations about the single largest component in their estimate, the number of Palestinians/Jordanians in Saudi Arabia. In Table 14, pp. 138-139 of their *International Migration and Development in the Arab Region* (Geneva: ILO, 1980), they gave this as 536,800, which makes Palestinians and Jordanians constitute over one-third of the entire foreign population of Saudi Arabia. In *Ibid.,* Table 10, p. 134, they suggested that 175,000 workers of Palestinian/Jordanian origin were in Saudi Arabia in 1975. From my own analysis of the distribution of Palestinians throughout the world, this figure appears to be excessive. In the study I did for UNESCO, I examined both the age distribution of Palestinians/Jordanians in Saudi Arabia as shown in the Saudi Census and the number of Palestinian/Jordanian students enrolled in school as shown in the Saudi *Education Yearbook* and attempted to estimate the total size of the population from the enrollment ratio. On this basis I reached an estimate for 1976-77 that did not exceed 120,000-150,000 residents of Palestinian origin, of whom less than a third were in the labor force. In short, Birks and Sinclair grossly overestimated the number of Palestinians in Saudi Arabia and therefore also exaggerated the total number of foreign workers and residents in that country in 1975. Subsequent to the writing of this paper I received a communication from Birks indicating that they have now revised downward their estimate of the number of Palestinians/Jordanians in Saudi Arabia.

[11] See Saad Eddin Ibrahim, "Oil Migration and the New Arab Social Order," mimeographed report dated June 1980, p. 45, Table IV, and note to our Table 2 for his sources.

[12] Exact figures are impossible to obtain and I suspect these estimates are too low. Egyptian data on Egyptians with *official* contracts abroad reveal a tenfold increase between 1970 and 1978, with substantial spurts in 1971-72 and again in 1976-77. They also indicate a shift in percentage terms away from high-level manpower. See National Bank of Egypt, *Economic Bulletin,* Vol. XXXII, Nos. 3-4 (1979), pp. 261-290.

[13] Birks and Sinclair, "The Kingdom of Saudi Arabia and the Libyan Arab Jamahiriya: The Key Countries of Employment," cited earlier, Table 74, p. 82, based on Libyan Arab Jamahiriya, Immigration Department, Secretariat of the Interior, *Immigrant Populations in Libya* (Tripoli, 1976, in Arabic), and Ministry of Planning and Scientific Research, *Work Permit Statistics* (Tripoli, mimeographed, 1976, in Arabic).

[14] From Census of Kuwait, 1970, reproduced in *Annual Statistical Abstract 1978,* pp. 23-24, cited above.

[15] My own computations from the 14 separate provincial returns that constitute the Saudi Census of 1974. I have used the table showing employees of 12 years and older by nationality and sector of employment and have cumulated males and females employed in the provinces.

[16] The higher figure was given in a recent *New York Times* article (February 23, 1981), p. 4.

[17] See A. Al-Moosa, "Non-Arab Immigration to Kuwait with Special Reference to Asian Immigrants," in *Journal of the Social Sciences* (Kuwait), 8, January, 1981, p. 24.

[18] It is interesting to note that of the Palestinian/Jordanian population in Saudi Arabia counted by the Census and classified by length of residence, fully one-half had been living in Saudi Arabia since before 1970. Whereas the number of Egyptians had increased markedly during the relatively short period 1973-74 (the start of the "boom"), the number of Palestinians/Jordanians had increased much less. Only one-fourth had arrived during the year before the census. I have calculated these percentages from data in the fourteen Census enumeration reports of the separate provinces of Saudi Arabia. A table repeated for each province cross-tabulates foreign residents in the province by nationality and duration of residence. It is these tables that I have used to calculate the relative recency of Egyptian and Palestinian migration to Saudi Arabia. It should be noted that the number of persons for whom duration-of-residence data are available is somewhat smaller than the totals by nationality that are presented in tables showing nationality by age. I assume that the census processors have omitted from the former table children of foreign nationals who were born in Saudi Arabia, but I have not been able to verify this.

[19] See Atif Kubursi, "Arab Economic Prospects in the 1980s" (Institute for Palestine Studies, Beirut, 1980), Table 2, p. 20.

[20] See p. 17 of Ministry of Overseas Development, Middle East Division, *The First Population Census of Qatar, April/May 1970* (mimeographed).

[21] See their *International Migration and Development in the Arab Region,* cited above, Table 12, p. 136.

[22] *Ibid.,* Table 32, p. 148.

[23] *Ibid.,* Table 47, p. 157.

[24] Al-Moosa, *op. cit.,* pp. 2, 26.

[25] See, for example, Basheer Nijim, "The Saudi Arabian 1975 Five-Year Plan: National Integration and Urbanization," mimeographed paper dated April 1976. Additional information on the new developments is available, *inter alia,* in Saad Eddin Ibrahim, *op. cit.,* pp. 144 *et seq.,* who discusses the Jubail and Yanbu complexes in terms of "enclave development projects" designed to insulate foreigners from the surrounding society; and in Birks and Sinclair, "The Kingdom of Saudi Arabia and the Libyan Arab Jamahiriya . . .," p. 20.

[26] See Alan Richards and Philip L. Martin, "The Laissez-Faire Approach to International Labor Migration: The Case of the Arab Middle East," *Working Paper No. 80-10,* University of California, Davis, Department of Agricultural Economics (mimeographed), 1980, p. 14.

[27] Birks and Sinclair, *International Migration and Development . . .,* esp. p. 113.

[28] Saad Eddin Ibrahim, *op. cit.,* p. 144.

[29] See, for example, Table 10, p. 290, of National Bank of Egypt, *Economic Bulletin,* Vol. 32, Nos. 3-4, 1979 for data on this.

BIBLIOGRAPHY

Abu-Lughod, Janet. "Demographic Characteristics of the Palestinian Population." Special Technical Report prepared for UNESCO in connection with the Palestine Open University Feasibility Study (mimeographed, February 1980).

_____ . "The Demographic Transformation of Palestine," in Ibrahim Abu-Lughod, ed., *The Transformation of Palestine*. Northwestern University Press, Evanston: 1971.

Al-Moosa, A. "Non-Arab Immigration to Kuwait with Special Reference to Asian Immigrants." (Kuwait) *Journal of the Social Sciences* 8 (January 1981), pp. 1-42.

Birks, J.S. and C.A. Sinclair. *Arab Manpower*. St. Martin's Press, New York: 1980.

_____ . *International Migration and Development in the Arab Region*. International Labor Office, Geneva: 1980.

_____ . "The Kingdom of Saudi Arabia and the Libyan Arab Jamahiriya: The Key Countries of Employment." Working paper of the International Labor Office, Geneva: mimeographed, May 1979.

_____ . "The Nature and Process of Labour Importing: The Arabian Gulf States of Kuwait, Bahrain, Qatar and the United Arab Emirates." Working paper of the International Labor Office, Geneva: mimeographed, August 1979.

Cottrell, Alvin et al., eds. *The Persian Gulf States: A General Survey*. The Johns Hopkins Press, Baltimore: 1980.

Fadhil, Mahmoud Abd al-, *Oil and Arab Unity,* in Arabic. Center for Arab Unity Studies, Beirut: 1979.

Haddad, Hassan and Basheer Nijim, eds., *The Arab World: A Handbook*. Medina Press, Wilmette: 1978.

Ibrahim, Saad Eddin. "Oil Migration and the New Arab Social Order." Mimeographed report dated June 1980.

Kubursi, Atif. "Arab Economic Prospects in the 1980s." Institute for Palestine Studies, Beirut: 1980, pp. 5-25.

National Bank of Egypt, "Temporary Emigration of Egyptians for Working Abroad Particularly in Arab Countries." *Economic Bulletin,* Vol. XXXII, Nos. 3-4 (1979).

Nijim, Basheer. "The Saudi Arabian Five-Year Plan: National Integration and Urbanization." Mimeographed paper dated April 1976.

Richards, Alan and Philip L. Martin. "The Laissez-Faire Approach to International Labor Migration: The Case of the Arab Middle East." Working paper prepared at the University of California, Davis: No. 80-10, undated but 1980.

United Nations Economic Commission for Western Asia. Series on the Population Situation in the ECWA Region dealing with specific countries. United Arab Emirates (Beirut: 1980); Bahrain (Beirut: 1979); Qatar (Beirut: 1980); Jordan (Beirut: 1980); Kuwait (Beirut: 1980).

United States-Saudi Arabian Joint Commission on Economic Co-operation. *Summary of Saudi Arabian Five-Year Development Plan (1975-1980).* Mimeographed report dated 1975.

Censuses of Qatar, Saudi Arabia, Israel, Kuwait, Syria, Jordan.

M ODERNIZATION, OIL, AND THE ARAB COUNTRIES *Dankwart A. Rustow*

Modernization, according to a widely accepted definition I proposed in 1967, means "widening control over nature through closer interaction among men."[1] It became a worldwide process as a result of the European voyages of discovery of the fifteenth and sixteenth centuries. By the nineteenth century it had generated a technological and social dynamism that has involved all of humanity and that has extended human control to material resources on all continents and in all oceans. A further acceleration of modernization has taken place since the end of World War II, including an extended division of labor, a global energy economy, and a tighter financial integration than ever before.

Modernization, it is important to remember, is not a synonym for moral progress: it does not provide any automatic prescriptions for individual happiness or social justice. Men and women in traditional, pre-modern societies are more likely to fall victim to natural catastrophes, malnutrition, tuberculosis, or childbed fever. In an era of global modernization they are more likely to be killed in highway accidents, or by gunfire or atomic bombs; or to suffer from high blood pressure, insomnia, or nervous breakdowns. As modern man frees himself from the shackles of nature he becomes entangled in a web of human relations; as he achieves mastery over nature he risks becoming enslaved by other men.

Nor is modernization to be confused with westernization. Human cooperation for control of the forces of nature is the basis of all civilization. The Middle East, along with China and India, was in the forefront of the prehistoric revolution of irrigated agri-

Dankwart A. Rustow holds a PhD from Yale University and presently is a Distinguished Professor of Political Science at the Graduate School, City University of New York. Dr. Rustow has also taught at Princeton and Columbia universities, held a senior staff position at the Brookings Institution, and served as a consultant to the Department of State and the Rockefeller and Ford foundations. Among his published works are *A World of Nations, Middle Eastern Political Systems,* and "U.S.-Saudi Relations and the Oil Crisis of the 1980s" *(Foreign Affairs).*

culture and of domestication of plants and animals. In the sixteenth century A.D. the Turkish Ottoman and Chinese Manchu empires had attained levels of technology and of complex but stable social organization unrivalled in the Christian West of the Middle Ages or the Renaissance. What made the West into the spearhead of world modernity was its readiness to exploit on a grand scale such inventions as navigation by compass, warfare by gunpowder, and printing by movable type. In sum, what distinguished the Europeans from other civilizations was their mobility, firepower, and ability to communicate.

Nevertheless, in the very act of extending the process of modernity to the far corners of the earth, Europe inexorably undermined its own temporary monopoly. Today, Soviet sputniks, American computers, Japanese automobiles, and transistors made in Hong Kong are features of a single global technology, and most of these are traded in a single global market. Human life on all continents has come to be dominated, more or less, by this modern technology and by the typically modern attitudes of secularism, materialism, empiricism, acquisitiveness, and restless innovation.

None of these attitudes were innate or traditional in the West; they were just as alien to medieval Christianity as they have been to traditional Confucianism, Hinduism, or Islam. Each major traditional civilization, in Europe or on any other continent, thus has had to face the challenge of replacing traditional with modern values, or else effecting some sort of reconciliation — with Europeans and Americans opting mostly for replacement and Japanese for synthesis. As Charles Issawi reminds us in this volume, there is much that contemporary Middle Easterners can learn from the Japanese pattern of combining advanced technology and economic organizaton with continued, or even deepened, attachment to traditional intellectual, artistic, and religious values.[2]

The Arab Middle East played a unique and important role in each of the two major phases of modernization just distinguished, that of European imperialism after the sixteenth century and that of global economic integration in recent decades.

Of all the major world regions, the Middle East has had the longest and most varied relations with Europe. For Europeans, the Middle East was always part of the "known world" — unlike the Americas or Japan, it did not have to be "discovered" or "opened up" by the arrival of ships on distant shores. In the historic political and cultural struggles around the Mediterranean, the Middle East was clearly in the ascendant throughout the millennium after Muḥammad. The Arabs learned their science and philosophy from ancient Greece and passed them on to the Europeans of the Renaissance. But as the dividing lines stabilized in the fifteenth and sixteenth centuries, the Islamic Middle East turned inward, and Christian Europe outward and overseas.

As a result, the Middle East came to be the very last region to feel the full impact of western imperialism. The Americas were conquered in the sixteenth to eighteenth centuries, Southern Asia in the seventeenth and eighteenth, and Tropical Africa in the nineteenth, whereas East Asia largely escaped such conquest. In the Middle East, western imperialist pressure began with Napoleon's intrusion into Egypt in 1798 and culminated in the occupation of Egypt and the Fertile Crescent between 1882 and 1920. This late arrival of European imperialism meant that the full western impact came at a time when educated Middle Easterners had already been converted to modern and western values of liberalism and nationalism, positivism and romanticism, rationalism and pragmatism. Conversely, westerners had had time to reflect ruefully on imperialism as "the white man's burden" and to disguise their colonies as "protectorates" or "mandates." What the Middle East came to experience was, in Bernard Lewis's words, a "halfhearted pussy-footing imperialism — an imperialism of interference without control that would neither create nor tolerate stable and orderly institutions."[3]

The imperialists not only arrived late but also departed early. The British withdrawal from Egypt in 1946 and Palestine in 1948 marked a crucial early phase in the European retreat from Asia and Africa, and the evacuation of British forces from the emirates of the Gulf completed that process for the Middle East. In sum, it was in the Middle East that European imperialism won most of its last victories and suffered many of its earliest defeats — an experience that has left behind a good deal of bitterness on both sides.

While the imperialist onslaught lasted, it left Middle Eastern leaders and movements with a number of difficult political choices — the most obvious one being between submission and resistance. For the Wahhabis in their remote location on the Arabian peninsula, resistance worked in the nineteenth century, and for the Kemalists in Turkey it worked under particularly favorable circumstances in 1919-23. But resistance failed for Shaykh Shāmil in the Caucasus in the 1860s, for the Mahdiyyah in the Sudan in the 1890s, and for the Sanūsiyyah in Libya in the 1920s.

A tempting and even riskier option was to try to manipulate the imperialists, specifically to encourage the advent of a remote imperialist as a counterweight to the imperialist already close at hand. Thus, the late Ottomans allied themselves with imperial Germany, the better to resist British, French, and Russian pressures — and were saved from becoming a German protectorate by the timely collapse of the Hohenzollern empire in 1918. Thus, Gamāl 'Abd al-Nāsir called in the Soviets to help oppose the British and the Americans — and his country was saved from what came to be considered its Soviet "occupation" only through Anwar al-Sadāt's bold change of course in 1972.

The danger of the manipulative tactic, of course, is that one may exchange a tired and decadent imperial master for a more powerful and vigorous one — as did the Syrians and Iraqis who joined the Arab revolt against the Ottomans in 1916, only to see their countries converted into British or French mandates a few years later. Another risk is that the imperialist powers, instead of keeping each other at bay, may agree on partition, as Russia and Britain did over Iran in 1907 and again in 1941. Perhaps the worst of all choices turns out to be a vacillating course between resistance and submission — such as that of the Egyptian Wafd party, which first organized national resistance to British rule, then accommodated to it, and at last ratified its continuation; or that of the Palestinian Arabs under the British mandate, who rebelled belatedly after a decade and a half of quiet accommodation.

And yet, when pursued with skill and in favorable circumstances, such maneuvering among the powers can become a strategy for political survival. Thus, Jordan's King Ḥusayn, after securing the departure of British forces, asked for their return in the crisis of 1958; obtained support from the United States and even Israel in warding off the threat from the PLO and Syria in 1970; and for over a quarter of a century has secured his rule by carefully keeping in touch with each shifting political trend in the region. Half a century earlier, Mustafa Kemal Atatürk's strategy in the Turkish war of independence, though based mainly on resistance, also included skillful diplomatic maneuvering, with successive contacts with the Soviets, French, and Italians until Britain and Greece remained as the only opponents.

For the imperialists, too, there are tactical choices to be made — though the risks for them are obviously negligible by comparison. Because of the focal location of the Middle East at the juncture of three continents and two oceans, the region has never been far from the whirlpool of international conflict; in contrast to, say, Siberia, parts of South America, or Australia, it never became the secure or unquestioned preserve of a single colonial power. Imperial rivalries over the Middle East could take many specific forms: each of several powers might seek to keep out the others; two or more of them might jointly invade, or partition, some part of the Middle East; or powers outside the Middle East might try to loosen the grip of those already established in part of the region. Until World War I, these rivalries among the powers helped preserve the independence of large parts of the Middle East. Then, in the period between the two World Wars, those same rivalries hastened conquest and partition. Finally, since 1945, the rival pressures of Russia and the United States helped to speed Britain's withdrawal from the region and to prevent the installation of either superpower as the new imperial ruler — thus securing for the region a precarious margin of political independence unprecedented in this century.

Specifically, United States policies to prevent Soviet expansion in the region were successfully pursued under the Truman Doctrine of 1947, whereas United States pressure for British withdrawal was most readily evident in Palestine in 1948 and again in securing the evacuation of Suez in 1956. Within the relative power vacuum thus created, Middle Eastern countries have been able to pursue shifting alignments (e.g., Egypt in 1955 and 1972-77; Iran in 1953 and 1979; Iraq in 1958 and 1980). There has also been a massive inflow of modern weapons, unprecedented in earlier periods or in other Third World regions, and a periodic sharpening of intra-regional conflicts and rivalries. This militarization of the Middle East has opened up a vast disproportion between military means and political ends[4] — a disproportion most clearly evident in the protracted course of the Arab-Israeli conflict. Anwar al-Sadāt's dramatic visit to Jerusalem in 1977 helped secure at least in part the Arab aim of return of occupied territories, where two decades of belligerence and escalating arms supplies had failed to do so. And a corresponding policy of armament and intransigence brought Israel no closer to the goal of secure and recognized boundaries, and indeed has confronted the Zionist ideal of an egalitarian Jewish society with the reality of a binational two-class society in which prevailing population growth rates bring about a steady increase in the size of the suppressed Arab minority. The militarization of the region has also meant a growing political role for the military, to the point where generals and colonels have emerged as the rulers in most Arab countries and the coup d'état has become the most frequent method of succession. Even in Israel's democratic system, it is not uncommon for generals to retire early to seek a second, political career.

*　　*　　*

Modernization, it was noted earlier, has entered a particularly intensive phase in the decades since World War II. Yet that overall process is marked by a curious inner contradiction. Global politics has become increasingly decentralized. Colonial empires have been dissolved and a multitude of sovereign states proclaimed in their stead, and membership in the United Nations has more than tripled since the organization's founding. The tight bipolar situation of the cold war of the 1950s has given way to a more complex interaction, as Western Europe (including West Germany, France, and Great Britain), China, and Japan have joined the United States and the Soviet Union as independent players. And at certain times or on certain issues, any one of a score of other countries — as large as Indonesia or as small as Israel or Libya — may play an important or even decisive international role. Global economics, on the contrary, has moved toward integration and unification. International trade has grown on an unprecedented scale; transport by sea and travel by air have intensified; multinational corporations have expanded their activities; international banking and finance have spread their web across the continents; and a growing stream of workers has moved across frontiers — from Mediterranean countries to central and northern Europe, from the Caribbean region to the United States, and from the populous countries of the Middle East and Asia to the oil-rich and sparsely populated countries of the Gulf. In sum, as more and more nations have proclaimed their sovereign independence, they have found themselves enmeshed in an ever tighter network of technological and economic interdependence.

Nowhere are those opposite trends as starkly palpable as in the Middle East. The period of imperialist withdrawal in the quarter century from 1946 to 1971 happened to coincide with the rapid development of the Middle East's petroleum resources. In 1950, petroleum accounted for only 30 percent of the world's energy consumption, and the Middle East (including North Africa) for only 15 percent of the world's petroleum production — giving the region a share of less than 5 percent in global energy output. By 1970, petroleum had become the world's prime fuel, accounting for nearly half the world's energy, and the Middle East had become the prime petroleum region, supplying 39 percent of the world's petroleum, as much as 69 percent of petroleum in international trade, and a solid 18 percent of the world's total energy.[5] As the Middle East became politically independent of the West, the leading western countries and Japan became economically dependent, in ever larger measure, on petroleum from the Middle East. While many Middle Eastern governments found that arms races brought them no closer to their political or even military goals, other Middle Eastern governments found in the political economy of petroleum a rare opportunity to assert their power.

How drastically the Middle Eastern oil scene has changed

in two decades is readily apparent from a comparison of the oil crises of 1951-53 and 1970-71. In 1951, when Prime Minister Muḥammad Muṣaddiq decreed the nationalization of Iran's oil, the concessionaire company, an affiliate of British Petroleum, withdrew its technicians; Britain dispatched naval units to the region and the Royal Air Force escorted tankers with Iranian oil into port at Aden, then still a crown colony, where BP's lawyers stood ready to have the cargo confiscated. Meanwhile, BP and other multinational oil companies vastly stepped up their oil exploration and production in neighboring countries such as Iraq, Kuwait, and Saudi Arabia. Middle Eastern production as a whole increased rather than declined, and more new oil was discovered in the Arab countries of the Gulf than had ever flowed from Iranian wells in the previous four decades.[6] Indeed, this intense spurt of petroleum activity in the early 1950s markedly contributed to making the Middle East the world's leading petroleum region.

In 1970, Libya's Colonel Mu'ammar al-Qadhdhāfī took advantage of a tight market and of the temporary disruption of a pipeline from Saudi Arabia to the Mediterranean to press his demands on the oil companies. Muṣaddiq had sought control over a single company's country-wide concession in Iran, and abroad had faced an interlocking network of seven major companies. Qadhdhāfī instead was dealing with more than a dozen different companies, majors and minors, and was careful to concentrate his initial pressure on the weakest ones. There was little solidarity between the major companies, such as Exxon, Mobil, and BP, and the "independents," such as Occidental and Marathon, whom the majors looked upon as interlopers. On the other hand, there was effective solidarity among Middle Eastern oil-producing countries, joined since 1960 (with Venezuela) in the Organization of Petroleum Exporting Countries.

OPEC's successes since 1970 have largely been due to the discovery and consistent application of six major strategic principles.

(1) The very first rule of conduct on which OPEC members agreed was that *no company in dispute with any member government*

would be allowed to increase production in any other OPEC country. In this way, the threat of shutdown that BP had used against Musaddiq could be turned against the companies instead.

(2) Next, OPEC developed a "best of current practices" doctrine,[7] whereby *any member country stood ready to claim any advantage negotiated by any fellow member,* such as higher posted prices, higher tax rates, or partial government ownership. Instead of allowing companies to reduce them to the lowest common denominator, OPEC members, quite on the contrary, raised their demands against the companies to the highest common multiple. This implied that OPEC governments broke ranks not to retreat but to leapfrog ahead. Thus, in 1970-71 there were several rounds of negotiation in which the Mediterranean producers (Libya and Algeria) and those of the Gulf outbid each other. In effect "OPEC managed to put competition itself in the service of monopoly!"[8]

(3) In the aftermath of the Iranian crisis, "50-50" profit sharing between companies and governments had become the rule through the Middle East. To increase the absolute size of their half-share, governments such as those of Saudi Arabia and Iran had consistently pressured the companies to increase production. Indeed, the purpose of the Libyan royal government in allocating a score of separate concessions to different companies or consortia was to ensure that the country's production would rise rapidly. Since the companies throughout the 1960s were bent on recouping their larger payments to governments by expanding their markets, production indeed increased rapidly. Qadhdhāfī's keen power instincts, nevertheless, led him instead to grasp a third principle: that a government's *income could be more effectively raised by increasing* not the number of barrels produced but *the rate of revenue per barrel.* A seller's income is the product of price multiplied by quantity: $I = P \times Q$. In the past, the governments had sought to increase Q, thereby in effect pitting one Middle Eastern oil government against another. Qadhdhāfī obtained a far greater effect by increasing P — thereby pitting governments against companies, or rather both of them against oil consumers; and ever since, OPEC members have continued to mind their P's and Q's.

(4) Soon, however, OPEC members came to view the *multi-national companies not as the governments' adversaries but as their junior partners.* As OPEC's "Declaratory Statement of Petroleum Policy in Member Countries" of 1968 had put it, the governments would "as far as feasible . . . develop their hydrocarbon resources directly"; but where they needed to rely on the services of multinational companies, such services would carry "a reasonable remuneration" — and no more.[9]

(5) This reversal of relations became evident in the companies' pricing policy. Throughout the 1950s and 1960s, they had absorbed higher payments to the governments of Venezuela and the Middle East by cutting into their own revenues per barrel, lowering prices, and increasing turnover.[10] (It was precisely as a result of those price cuts that petroleum by the mid-1960s came to replace coal as the world's premier fuel.) Then, as OPEC's pressure mounted in the early 1970s, the companies had little choice but to pass OPEC's tax increases on to their customers, thus abdicating their cherished traditional privilege of setting prices. Nonetheless, *the relationship between companies and governments was transformed* from a zero-sum game, where each side loses whatever the other gains, *into a positive-sum game,* where both can gain at once.

As OPEC revenues per barrel mounted from about $1 in 1971 to $10 in 1974 and $34 in 1981, the benefit to the governments became obvious. Yet the companies' income per barrel from OPEC production, after suffering a sharp decline in the 1960s, began to stabilize at around 30 to 40 cents a barrel starting in the mid-1970s. The companies' major gain, meanwhile, has been the vast appreciation in the value of their underground reserves in non-OPEC countries, particularly the United States. Stobaugh and Yergin have estimated that, at OPEC prices, the value of those underground proven reserves in the United States increased $200 billion in 1973 to as much as $2 trillion in 1980 — a tenfold increase.[11]

(6) There is one crucial question of strategy on which OPEC countries' interests have come to differ since the late 1970s. *Those with large populations and modest oil reserves have sought to maxi-*

mize incomes in the short-run; those with small populations and huge reserves have taken the longer view. In the first category have been countries such as Nigeria, Algeria, Indonesia, and Venezuela, with a reserves-to-production ratio of 20 years or less. Their oil reserves are sure to run out before the industrial world has shifted from petroleum to other fuels. Hence their interest is to charge what the traffic will bear now, and invest the proceeds for future generations. In the second category have been countries with small populations and oil reserves that are likely to last well into the twenty-first century, notably the Gulf countries. It is not in their interest to force the consumer countries into any large-scale programs of substitution; to drive too hard a bargain now might make their remaining underground oil worthless forever. Hence Saudi Arabia, as the leader of this second group, has advocated a policy of moderate increases that, in effect, would index the oil price to world inflation and to economic growth in the major consumer countries.[12]

OPEC members, in short, have established a pattern of solidarity and escalation (1-2) of obvious benefit of all members; have concentrated on raising unit income (3); have redefined their relationship with the companies as a mutually beneficial partnership (4-5); and have differed on maximizing income over the shorter or longer run (6).

OPEC'S key strategist in redefining relations with the companies was Shaykh Aḥmad Zakī al-Yamanī, the Saudi petroleum minister who also was the chief author of the 1968 OPEC policy declaration. Saudi Arabia's role was crucial in engineering the price leap of 1973-74, and since then the Saudis have made no secret of their preference for small and orderly price increases. When demand dropped, as in the recession of 1975, the Saudis were able to defend the OPEC price by drawing on their ample financial reserves and taking a disproportionate amount of the necessary production cuts. When other OPEC members insisted on a higher price, as in 1977, Saudi Arabia was able to use its spare production capacity to draw away the customers of the "price hawks" and convert their price increase into a net loss in income.[13]

The one occasion when the Saudis were conspicuously unable to control the price was after 1979, when their spare capacity was unequal to compensating for the total shutdown in Iran or to keeping up with the frantic buying spree of anxious traders and eager speculators. It took more than two and a half years for the Saudis to reimpose price unity on OPEC, at about two and a half times the 1978 price levels. It should be noted, however, that the Saudi position is likely to be stronger in the future. With demand for OPEC oil down to 21 million barrels a day (mbd) in 1981 and possibly due to decline further, and a Saudi "normal" production rate of perhaps 6 mbd in the early 1980s, Saudi Arabia will be able to double its production at a single stroke, thus beating its OPEC confederates in any possible price war, or alternatively making up for any production shutdown in two or three other countries.[14] Incidentally, the "long-term strategy" of small price increases advocated by the Saudis would also imply small and orderly decreases in income in a declining market, and thus may well recommend itself for a rainy day.

The bold and yet responsible oil policy that Saudi Arabia has pursued, which recognizes the community of interest not only among Third World oil exporters, but also between OPEC and the oil companies, and between oil-exporting and oil-importing countries, is a prima-facie indication of the rapid progress of modernization among the elites of the Arab Middle East. Cultural bias at times has led western observers to underrate this achievement — just as wishful thinking often leads them prematurely to predict OPEC's demise.[15] Perhaps it is appropriate to reemphasize what John Mugno and I wrote in 1976 — that the OPEC revolution has resulted in the largest transfer of income in the world's financial history and "that no group of governments comes by $100 billion a year in a fit of absentmindedness."[16]

*   *   *

Modernization, we noted at the outset, increases both human control and human dependence. The current phase of modernization in the Arab oil countries is due to a rare constellation of outside forces that afforded Middle Easterners an unprecedented interval of political independence and economic power. Yet inexorably those same forces in the late twentieth century are propelling those same Middle Easterners and their children into even greater dependence on outside forces over which they have only partial control.

The current flow of oil income depends in part on patterns of energy consumption, substitution, and conservation in Europe, Japan, and the United States that are in a process of change. The 1979 price explosion resulted in a decline of demand for OPEC oil of as much as one third. How long will oil remain the world's major fuel, and how long will OPEC continue to set its price?

Other forms of dependence are evident in the current process of domestic social and economic change. Will modernization in Saudi Arabia mean the building of a more educated, prosperous, and cohesive Saudi society in the future? Or will it mean Korean construction crews building housing for Egyptian drilling teams that will enable a Lebanese accountant to deposit a check in Switzerland with which to pay a U.S. consulting firm that will make plans for the arrival of more Koreans, Lebanese, Egyptians, and Americans?

In the Middle East, will regional conflict continue at a tolerable level that on balance promotes the cause of the oil countries — such as the 1973 Arab-Israeli war that provided the occasion for the first major price rise or the Iranian revolution that prompted the second? Or will there be conflicts — such as a gradual Sovietization of Iran, naval warfare in the Gulf or the Strait of Hormuz, or a political upheaval in Saudi Arabia — that will endanger or destroy the oil price stability that Saudi policy has been at such pains to restore?

Beyond the Middle Eastern region, will there be a global order of political tolerance and accommodation? If so, the Middle East has more diversity to be tolerated and more conflicts to be resolved or accommodated than any other region. Will superpower rivalry, or attempts at unilateral expansion by one of the powers, bring the world to the brink of thermonuclear war? If so, it is easy to construct a number of Middle Eastern scenarios of uncertainty, gamble, miscalculation, and escalation that could lead to precisely such a confrontation. Or will the present capitalist order, based on the post-1945 *pax Americana,* continue with its uneven but powerful economic momentum? If so, few regions will have such large financial and economic assets to contribute as does the Middle East.

Many of the issues and alternatives just listed clearly seem beyond the control of Middle Eastern nations and their leaders, who will at best be able to navigate amidst the shoals, eddies, and swirls. But remember that such simple technical operations as the management of the Suez Canal or of the Saudi oil fields also were thought to be beyond the control of Middle Easterners as recently as thirty years ago — or rather were withheld from their control by the imperialist world order of that day.

Modernization means, above all, the ability to learn, and recent learning processes in the Middle East have been rapid and effective beyond all expectation. The ruling elites of Middle Eastern countries learned in the 1950s and 1960s to take advantage of the international play of forces so as to assert their own political independence, and in the 1960s and 1970s to maximize the returns from their underground oil resources in their own long-range economic interest. In the 1970s and 1980s they are learning to transform the revenues flowing in from abroad into rapid economic development at home and effective investment overseas. There is every reason to believe that those same elites or their successors will learn to cope with the further challenges of modernization in the late twentieth and the twenty-first centuries: keeping regional conflict from getting out of bounds, preventing the Middle East from falling prey to any new imperialism, investing today's oil revenues to secure a better life for their descendants in the post-oil era, and combining the social and technological imperatives of today and tomorrow with the timeless Islamic and Arabic values inherited from the past.

NOTES

[1] Dankwart A. Rustow, *A World of Nations* (Washington: Brookings, 1967), p.3.

[2] Charles Issawi, "Why Japan?" (pp. 283-300 below).

[3] Bernard Lewis, "Democracy in the Middle East: Its State and Prospects," *Middle Eastern Affairs,* Vol. 6, No. 4 (April 1955), p. 105.

[4] Dankwart A. Rustow, "Political Ends and Military Means in the Late Ottoman and Post-Ottoman Middle East," in V.J. Parry and M. Japp, eds., *War, Technology, and Society in the Middle East* (London: Oxford University Press, 1975), pp. 386-399.

[5] For 1950 data see Joel Darmstadter *et al, Energy in the World Economy* (Baltimore: Johns Hopkins, 1971), pp. 21, 23; for 1970 see *BP Statistical Review of the World Oil Industry* (London: BP, 1981), pp. 18, 27, 32.

[6] On the Iranian crisis and the rise of OPEC see Dankwart A. Rustow and John F. Mugno, *OPEC: Success and Prospects* (New York: NYU Press for the Council on Foreign Relations, 1976), Chapter I.

[7] *Ibid.*, pp. 21ff.

[8] Dankwart A. Rustow, *Oil and Turmoil: America Faces OPEC and the Middle East* (New York: Norton, 1982), Chapter 4.

[9] The "Declaratory Statement" is reprinted in Rustow and Mugno, *op. cit.*, pp. 166-172; the passage is from art. 1.2.

[10] Thus, between 1960 and 1970 the seven major companies' net revenues fell from 53 to 38 cents per barrel, but prices were cut by nearly one half and turnover tripled. As a result, OPEC's aggregate annual revenues rose from $2.2 to $7.8 billion, and those of the companies from $1.6 to $2.7 billion. *Ibid.*, pp. 130ff.

[11] Robert Stobaugh and Daniel Yergin, "Energy: An Emergency Telescoped," *Foreign Affairs*, Vol. 58, No. 3 (Spring 1980), p. 87.

[12] On the pricing formula of OPEC's "long-term strategy" see D. A. Rustow, *Oil and Turmoil, op. cit.*, pp. 176ff.

[13] On the 1977 price war see D.A. Rustow, "Middle East Oil: International and Regional Developments," in C. Legum and H. Shaked, eds., *Middle East Contemporary Survey*, Vol. 2, 1977-78 (New York and London: Holmes & Meier, 1979), p. 310.

[14] On the 1979-81 crisis and differences within OPEC see D. A. Rustow, *Oil and Turmoil, op. cit.*, Chapter 6.

[15] For recent predictions of OPEC's demise see, e.g., S. Fred Singer, "An End to OPEC?", *Foreign Policy*, No. 45 (Winter 1981-82), pp. 115-121.

[16] Rustow and Mugno, *op. cit.*, p. vii.

WHY JAPAN?
Charles Issawi

Why indeed Japan? Why did Japan alone among the countries of Asia, Africa, and Latin America "make it" in the nineteenth and early twentieth centuries? Why not the Arabs? Why not, for instance, Iraq, whose potential was, and still is, so great? It has been said that "Brazil is the land of the future, but then it has been for the last 300 years." And so has Iraq: one could cite numerous accounts written during the last 150 years that are ecstatic about Iraq's economic possibilities, because of its combination of fertile soil, mineral wealth, navigable rivers, and proximity to India, Turkey, Iran, and other economic centers.

Or why not Egypt, which was the Arab country that, all things considered, was the best placed for modernization? This question has been raised before. In 1952, at the end of a discussion of the course of Egyptian history in the second half of the nineteenth century and of possible alternatives, this author wrote: "If during that time she had had a government that was both national and enlightened . . . Egypt might have emerged into the twentieth century as a small scale Japan."[1] As Manon and Des Grieux sang wistfully about their dream house, "Qui n'a pas fait des rêves?" Some fifteen years later, Roger Owen took the matter up much more thoroughly and discussed the numerous factors that enabled Japan to achieve rapid all-round development.[2] This paper will follow in his footsteps, but will continue a little further, and point out some other features of the landscape.

A few scattered indicators taken at various times in the nineteenth century might have suggested that Egypt was, in fact, doing

Charles Issawi earned an MA from Oxford University and is currently the Bayard-Dodge Professor of Near Eastern Studies at Princeton University. Professor Issawi has also taught at Columbia and Harvard universities and has served as president of the Middle East Studies Association, a consultant to the United Nations, and a member of the Council on Foreign Relations. He has also worked for the Egyptian Ministry of Finance and the National Bank of Egypt. Among his published works are *Egypt at Mid-Century, The Economic History of the Middle East 1800-1914,* and *Oil, the Middle East and the World.*

rather better than Japan. Take for instance the two countries' understanding of what was happening in Europe. In the eighteenth century, the Japanese had a much deeper interest in and clearer notion of European science and technology than did the Arabs (or Turks), but by the 1830s, thanks to Muhammad Ali's educational missions and the foreign schools established in Lebanon and Egypt, the position was reversed. Al-Tahtawi's *Takhlis al-Ibriz fi Talkhis Baris,* published in 1834, shows a firm grasp of French society and politics, and in particular of the 1830 Revolution. The Armenian Yusuf Hekekyan, who was put in charge of the Egyptian Engineering School in 1830, was, as his delightful and instructive papers show, as Anglicized as it was possible for a foreigner to be.[3] In contrast, in Japan "Fujita Toko, a prominent but poorly informed nationalist, concluded in 1826 on the basis of similarities in clothing styles that Holland had lost its independence to Russia and that Japan was now threatened by a monolithic Roman Catholic West."[4]

Or consider the following western judgment on Japan, exactly one hundred years ago, in 1881. "Wealthy we do not think it will ever become: the advantages conferred by Nature, with the exception of the climate, and the love of indolence and pleasure of the people themselves forbid it. The Japanese are a happy race, and being content with little are not likely to achieve much."

Or this one: "The national banking system of Japan is but another example of the futility of trying to transfer Western growth to an Oriental habitat. In this part of the world principles, established and recognized in the West, appear to lose whatever virtue and vitality they originally possessed and tend fatally towards weediness and corruption."[5] And, according to Marius Jansen, around 1900 Kipling declared "the Japanese should have no concern with business. The Jap has no business savvy." This surely offsets the numerous disobliging remarks about the Arabs and Egyptians, of which here is one example by Lord Cromer:[6] "The mind of the Oriental, on the other hand, like his picturesque streets, is eminently wanting in symmetry. His reasoning is of the most slipshod description. Although the ancient Arabs acquired in a somewhat high degree the science of dialectics, their descendants are singularly deficient in the logical faculty. They are often incapable of drawing the most obvious conclusions from any simple premises of which they may admit the truth." Or even better, this gem: "The Oriental has a remarkable capacity for assimilating to himself the worst and rejecting the best parts of any European civilization with which he may be brought in contact."[7]

But why dwell on what the Egyptians and Japanese thought of Europe, or what Europe thought of them? For a social scientist, there are other, more objective, indicators of economic development. In 1913, Egypt's per capita gross domestic product was slightly higher than that of Japan, and its foreign trade (imports plus exports) per head of population was twice as high. In relation to both its inhabited area and population, Egypt's railway network was also far more extensive than that of Japan.[8] Surely all that means something.

It does, but other figures tell a different story, notably those on education, health, birth and death rates, industrial production, capital formation, and the development of various economic institutions. It was the latter that were to prove decisive. Before analyzing them more closely in trying to understand the nature of the "Japanese miracle," however, let us once more consider which of the prerequisites of modernization existed in Egypt in the nineteenth century.

There was, first, Egypt's extraordinary homogeneity. Egypt had no ethnic or linguistic minorities and only a small, and thoroughly assimilated, religious minority. Its population was almost totally sedentary and, in addition, very homogeneous in its social characteristics. The contrast between Egypt and other parts of the Middle East and North Africa in this respect is immense, but Egypt also compares very favorably with most countries in other parts of the world, including many in Europe.

Second, due in part to its compactness, its sedentariness, its river transport, its irrigation system, and its bureaucratic tradition, Egypt has for at least 6,000 years been under centralized government control. This control broke down in the eighteenth century, but was swiftly reestablished by Muhammad Ali and has continued to increase to our day. Here again, one cannot overstress the contrast between Egypt and Syria, Iraq, and the Maghreb. Egypt is a governable country, and that is surely an indispensable condition of modernization.

Third, Egypt had a substantial agricultural surplus. In 1844, long before any rise had been registered in wheat yield, the latter was an estimated 1,000 kilograms per hectare. This figure was about equal to those for France and Germany, and well above those for northern, central, and eastern Europe.[9] It was perhaps twice as high as yields in other parts of the Arab world. Output per farm worker must also have been fairly high, since population was sparse and land abundant. Egypt's cultivated area was about 3,000,000 acres and the number of male farm workers may have been around 1,000,000, implying that each worker had an average of some 3 acres of land at his disposal. With the introduction of cotton, which led to perennial irrigation and double-cropping, both output per acre and output per man increased severalfold. Patrick O'Brien has studied this question in depth, and we can summarize his conclusions as follows: Between 1821 and the end of the century, farm output per acre rose nearly 12½ times, and per head of rural population over 6½ times.[10] This represents a very large surplus which, if it had been used, could have provided the capital required for quite rapid development.

Fourth, Egypt had an advantage that was almost unique in the Middle East and North Africa, though fairly common in more humid regions: excellent internal waterways. The Nile, with its branches and irrigation canals, penetrates every part of the inhabited area. Moreover, the prevailing winds are northerly, which means that boats can sail upstream and float downstream. Thus, it has always been possible cheaply to transport agricultural produce to the towns (Alexandria, Cairo, and others), and to export the surplus. Furthermore, Egypt was quick to modernize its transport. The port of Alexandria, connected to the Nile by the Mahmudiyya canal in 1819, was by far the best in the Middle East and North Africa and one of the two or three leading ports in the Mediterranean. Other good ports were soon built at Suez and Port Said. Egypt had a railway before Sweden or central Poland, and long before Japan. By the end of the nineteenth century its rail network, whether measured relative to inhabited area or population, was one of the densest in the world.

Fifth, thanks to its bureaucracy, its long-established fiscal traditions, and its numerous agricultural cadastres and surveys, repeated over the centuries, the Egyptian government was able to extract a large proportion of the agricultural surplus. In the eighteenth century, taxes were rather high on both agricultural and commercial incomes, and under Muhammad Ali they rose steeply. Indeed, Muhammad Ali's methods were very close to those of the Soviet government in the 1930s: they consisted of compulsory purchase of farm produce at low prices and resale to urban consumers or foreign exporters at much higher prices, the government pocketing the difference. Like the Soviets, Muhammad Ali used most of the funds thus obtained for armaments, but also like them he invested large amounts in transport, industry, education, and other economic activities. His example shows what could have been done in the field of development.

Finally, in 1800 Egypt was, by contemporary standards, a highly urbanized country. Cairo had over 200,000 inhabitants, a large figure for that time, and other towns of 5,000 inhabitants or more had a total population of about 150,000. In other words, some 10 percent of Egypt's population lived in towns.[11] This percentage was at least equal to that for France in 1800 and higher than that for other European countries with the exception of Great Britain and the Netherlands.[12] All students of modernization agree that a large urban base is an indispensable precondition of the process.

At this point, one may be tempted to ask the question freshmen students of economics sometimes put to their professor: "If you are so smart, why aren't you rich?" Why didn't Egypt become rich? One can best answer this by seeing why Japan did. Japan had five major advantages denied to Egypt as well as one minor one — somewhat more abundant and varied natural resources. The latter point can be dealt with briefly. In absolute terms, Japan is poor in resources, and its man-land ratio was far higher than that of Egypt, but it had small reserves of coal, iron, and copper, on which it relied heavily for many decades. It has abundant water power, which it harnessed at an early stage, supplying electricity not only to the factories and railways but also to the village craftsmen. Some rivers were navigable, though improvement was often necessary. And its long shoreline offered great opportunities for coastal navigation, of which the Japanese have always taken full advantage. This enabled Japan to save on railways, which require such heavy capital investment; it was only at the very close of the nineteenth century that Japan's total railway mileage exceeded that of Egypt, with its far smaller inhabited area and population. As for the major factors, they were a favorable location that reduced the danger of foreign interference; a social cohesion unmatched in the world; far more developed human resources; an early orientation toward economic growth and a much greater sense of curiosity; and an extraordinarily wise leadership, which seems to have had an uncanny knack for taking the right economic measures. These topics are discussed in more detail below.

Whereas Egypt is at the very center of the world — at least the Old World, which is what has counted — Japan is at the very edge. This means that the aggressive imperialisms of the nineteenth century — British, French, and Russian — could reach Japan only at the end of a very long line of communications, where their impact was greatly attenuated. If Japan had been situated, like Egypt, at the junction of three continents, would it have been able to preserve its independence and shape its own destiny? Perhaps — after all Turkey succeeded (albeit just barely) in preserving its political independence, though certainly not its economic freedom of action, and 30 million tough Japanese would have given any imperialist pause. Even as it was, though, the Japanese had to accept the "Unequal Treaties" with the West. This meant that until the late 1890s Japanese customs duties could not be raised above a nominal 5 percent, and full autonomy was not achieved until 1911; moreover, until the late 1890s foreigners had the right to be judged in their own consular courts and not in the Japanese tribunals. But, being Japanese, they managed to carry out an amazing economic and social transformation even with that handicap. Egypt, on the other hand, had to wait until 1930 for the lapse of the Commercial Treaties which deprived it of tariff autonomy and until 1937 for the abolition of the Capitulations, which severely restricted its fiscal, administrative, and judicial freedom of action. Egypt experienced forty years of British occupation, a period that saw many real improvements but, on balance, gave an unhealthy twist to economic and social developments.

Another advantage of Japan's location should also be mentioned. Japan enjoyed three centuries of peace and, until it started its own form of rather profitable imperialism in the 1890s, its expenditure on armaments was low. In contrast, under both Muhammad Ali and Ismail, Egypt spent large amounts on defense, leaving that much less for development. Ottoman expenditure on armaments and war was immense.[13]

Some readers may feel that the external factor is sufficient to explain Japan's superior performance. Indeed, Galal Amin claims in his very interesting recent book *Al-Mashriq al-'Arabi wa al-Gharb* that foreign pressure fully explains the failure of both the Arab developmental initiative of the 1820s through 1840s, led by Muhammad Ali, and the one of the 1950s and 1960s, led by Gamal Abd al-Nasir. I do not agree. Indeed, in almost every respect except the technological, Japan had largely been modernized before it was "opened up" by the United States and Europe in the 1850s and 1860s, and this, above all, explains its unique performance. In Bertrand Russell's apt phrase, Japan was an "economically but not culturally backward" country.[14]

First and foremost, Japan exhibited *cohesion,* to a degree unmatched in the world. Japan's ethnic, linguistic, and religious homogeneity is probably greater than that of any other country. The only threat posed to this homogeneity — the rapid spread of Christianity in the sixteenth century — was summarily and brutally dealt with by the Tokugawa government and, for good measure, Japan retreated into strict isolation for some 250 years, and had to be pried out by warships. But Japan had, and still has, more than homogeneity. Again to an unparalleled degree, it has social cohesion — what that amazing man Ibn Khaldun called *'asabiyya.* He saw, what so many Anglo-Saxon social scientists are still determined not to see, that *'asabiyya* is the foundation of a country's greatness and prosperity, and Japan would have struck him as a textbook example. It also struck another genius, Thorstein Veblen, who in 1915 wrote a most perceptive essay on "The Opportunity of Japan,"[15] placing its bid for world power a generation away — close enough, as it turned out. Japanese history is full of examples of self-sacrifice and devotion to duty proclaimed by this cohesion, from the *samurai* and *kamikaze* warriors to the Toyota and Sony workers. Cohesion also explains both the sense of obligation felt by firms toward their staff, which results in the so-called "life employment" system, and the consensus sought, at many levels, before decisions are taken. But there is one more thing to say on this subject. Not only was the nineteenth-century Japanese population cohesive and obedient, but the oligarchy that carried out the Meiji transformation in the 1870s and 1880s was very homogeneous, having a common geographic and social origin, similar ages and backgrounds, and similar values.[16]

Let us now turn to Japan's human resources. These may be studied under four headings: education, health, birth control, and the education and employment of women. In the eighteenth century and the first half of the nineteenth century Japan made enormous strides in educating its commoners, by founding thousands of schools throughout the land. By the 1850s "an estimated 40 percent of the male population and 10 percent of the female had achieved some degree of literacy." In the cities the figures were much higher, being put at 75 to 85 percent. At this point it is worth noting that, in contrast to many other countries, the nobility not only did not oppose but seems to have encouraged the spread of education among commoners. One result was a very large publishing industry; in the 1780s some 3,000 titles were being published each year, editions of over 10,000 were not uncommon, books were cheap, and both free and commercial lending libraries were active.[17] These figures compare very favorably with Western Europe. With the Meiji Restoration and the beginning of rapid modernization, education surged forward. By 1907 over 97 percent of children of school age were attending primary school, and illiteracy had been to all intents and purposes wiped out.

One hardly needs to point out the contrast between this record and that of the Arab countries. In 1907, 93 percent of Egyptians were illiterate and, except in Lebanon and Syria, the situation in the other Arab countries was even worse. And even today, the Arab countries have not reached the degree of elementary schooling achieved by Japan eighty years ago. The rapid development of natural resources that took place in the Arab world has not been accompanied by a proportionate development of human resources. Egypt imported its middle class *en bloc,* in the form of Europeans, Greeks, Syro-Lebanese, Jews, and Armenians. In North Africa the dichotomy was even sharper, since the French or Italians supplied not only the middle class but also the skilled working class. The oil countries of the Gulf are witnessing a similar process today. Only Lebanon and Syria experienced a development of human resources that matched their rather slow economic growth.

Japanese education was based on state schools, but it is worth noting that half the universities were private. Also worth noting is the heavy emphasis on practical and technical subjects.[18] In contrast, except under Muhammad Ali, Arab education has stressed the humanities and law.[19]

Health may be dealt with very briefly. In the nineteenth century, conditions of hygiene in Japan seem to have been distinctly superior to those prevailing in the Middle East or other developing regions, and the death rate was around 25 per 1,000, compared to over 40 in the Middle East and North Africa. This implies much less wastage, in both human and economic terms. By the 1920s Japan's death rate had fallen below 20 — a figure not reached in the Arab world until the 1950s — and in the early 1950s the Japanese rate fell below 10, a figure typical of advanced countries.

The matter of birth rates is more interesting. For some 150 years Japan managed to keep its population constant at 30 million, partly becaue of the usual Malthusian checks of war, pestilence, and famine but also because of deliberate control by means of abortion and infanticide. In the second half of the nineteenth century birth rates seem to have risen slightly, but at their highest they were well below those in the Arab world, about 35-40 per 1,000 compared to, say, 45-50, and fell slowly to about 30 in the late 1930s. After World War II Japan's birth rate plunged more precipitously than that of any country on record and soon settled at the European level of 15, whereas Arab rates have remained at 40-50, producing an explosive population growth.

As regards the position of women, no one would claim that Japanese women were, or are, among the most emancipated. It is, however, a fact that at an early date the Japanese began to make good use of their womanpower — or, if one prefers, to exploit their women. "By the 1890s, women outnumbered men workers in the factories" and were employed, in substantial numbers, "as office workers, telephone operators, teachers and receptionists . . . . Girls' primary school attendance rates began to equal boys'." Progress at the middle and higher school level came a decade or two later.[20]

It was not only social development that had long roots in Japan's history. The same was true of economic development. Two different aspects should be distinguished: Japan's early interest in and quick absorption of western science and technology; and the purely indigenous, spontaneous development of the Japanese economy in the seventeenth and eighteenth centuries.

As early as the sixteenth century, European visitors to Japan "usually reported lively curiosity about Western civilization on the part of the Japanese."[21] After foreigners had been excluded, a peephole on the outside world was provided by the small, isolated Dutch colony on the island of Deshima. Late in the seventeenth century some Japanese started learning Dutch and in the eighteenth century they began systematically to study Western technology, science, and painting; soon a small number of Japanese had become familiar with the Copernican and Newtonian theories, as well as with anatomical science, including the theory of the circulation of the blood. At the same time, some artists began to draw and paint in perspective. By 1811, a Japanese scholar was urging his countrymen to study all kinds of learning. "Foreign though they are, they can help Japan if Japanese study them and select their good points. It is thus quite proper to speak of Chinese learning, and even of Indian and Dutch learning, as Japanese learning."[22]

As the nineteenth century wore on, western learning was adopted wholesale, and at first very indiscriminately. Western textbooks were translated and used in schools, not always with good results, foreign advisers and teachers were imported in large numbers, and in the universities many subjects were taught in foreign languages. But in the 1880s a reaction set in, new textbooks were provided, Japanese teachers replaced foreigners, and Japanese became the language of instruction.[23] Meanwhile, the numerous Japanese who travelled abroad were as observant as their present-day descendants; for lack of Nikon cameras they brought with them sketch books, and sketched almost everything they saw. By contrast, this author does not know of a single reported case of a Middle Easterner drawing anything he saw in Europe or America in the nineteenth century.

Japanese economic development was not wholly dependent on the impetus provided by contact with foreigners. Even before the latter became important, the Japanese achieved great success in certain important fields. Take handicrafts. As anyone who has been to a museum knows, Japanese crafts were highly sophisticated, and they were widespread not only in the cities but in the countryside. Moreover, because of Japan's isolation, these crafts were exposed to the devastating competition of European machine-made goods far later than were those of the Middle East, India, or Latin America. They also survived much longer because of the peculiar pattern of Japanese development. The Japanese soon picked up European production methods but retained their traditional consumption habits until very recently, whereas the people of the Middle East soon learned to consume *alla franga* but are only just beginning to adopt western production methods. As a result, many Arab handicrafts soon lost their domestic markets, whereas their Japanese counterparts did not. But there is another point: to an unequalled degree, Japan made use of its handicrafts and village industries in its industrialization. Particularly in silk and cotton textiles, which for a long time accounted for the bulk of industrial employment and output, but also in many other areas, including machinery and equipment, a large part of the work was done by subcontracting to small workshops in villages or towns or even to peasant households.[24] One need hardly point out how beneficial was this type of industrialization in terms of employment, saving of capital, and conservation of skills. Unfortunately, there has been little like it in the Arab world.

Still more favorable for development was traditional Japanese agriculture. In view of Japan's very exiguous area and its large population, for centuries sustained efforts had been made to raise output per acre by using better methods, selecting seeds, experimenting with various types of organic fertilizers, introducing new cash crops, and so forth. One book on sericulture had a first printing of 3,000 copies, and many books went through several editions. The spread of literacy through rural Japan, without which the technical literature on farming could not have flourished, is a fascinating story not yet fully known.[25] As a result, Japanese yields were among the very highest in the world and rose steadily; indeed, they were well above those prevailing in most developing countries today. When Japan began its modern development, after a few misguided efforts to introduce western agricultural machinery and farm practices it was found possible to increase output, steadily and appreciably, by continuing along the traditional lines and incorporating the findings of contemporary agricultural research.[26]

Tokugawa Japan was a highly urbanized country. By 1720 Tokyo had about 1,000,000 inhabitants (Peking and London being the only other cities of that size in the eighteenth century), Osaka and Kyoto had about 400,000 each, and some 12 percent of the total population lived in towns of over 10,000 inhabitants, a figure higher than that for all but three or four European countries.[27] Moreover, the nobility was forced to reside in the capital, which further increased urban purchasing power. As a result, a large proportion of the agricultural and handicraft produce of the villages had to move to the cities, in payment of rent and taxes. This greatly stimulated the commercialization of the economy and gave rise to a large class of merchants and financiers. Double entry bookkeeping, some of it on a very high level, was practiced and what was probably the world's first department store was established by the Mitsui family in Tokyo in 1683; the late Ivan

Morris told me that their promotional devices included the distribution of free umbrellas. In finance there were "exceptionally
highly developed" credit institutions and instruments including
paper money, checks, and even "futures transactions in rice" in
Osaka in 1730.[28]

Let us touch once more on the matter of attitudes. The
samurai shared a military ethic which proved highly effective on
the battlefield. But in a larger part of the Japanese population a
different ethic prevailed, a work and profit ethic. The titles of
some of the children's books used in schools are eloquent: in the
towns, *Commercial Reader,* 1693; *Wholesaler's Reader,* 1772;
Navigation and Shipping Reader, 1823; *Good Business for the Clothi-
er,* 1825; in the villages, *Agricultural Reader,* 1762; *Farmer's Reader,* 1766; *Increased Profits for Farmers,* 1811; *Bumper Crops,*
1836.[29] No wonder, after all this, that (like parts of Europe and
unlike the Middle East and North Africa) Japan experienced overall economic growth, estimated at somewhat less than 1 percent a
year between the early 1700s and 1860, despite a virtually constant population.[30]

We now come to our last topic: Japan's extraordinarily *sound
economic strategy* when it did decide to modernize, in the 1870s.
Three closely related aspects may be distinguished: sparing use of
capital and local generation of investment funds; the optimum
utilization of the factor mix; and the right sequence of processes
and stages.

First of all, by the end of the 1880s Japan's investment rate
was over 11 percent of GNP, and the ratio rose steadily to over 20
percent by 1920 and to 40 percent by 1960.[31] These figures are
staggering and have no counterpart anywhere in the world except
for the Soviet Union under Stalin. By contrast, in Egypt the rate in
1913 was distinctly under 10 percent and in the 1950s and 1960s
averaged well under 15 percent. Except for the oil countries during or after the 1950s, the figures for the other Middle Eastern
countries were no higher.[32] However, the matter does not end
there. By the 1870s Egypt had accumulated a foreign debt of $500
million and by 1913 the figure had doubled. Japan began borrowing much later, but by 1913 it too had a foreign debt of $1,000

million. But, first, its population was four times as large as that of Egypt and its economy was more developed; second, whereas the bulk of Egypt's public borrowings had been wasted, and a significant part of its private borrowings misinvested, the Japanese had used almost all their borrowings for highly productive purposes. Turkey and Iran were in much the same situation as Egypt. And, coming to the last few decades, in the non-oil-producing countries of the Middle East a large proportion of investment funds has come from foreign aid.[33]

As regards the factor mix, Japan has always been short of land and, until the last few years, capital was also scarce. Its one asset was good but cheap labor, and of that it made the fullest use. In agriculture, after the previously mentioned brief and unsuccessful experiments with American and European machinery and techniques, Japan reverted to its labor-intensive methods, using huge inputs of labor per acre but also taking the fullest advantage of the discoveries of western and indigenous agricultural research. The result was the highest output per acre in the world, even higher than Egypt's. As in Egypt, output per man remained low but total agricultural production rose rather quickly, and, because of the rise in population, millions of workers were released for employment in other sectors. For many decades agriculture was able to fulfill the role demanded of it: to feed the growing population and to provide the exports needed to earn the foreign exchange required for industrialization.

Industry also developed in a peculiar way. First, as noted earlier, great use was made of existing handicraft skills in the villages and small towns by means of an extensive system of subcontracting. Second, there was the predominance of small workshops equipped with electric and other motors but using labor-intensive methods and having a relatively low output per man. As late as 1934, shops with less than 5 workers accounted for 42 percent of factory output, and among factories those with 5-9 operatives represented 57 percent of the total.[34] Third, for a long time the emphasis was on industries that required little capital but employed many workers, chiefly textiles. To illustrate, at the turn of the century an up-to-date steel plant cost the relatively huge sum of $28-30 million, whereas a modern cotton spinning factory cost $250,000, and small silk filatures or cotton mills cost far less.[35] Hence the initial concentration on silk and cotton textiles, which were soon exported in large quantities; by 1913, half the cotton processed in Japan was being sold abroad, as yarn or cloth.[36] Until the last couple of decades, Japanese industries had lower capital, lower horsepower, and lower output per man than European, not to mention American, industries but that was precisely what the factor mix required.[37]

As regards sequence, Japan at first relied heavily on foreign trade, exporting silk and other raw materials to earn the badly needed foreign exchange. Until the turn of the century, foreign enterprise in Japan was discouraged and foreigners were not allowed to own land or mines. But foreign experts were employed, in large numbers, and Japanese went abroad to study. More important, foreign trade became, in Lockwood's apt phrase, "a Highway of Learning."[38] The Japanese imported textiles, copied them, and soon exported large quantities. They then imported machinery, and copied the machines. They realized the importance of shipping, built a fleet of 1,500,000 tons by 1913 — a figure just being attained by a few Middle Eastern countries — and started building steamships. At the turn of the century they started encouraging high-technology foreign firms like General Electric, Armstrong-Vickers, Siemens, Ford, and others to come in and learned from them, but saw to it that foreigners did not control too large a section of the economy. By the 1930s they had built up a large heavy industrial base, which was put to effective use in World War II.[39] After 1945 they resumed their educational process, this time concentrating on high technology products and giving up armaments at the very moment when the Arabs became fascinated with them and began to devote huge sums to defense. One cannot but contrast this assiduity and persistence with all the lost opportunities in the Middle East in the last 150 years.

Finally, a word about the role of the government in economic development. Government intervention included both overall direction and help in specific fields. A good early example of the former is the Matsukata deflation of 1881, which ended the inflation and monetary disorders that had followed the opening up of Japan and established the financial basis for the country's take-off.[40] Government accounted for some 30 percent of total investment in the period 1887-1936.[41] In addition to building railways, providing other overheads, and subsidizing important branches of activity, the government itself pioneered many industries, setting up model factories which it then turned over to private enterprise.[42] All this is not unusual; it has been practiced, at various times, in both Europe and the developing countries. What is unique, however, is the relation between state and business. Whereas in the United States this is thought of primarily in adversary terms, resulting in that country's present situation of stalemate and drift, and whereas in most developing countries, including those in the Middle East, the state soon rushes and takes over the private sector, in Japan there exists that amazing symbiosis enviously referred to by its discomfited rivals as "Japan Inc." This brings us to our starting point, Japanese *'asabiyya.*

Can one point to more general causes of Japan's success? I myself am inclined to attach much importance to the fact that Japan was perhaps the only country outside Europe to have had genuine feudalism, and that, as Marx saw so clearly, feudalism seems to be a very good preparation for capitalism. The only country approaching this in the Middle East is Lebanon, and perhaps it is no coincidence that Lebanon took to capitalism like a duck to water.

Another interesting observation has been made by Roy Mottahedeh on the contrast between the curiosity shown by Europeans and Japanese about foreign cultures (first Islam and then the Orient for Europe, first China and then the West for Japan) and the lack of curiosity on the part of the Arabs, Turks, and Chinese about European or other cultures. His explanation was that such a curiosity was the result of a combination of a sense of moral superiority and intellectual inferiority, while the Muslims and Chinese, in contrast, had not only a sense of moral superiority but also a mistaken one of intellectual superiority.

In any case, the Arabs missed the nineteenth century capitalist bus which the Japanese boarded so successfully. But there are other buses, and today the Arabs have opportunities that neither the Japanese nor anyone else could have imagined. One hopes that they will make good use of them and find their own roads to development. In doing so, they would be well advised to ponder the experience of Japan and to take some of its lessons to heart.

NOTES

[1] Charles Issawi, *Egypt at Mid-Century* (London, 1954), pp. 19-20.

[2] E.R.J. Owen, *Cotton and the Egyptian Economy* (Oxford, 1969), pp. 356-64.

[3] Ahmed Abdel-Rahim Mustafa, "The Hekekyan Papers," in P.M. Holt, ed., *Political and Social Change in Modern Egypt* (London, 1968), pp. 68-75.

[4] C.E. Black *et al.*, *The Modernization of Japan and Russia* (New York, 1975), p. 27.

[5] Quoted in G.C. Allen, *A Short Economic History of Modern Japan* (London, 1946), p. 2.

[6] Earl of Cromer, *Modern Egypt*, vol. 2 (New York, 1908), pp. 146-47.

[7] *Ibid.*, vol. 2, p. 239.

[8] For figures see Charles Issawi, "Asymmetrical Development and Transport in Egypt, 1800-1914," in William Polk and Richard Chambers, eds., *Beginnings of Modernization in the Middle East* (Chicago, 1968).

[9] Helen Rivlin, *The Agricultural Policy of Muhammad Ali* (Cambridge, Massachusetts, 1961), p. 262; Jerome Blum, *The End of the Old Order in Europe* (Princeton, 1978), pp. 144-45.

[10] P. O'Brien, "The Long-Term Growth of Agricultural Production in Egypt: 1821-1962," in Holt, *op. cit.*, pp. 162-95.

[11] For a recent and exhaustive study see Justin McCarthy, "Nineteenth Century Egyptian Population," in Elie Kedourie, ed., *The Middle Eastern Economy* (London, 1976), pp. 1-39.

[12] For a discussion see Charles Issawi, "Economic Change and Urbanization in the Middle East," in Ira Lapidus, ed., *Middle Eastern Cities* (Berkeley and Los Angeles, 1969), pp. 102-19, reprinted in *idem, The Arab Legacy* (Princeton, 1981).

[13] See figures in Charles Issawi, *The Economic History of Turkey, 1800-1914* (Chicago, 1980), pp. 3-4, 324.

[14] Quoted by Herbert Passin, *Society and Education in Japan* (New York, 1965), p. 6.

[15] Thorstein Veblen, *Essays in our Changing Order* (New York, 1943).

[16] Black *et al.*, *op. cit.*, p. 149.

[17] *Ibid.*, pp. 106-9; Passin, *op. cit.*, pp. 11-61; Nan [Ivan] Morris, *The Life of an Amorous Woman* (London, 1964), pp. 26-27.

[18] Black, *op. cit.*, pp. 219-20, 239.

[19] For a breakdown of Egyptian educational missions, see Charles Issawi, *Egypt at Mid-Century* (London, 1954), p. 51.

[20] Passin, *op. cit.*, p. 97.

[21] Black, *op. cit.,* p. 34.

[22] Donald Keene, *The Japanese Discovery of Europe, 1720-1830* (Stanford, California, 1969), p. 159 and *passim.*

[23] Passin, *op. cit.,* pp. 69-95.

[24] William Lockwood, *The Economic Development of Japan* (Princeton, 1954), pp. 480-90.

[25] Thomas C. Smith, "Okura Nagatsune and the Technologists," in A.M. Craig and D.H. Shively, eds., *Personality in Japanese History* (Berkeley, 1970).

[26] Thomas C. Smith, *Agrarian Origins of Modern Japan* (Stanford, California, 1959); James I. Nakamura, *Agricultural Production and the Economic Development of Japan* (Princeton, 1966).

[27] Black, *op. cit.,* pp. 82-85.

[28] M. Miyamoto *et al.,* "Economic Development in Pre-historical Japan," *Journal of Economic History,* December 1965; E.S. Crawcour, "Changes in Japanese Commerce in the Tokugawa Period," in John Hall and Marius Jansen, eds., *Studies in the Institutional History of Early Modern Japan* (Princeton, 1968), pp. 198-202; *idem,* "The Tokugawa Heritage," in William Lockwood, ed., *The State and Economic Enterprise in Japan* (Princeton, 1965), pp. 17-44.

[29] Passin, *op. cit.,* p. 32.

[30] Black, *op. cit.,* p. 60.

[31] K. Ohkawa and H. Rosovsky, "A Century of Japanese Economic Growth," in Lockwood, *The State,* p. 90.

[32] See my *Economic History of the Middle East and North Africa* (New York, 1982), Chapter IX.

[33] *Ibid.*

[34] Lockwood, *Economic Development,* pp. 2-178, 202.

[35] *Ibid.,* p. 33.

[36] *Ibid.,* p. 31.

[37] See figures for 1934 in *Ibid.,* p. 178-81.

[38] *Ibid.,* pp. 320-34.

[39] "Japan thus entered the war with an aircraft industry 50 percent equipped with foreign-built tools, and staffed with technicians trained in American plants and engineering schools," *Ibid.,* p. 331.

[40] Ohkawa and Rosovsky, *op. cit.,* pp. 65-66.

[41] David Landes, "Japan and Europe: Contrasts in Industrialization," in Lockwood, *The State,* p. 100.

[42] *Ibid.,* also Lockwood, *Economic Development,* p. 326.

THE POOR RICH ARABS
Hisham Sharabi

The Arab world today, considered strictly in terms of its vast resources, would seem assured of rapid development and a prosperous future. By 1985, the assets of the major oil-producing countries in the region, estimated now to be nearly $300 billion, are expected to reach the $650 billion mark. Over the same period the revenue from oil will amount to an estimated $1,300 billion. This means that in the next five years the Arabs will have at their disposal awesome wealth to use for developing their society. This phenomenon has no parallel in history. No other society has acquired the means to transform itself so easily without paying the price of long and painful primitive capital accumulation.

Yet what is happening in the Arab world today belies these exciting figures. Between 1973 and 1980, 90 percent of revenue from oil was spent on nonproductive goods and services and only 10 percent was productively invested. Indeed, viewed from the standpoint of the ordinary citizen, daily life in the Arab world appears incoherent and mystifying. It is characterized by misery in wealth, by underdevelopment in development, by weakness in strength. Of the region's nearly 160 million people, perhaps 2 percent live in luxury and splendor; some 10 percent, the small middle class, enjoy relative ease and comfort; and the majority, close to 90 percent, struggle for mere survival. No wonder, to the ordinary citizen, so close to yet so far from the fabulous wealth, reality appears incomprehensible, surrealistic.

In the book *Global Reach,* which deals with multinational corporations in the Third World, Richard Barnett and Ronald

Hisham Sharabi earned a PhD in the History of Culture at the University of Chicago. Dr. Sharabi is the Umar al-Mukhtar Professor of Arab Culture and a Professor of History at Georgetown University. He has taught at the American University of Beirut and is a former President of the National Association of Arab Americans. At present, he is editor of the *Journal of Palestine Studies.* He has written extensively on the Arab world; among his works are *Nationalism and Revolution in the Arab World* and *Palestine and Israel: The Lethal Dilemma.*

301

Muller portray what a modern Gulliver might find in a typical underdeveloped nation; in so doing, they accurately describe the conditions experienced by many people in some Arab countries:

"One out of every ten thousand persons lives in a palace with high walls and gardens and a Cadillac [read Cadillacs and Mercedes] in the driveway. A few blocks away hundreds are sleeping in the streets . . . Around the corner, tens of thousands are jammed in huts without electricity or plumbing. Outside the city most of the population scratches out a bare subsistence . . . The stock market is booming, but babies die . . . There are luxurious restaurants and stinking open sewers. The capital boasts late-model computers and receives jumbo jets every day, but more than half the people cannot read . . . For them disease, filth, and sudden death are constant companions."

It has been pointed out that despite certain differences, the situation in some Arab countries today resembles that which prevailed in Iran during the last years of the Shah's reign. Yet both conservative and progressive regimes are responding to this situation in ways that show that the Iranian lesson has not been properly learned by the ruling elites. Instead of introducing meaningful reform, they apply more security measures, failing to realize, as the Shah finally did when it was too late, that when self-preservation becomes the overriding concern of government, repression solidifies into irreversible policy: coercion leads to more coercion, and contradictions, instead of being overcome, sharpen and become more and more difficult to resolve. It would be self-deluding to think that Islamic militancy in the Arab world (and in Islamic countries generally) can be blunted simply by coercive measures and state puritanism. In form, popular indignation is certainly Islamic, but in content, it is clearly social and political.

This malaise is by no means characteristic only of Arab countries; it afflicts most of the countries of the Third World. It is largely the product of the influence — social, economic, and political — of the industrialized countries, of consumerism, of the greed for profit, of the corrupting impact of multinational corporations. The revolution of rising expectations has now become the revolution of mounting frustrations; it has led to the present era of unstoppable instability.

History sometimes moves backward. We may today be witnessing such an instance of regression in the Arab world. Under the impact of an increasingly tough imperial policy, concerned only with security and economic and energy interests, and supported on the ground by an aggressive and expanding colonizing movement, a hundred years of Arab progress aimed at securing modernization, secularism, unity, and democracy seem to be giving way to fragmentation along sectarian and ethnic lines, ideological and religious narrowness, and anachronistic social and political tendencies. But history shows that temporary regression tends to strengthen the radicalization of society and thus, paradoxically, to hasten social transformation, but in violent instead of peaceful ways.

What happens in the Arab countries concerns not only the Arab world, but the whole globe, including the United States. As was pointed out above, the sources of the malaise from which the Arab world suffers are external as well as internal. Chief among the former is the way in which the United States has dealt with the region. This is not the place to discuss the overall social and political impact on the Middle East of U.S. policy, but a few observations are in order with regard to its effects on social transformation.

In its dealings with the Arab world, the United States is seen by more and more people there as cynical, manipulative, and coercive. They see it as treating the area only in terms of its own interests and its anti-Soviet crusade, with hardly any regard to the aspirations and interests of the people involved. The United States today may have many friends among the ruling elites, but it has fewer and fewer friends among the Arab people. Indeed, the popular frustration with the United States has now reached what is probably its highest point since World War II. In Washington, this may be dismissed with the same absentmindedness that has characterized official U.S. attitudes toward similar situations in other countries, including Iran, and the consequences are likely to be the same.

This growing anger is due to a variety of reasons, some obvious, others not easy to define. Some Arabs wonder whether it is an accident that the stereotyping of Arabs in the American media grows daily more aggressive and that the public attitude toward everything Arab becomes more and more hostile. How is one to explain the U.S. alliance, presumably to protect American interests in the Arab world itself, with the occupier of Arab lands? How is one to account for the lionization of precisely the one Arab leader whom Arabs almost universally regard as a quisling?

Many Arabs find it proper to ask whether it is really in the interest of the United States to oppose democratization in the Arab world on the grounds that the status quo in the region must be preseved at all costs, or to brand indiscriminately all demands for social change as subversive or pro-Soviet? Experience has shown that military approaches have never solved political problems and that repression and coercion, whether applied from within or from without, can bring only temporary stability and will in the end lead to collapse and unpredictable consequences.